Lessons *in* Love

FROM

A Course in Miracles

The holiest of all the spots on earth is where an
ancient hatred has become a present love.

Lessons *in Love*

FROM

A Course in Miracles

Truths and Meditations
on the Legendary Text

By Brad Oliphant

STERLING ETHOS
New York

STERLING ETHOS
New York

An Imprint of Sterling Publishing
387 Park Avenue South
New York, NY 10016

ISBN 978-1-4549-1135-7

Distributed in Canada by Sterling Publishing
℅ Canadian Manda Group, 165 Dufferin Street
Toronto, Ontario, Canada M6K 3H6
Distributed in the United Kingdom by GMC Distribution Services
Castle Place, 166 High Street, Lewes, East Sussex, England BN7 1XU
Distributed in Australia by Capricorn Link (Australia) Pty. Ltd.
P.O. Box 704, Windsor, NSW 2756, Australia

For information about custom editions, special sales, and premium and corporate purchases,
please contact Sterling Special Sales at 800-805-5489 or specialsales@sterlingpublishing.com.

Manufactured in China

2 4 6 8 10 9 7 5 3 1

www.sterlingpublishing.com

DEDICATION

In loving memory of my dearest mother, Barbara. All thanks to you, mom, for your

lasting support and constant love. My heart is yours. Walk in His light now and

know that you will forevermore be loved. Thanks to my father, Nugent, for coming

back into my life. I relish our newfound relationship. To Bart and Londa, my brother

and sister: how blessed I am to have had you both in my life. You have both been

cornerstones in my development. And to Tom, my stepfather, thank you for taking

such loving care of my mom. I am so grateful. You all have been my greatest teachers.

Until your knees finally hit the floor,
you're just playing at life, and on some level
you're scared because you know that you're just playing.
The moment of surrender is not when life is over.
It's when life begins.

Marianne Williamson

*As you look in,
you choose the
guide for seeing.
And then you look
out and behold
his witnesses.
This is why you
find what you seek.*

CONTENTS

ACKNOWLEDGMENTS

I would like to begin by thanking Gary R. Renard for taking a leap of faith in agreeing to write the Foreword to this book. His book *The Disappearance of the Universe* has been monumental to my evolving understanding. To Amy Torres: you have been crucial as I have studied the Course. Thank you for gracing me with a most loving Glossary. To Jon and Dolores Mundy: I am so honored to have met you both. Your presence is a joy to behold, for the both of you truly walk the walk and talk the love. Thank you for your gracious endorsement and for including me in your "MiracleMagazine." To Shanti: what a powerhouse of inspiration you are. I am blessed for having crossed your path. To Michael O'Brien: thank you for helping clarify so much in my life. How grateful I am for your touching endorsement as well. To Sherry Strong and Alexandra De Borchgrave: how thankful I am for your supportive words on my work. To Earl Purdy: your repetitive style of teaching got through to me when others could not. Your cheerful demeanor and jolly attitude continue to wake me from my sleep. And to Jennifer Hadley: your continuous efforts to collaborate with others and to help spread truth throughout the world is a testament unto itself. Thank you.

Furthermore, I would like to acknowledge a lady who planted the seed for my awakening some sixteen years ago—Marianne Williamson. Marianne's book, *A Return to Love,* was a colossal turning point for me in my search for truth. It triggered something inside me that helped open my eyes for the first time. I am forever grateful.

I also would like to thank several of my closest friends and colleagues who are walking this journey with me. Lili Berley: for pointing me in the right direction. Your loving guidance over the years led me to peace and happiness— thank you. To George Maestre: few words can describe the appreciation and love I have for you. Thank you for stepping up, and agreeing to seek out truth with me. Iso Argamin: you are someone who has inspired me from the beginning with your dedication to helping others. What a beautiful act of charity you demonstrate in your life—thank you as well. Lane Spigner: you have been a clean mirror for me to look into every time we meet. Your determination and willingness to continue learning have been an incredible support for me. To Tede, my prayer partner: you will forevermore be in my heart. Thank you for always showing me the face of Christ. To Pam Gettman (the wicked one— ha!): thank you for your gentleness, your innocence, and your loving disposition. You comfort me. To Noff and Liz Colabella: wow, where do I start? Liz, you bring sunshine into my life. How I adore you. Thank you for loving me and being present in my life. Thanks to you Noff for your brotherhood and always treating me like family. And to your children, Jay and Melissa, thank you as well. To Lee Harris: many thanks for inspiring me in so many areas on my journey. To Rory Donadio, who has given me the nickname "Course": you walked into my life when I was hopeless. You extended your hand and your love, without prejudice, and helped me find my way. You are my brother, and will always be one with me. To Michael Beiser: the laughter we share is medicine for healing. I honor our friendship and relish your gift of giving. To Pia and Cullen Orlean, for your devotion to spirit and your continued support over the years. Your love has strengthened me. And to Marta Hallett: thank you for helping this book get into the right hands.

There are so many others who have inspired and helped transport me into this place where I now stand: Doreen Birdsell, Kathy Bugglin, Joan and Eddie Olbrich, Laurin Jones, Dalai Hagiescu, Julio Espada, Tommy Merino, Annette Leach, Victoria Hagai, Michael Jones, Alyson Maloy, Helio and Maria Ascari, David Rose, Eleni, George, Zen, and Billy Fuiaxis. (You are my sister, Eleni. Please know this.)

To Ezra and Mieke, Mila, and Raffa Nanes. Thank you, Ez, for your friendship over the years. You have seen me through some of my most troubled days, and never turned your back. To Peter Lik: your photography work has been a leading contributor to a most recent display of creativity for me. Your ability to capture the raw essence of nature in its best light is beyond words—thank you for this. I hope to shoot with you one day. To Deva and Miten Premali: thanks for all your loving contributions you have spread throughout the world with your healing music—Namaste.

Thanks also to Rosemarie LoSasso and Judith Whitson at FACIM, for your guidance and helping hand. To Deborah Roberts, for helping guide me throughout this entire book's process.

To Kenneth Wapnick, in loving memory: many thanks to you for your loving and instrumental touch upon this legendary text, helping to bring clarity to its teachings like no other. To each and every translator who devoted their time to spreading this truth—thank you. By your efforts, you have helped join this world as one. And finally, to Sterling Publishing: thank you all for believing in my work and offering me this wonderful opportunity.

And to all those whose names I failed to mention: thank you for assisting me in knowing my Self. You know who you are.

In closing, all thanks to my beloved brother, Jesus: for You shined Your glorious light on me at my darkest hour and lit a path of hope before my feet. You have given me a way of life that I never knew was possible. Thank you for leading me to *A Course in Miracles*. It has set me free. I no longer desire to be a worldly problem solver, but want only to be my Father's vision holder. I will forevermore be your happy learner.

With love, your brother, Brad

A NOTE ABOUT LANGUAGE

Throughout this book, the Course and I both use masculine pronouns (*he, him, himself, Him*) to refer to God, God's Holy Spirit, Jesus, and to each individual Son of God. Masculine references like *brother,* both singular and plural, are also use throughout. Whenever these masculine pronouns and terms appear, please note that they are intended to encompass both masculine and feminine genders. Even though the Holy Spirit does not recognize gender, these terms and pronouns are only being used for teaching purposes!

Also, in referring to the *Son(s) of God,* the Course and I are both referring to Jesus and all human beings. *A Course in Miracles* views all of us as extensions of God's Love. We are all part of One Whole!

Finally, all text from *A Course in Miracles* is as it appears in its third edition. Author comments placed throughout have all been prefaced with the phrase *Author's Notes.*

FOREWORD BY GARY R. RENARD

As a spiritual student for the last thirty-four years, I've been fortunate enough to have had more than my share of mystical experiences. Many spiritual students don't have any, and that doesn't matter. They are not necessarily a sign of spiritual advancement; they are symbolic of the fact that the mind is awakening. But if you do not have mystical experiences, that doesn't mean that your mind is not awakening. It simply means that we don't all have the same experiences at the same time. Indeed, you may have had such experiences in your last lifetime. What does matter is your answer to such questions as these: Am I being more forgiving? Am I feeling more peaceful? More loving? More inspired? If you can answer "yes" to questions like these you can be assured that you are making tremendous spiritual progress.

The reason I bring this up is because, in my case, the mystical experiences I've had have usually been very visual. When I was four or five years old and I went to bed at night, I remember that I'd close my eyes and see a tremendous kaleidoscope of colors. These images fascinated me and filled me with wonder. I was probably one of the few children in the world who actually looked forward to going to bed at night. This stopped when I was six or seven, and never came back in that form.

Later, when I was twenty-seven, I embarked on a spiritual path, and a whole new series of visual experiences began to unfold for me. The last thirty-four years have held for me a wide variety of interesting, and sometimes wild visual scenes. These have been good experiences that have left me in awe—never unpleasant ones, unless they came in the form of bad dreams when I was asleep at night.

My optical prowess left me with a habit of staring at beauty, whether it be art, nature, or the female form. If a shape is beautiful, my eyes will find it. I'm sure the Pisces in me also has something to do with that. And when it comes to art, that certainly includes brilliant photography.

All of which brings us to this wonderful and elegant book by Brad Oliphant. When I look at the photographs herein, they transport me to the places and forms that are captured. Brad has a gift, and it is well displayed in these pages. If I had some sophisticated friends coming over for a visit, this is the kind of book I'd want on my coffee table. It has style and grace, and some of the best pictures you'll ever see.

I'm not an expert in photography, but I am an expert on visual beauty, both esoteric and practical. If you love any kind of art, you'll probably be drawn to the excellence of this book. I was, and I'll be happily recommending it to people for a long, long time. And as far as the illusion of time is concerned, there's a favorite quote of both Brad's and mine from my first book, *The Disappearance of the Universe,* that I'd like to share with you to end this Foreword:

Time heals not all wounds, but forgiveness will heal all time.

Gary R. Renard

YOU ARE AS GOD CREATED YOU.

The sounds of this world are still, the sights of this world disappear, and all the thoughts that this world ever held are wiped away forever by this one idea. Here is salvation accomplished. Here is sanity restored.

You are as God created you! Darkness cannot obscure the glory of God's Son.

The Son of God is you.

You stand in light, strong in the sinlessness in which you were created, and in which you will remain throughout eternity.

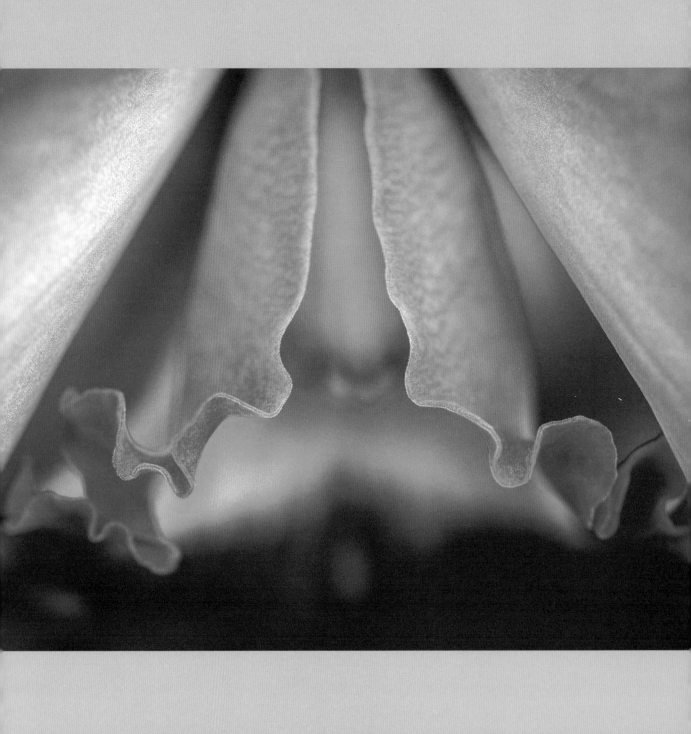

INTRODUCTION

There is a glow of a long-forgotten memory, an inward light calling us to awaken and come home—to know the peace and joy from which we were created. If for just one single moment in time—one "holy instant"—we would be still and become willing to listen, we would be impossible to move. And it is here that I begin my story.

Here I sit, to my own amazement, writing an introduction to my own book based on the teachings from *A Course in Miracles,* and accompanied by my photography. For it was not too long ago that I was lost, caught in a web of great despair and isolation, due to a twenty-five-year drug and alcohol addiction. I was left facing a wall of hopelessness beyond belief—a cloud of guilt so thick with shame that I saw no way out. Not even a crack of light. Suicide had presumably become my best option.

One cold November evening in the year 2008, I found myself kneeling, begging, and crying out for help from the depths of my being. I didn't know to whom I was crying out, for my only recollection of God was what had been taught to me from my Christian religious upbringing. Given this teaching, I cried out to Jesus, but with a wavering faith and unsure of who I was calling for. For having read and known the Bible, I personally had never been able to put my trust in a work apparently filled with many contradictions. Once I had been so comforted in my readings of the Bible, knowing that God's Love was unfailing and unconditional, only to read in another passage of God's wrath and punishment and condemnation. The Bible itself is filled with beauty, epiphanies, and testimonies of the highest level. However, with my limited understanding at the time, my heart was closed off because of my own confusion about the Bible and the false testimony others had given me, based on their own erroneous beliefs. Scripture of any kind, placed in the hands of those who have not yet sufficiently awakened to truth and understanding, is often used for egocentric and willful purposes. However, it does not really matter who seems to distort what, because, in truth, the only mind we need to change is our own.

Nonetheless, I cried out, desperate for relief from the agony of addiction and for a breath of life and a pathway out of my hell. I remember weeping so much that my face swelled beyond recognition. Then suddenly, as if a cloud had parted, I felt a surge of warmth and comfort come over me that I cannot explain to this day. I felt as if I were being held and protected. Having no sense of my body, I felt levitated. I felt the presence of Jesus. I will never be able to explain how I knew it was Jesus—I just knew with certainty. I felt nothing but an overwhelming sense of unconditional love: the love that my heart had always told me was true. And then I was given a message—one that did not come in the form of words or any language, but more like an inner intuition that said with perfect clarity:

I am here; help will come.

No sooner than had this presence arrived, it too had left. I was once again alone in my room, filled with uncertainty, but with an awareness that something had shifted within me. Something had changed—I felt renewed. I understand now that I received a miracle that night, one that had opened a pathway of truth for me, through which an abundance of grace and blessings gushed forth.

The following morning, the dark craving for alcohol and drugs—and the solution it once presented to me—had been lifted. Somehow I found myself clean and sober for a number of days and felt compelled to visit the beach at Fire Island, New York, for its warm sun-lit sandy beaches have always been a sanctuary for me. On my return train ride home, a lady approached me and asked if she could speak with me because she noticed I seemed troubled. This lady, whom I came to recognize as the "help that would come," introduced me to *A Course in Miracles*. And even though I was not aware of it at the time, this was the turning point in my life that ultimately reawakened my spiritual vision. Since then, I have found that my investment in the world, as well as my self-reliance, have both greatly diminished.

Upon opening the Course for the first time, I was amazed with its structure and magnitude, its poetic melodies, its Shakespearian resonances, and its symphonic motifs. But no sooner had I opened the book than I learned that its teachings were said to have been derived from an inner dictation from the Voice of Jesus. At first glance, I was discomforted by this, thinking it was another religion or

theology. This was not what I was searching for. Assuming it was a religious tome, I questioned its teachings and doubted that it would provide me with a helpful outcome. But the more I read, the more my heart began to crack open, believing that I finally had found what I had been searching for all this time—the truth that sets you free. I completed my first study of the Course in its entirety in two years with vigilance and determination. I can now say with complete certainty that not only is the Course from whom it states to be from, but it could not be from any other source. The consistency of truth and love inherent in the Course teachings awakened something inside me. Here were the interpretive teachings I had longed for.

During my studies, I learned that Jesus is not the only teacher of God, for our Creator has sent His Holy Spirit/the Voice of Love into this dream world in manifold forms to offer us His greatest teachings without fear. Jesus, or correctly named Y'shua, just so happens to be my teacher. You might even say that Jesus is my guru. For a guru is one who leads us from darkness and illusions, which is ignorance, into truth and light, which is understanding. Jesus states in the Course:

The journey that we undertake together is the exchange of dark for light, of ignorance for understanding. Nothing you understand is fearful. It is only in darkness and in ignorance that you perceive the frightening, and shrink away from it to further darkness.

This underscores the importance of establishing a relationship with our Inner Guide. For we cannot escape from the problems we ourselves have created; therefore, we are in need of one who knows the truth and can offer us freedom from our faulty choices. This teaching also emphasizes for me the importance of letting go of my past fears, embodied in certain words and terms the world had taught me. For in letting a new and loving definition take their place, I was finally able to see the light within them.

Religious leaders have often referred to Jesus as one of the ultimate spiritual leaders of all time, someone who should be bowed down to and revered. But I have come to learn that He was, in truth, one of the ultimate followers, demonstrating and teaching that we, too, could do as he did, and achieve even greater things. For in all His thoughts and actions, he put first and foremost the guidance of the Holy Spirit and God's Love. This alone was what he followed, teaching complete equality and the truth that God's Kingdom resides within each of us. This is why He is known today as the greatest teacher of love. Take a quick look through the Bible and nowhere does Jesus say, "Worship me." His call to us was "Follow me." There is a huge difference between the two. He was saying: "This is what is possible if you are willing to follow these principles, just as I have." Jesus demonstrated authentic spirituality, showing us that peace was always possible, regardless of what the outside world considered of value. Come riches or poverty, health or sickness—even in His crucifixion—He chose to place love at the center of His ministry. Peace prevailed simply because He remained true to the guidance of the Holy Spirit and to His convictions.

In the following four years, I engrossed myself in the teachings of the Course. I quickly discovered that its primary focus is on forgiveness, although it redefines forgiveness, as well as many other Christian terms. The terms *Atonement* and *Miracles* are also redefined, being all one and the same—they undo error (at their source),

thus allowing healing to take place. Terms such as *sin, hell, judgment, fear, guilt,* and many other human constructs are redefined as well. The Course even goes as far as to redefine this world. I once recoiled from words like *Atonement, judgment, sin, salvation,* and even the name *Jesus,* although it is now clear to me that this was simply due to the worldly definitions that I had ascribed to them. But having found these terms redefined with clarity, I was comforted and saw nothing but love. The words became meaningless, and left me with a sense of peace—a peace, as they say, "that surpasses all understanding." The Course maintains that *all terms are potentially controversial, and those who seek controversy will find it. Yet those who seek clarification will find it as well. They must, however, be willing to overlook controversy, recognizing that it is a defense against truth in the form of a delaying maneuver.* That said, I would like to encourage you, as you read along, to question every term that elicits any discomfort or past thoughts of fear, inviting you to open the Glossary at the back of this book to see how my friend and teacher Amy Torres has redefined them with loving accuracy.

The Course centers itself around a teaching based on nonduality, meaning there are not two of anything, but only Oneness—one Mind, one Spirit, one Source, one Love, and one Truth. All of these are all-inclusive and all-encompassing. This Oneness is unalterable and will forever remain unaffected by our apparent sense of separation and division, and our chaotic beliefs in different truths. Even the word *God,* which is solely a name given to the Source of all Life by humankind, somehow loses its meaning after having been labeled. For what we call God is nameless, formless, and genderless. The Course states, "that words are but symbols of symbol. They are thus twice removed from reality" and "nothing that is true need be explained." This is why our naming God according to our own understanding could never alter its truth. We call this Source by many names: She, He, Allah, Muse, Abraham, Buddha, Shiva, Zeus, or the Divine. These words have no meaning in themselves; however, they are helpful in placing meaning where it belongs. As the Course teaches: *How can "Divine Abstraction" be labeled?*

It is a self-study Course, and is not intended to become another cult or religion. Its sole purpose is to provide a way by which some people can find their own Inner Teacher.

There is no evangelism in the Course. It is not about getting the word "out" to the world. It is about getting the word "in" to the heart. Retaining the mind in the heart is "inwardness."

Living A Course in Miracles, by Jon Mundy, PhD

It is a Course in mind training; as a teaching of metaphysics, the Course states that "an untrained mind can accomplish nothing." The purpose of the *Workbook for Students* in the Course is to help correct our erroneous perceptions and train our minds to develop a different way of perceiving everything and everyone in the world. (This workbook is what sets the Course apart from other spiritual teachings.) After having our erroneous perceptions corrected, truth merely dawns on our mind by itself. The workbook's exercises are about adopting a different perspective on every point of view we have about the world. Right-minded perception is the result of miracles undoing fear and guilt within our mind. This, in turn, opens the gateway to knowledge and freedom,

helping to remind us of our true Selves and the memory of our Creator. The miracle "compares what you have made with creation, accepting what is in accord with it as true, and rejecting what is out of accord as false." Jesus correctly defines the miracle as being a correction, or a shift within the mind, rather than an occurrence that takes place outside of us in time and space. It inverts upside-down, fear-based perception, allowing love to take its place. Through miracles, problems don't get solved, they get dissolved, as we evolve into a greater awareness of Love.

The Course teaches us that there are only two thought systems to choose between—the ego's or God's—and only two emotions—fear and love. For there is no such thing as a neutral thought. We are either projecting fear and guilt, which is the thought system of our insidious ego—"the great deceiver"— one in the same as what the Bible refers to as the devil— or we are extending love, which is of God, the source of all life. It is up to us which one we choose. The ego separates; God unites. The gift that Jesus offers us is the gift of choice, to choose again. In this new choice, we receive His miracle, which frees us from illusions of fear and guilt and allows the peace of God to return to our mind. We either learn through fear, or through love—it's our choice.

The power of decision is your one remaining freedom as a prisoner of this world.

We are the ones who have conferred all the meaning on this world. In turn, we have created a meaningless world. In this worldview, truth is different for everyone; symbols rule and govern us and have given rise to a world of perception. Our perceptions have become our realities. All must go through this phase of learning, but the sooner the premise on which all this rests is called into question, the sooner we will reach our own turning point in life—one that will lead to correct perception of the world and one that will lean toward truth. Thus are separate goals and wills unified as we come to remember our true relationship with our Source. All the meaning we have placed upon this world and our Creator have become a mere shadow that is cast over truth—a veil of separation that hides our true reality of unity in love.

Through the gifts of freedom that this Course has offered me, the chains that used to bind me behind darkened walls of shame have all been broken. And after having been set free, I finally recognized that I was able to acknowledge sole responsibility for having placed the shackles around my own feet. Only by taking full responsibility for my thoughts and asking for continuous guidance from my Inner Teacher, have I been able to change the way I see myself and the world.

> *You will not break loose until you realize that*
> *you yourself forge the chains that bind you.*
>
> Arten, in *The Disappearance of the Universe,*
> by Gary R. Renard

And it is just that: changing our minds about the world. For the Course teaches that "the world is not left by death, but by truth." No one reaches Love with fear and guilt in his heart. Simply by our willingness to perceive everything differently from the teachings of the muse, who lives within us all, are we finally able to escape from fear and guilt and the recycling of our dreams of rebirth. The Course calls this muse God's Holy Spirit.

A shift of great proportions has happened within me; my brother's interest has now become my own. Never before have I thought this way. My heart now yearns to extend God's Love everywhere I go. It has been as if I have been allowed entrance into the senate of Truth, for this world has long kept secret the true laws that govern our lives. It has manipulated them and used them against us, for such is this world. Even religion has kept hidden what this Course has finally made clear to me: **God is love and is always extending nothing but His Love; everything else is of our own making.** Author Paul Ferrini, in his book *I am the Door,* perfectly encapsulates what *A Course in Miracles* is trying to help us see. It is this:

> *You are the dreamer of the darkness and*
> *the one who brings the light.*
> *You are tempter and savior rolled in one.*
> *This you will come to know if you do not know it already.*

Jesus teaches us this same truth in *A Course in Miracles*—"The enemy is you, as is the Christ." This speaks of the power of our decision making. We condemn ourselves, as we save ourselves, simply by our own choices. The Bible as well reinstates this truth with scripture stating: *Does a fountain send forth from the same opening both sweet and bitter waters? Can a fig tree, my brethren, bear olives, or a grapevine, figs? Who is there among you who is wise and has understanding? Then let him by his noble living show for this his good works that spring forth from humility of true wisdom. But if you have bitter jealousy and contention in your hearts, do not pride yourselves on this and thus be in defiance to the Truth. This superficial wisdom descendeth not from above, but is earthly and self-centered in man.*

I have come to know a peace and a joy that mystify me. I have tried to explain their beauty, but words fail me. For words are meaningless next to the Truth. Light has finally seeped through the cracks of my prison cell, reminding me of what has always been waiting patiently for me simply to ask for its return. I have transiently been removed from darkness. A weight that burdened me so heavily all my days has been lifted, and I have found that my step has been lightened to such a degree that I often seem to skim the ground as I walk. Do I still have dark days? Oh, yes! But I believe I have trained my mind enough to know when I am having insane and fearful thoughts, and have committed myself to asking for help from my Inner Teacher—who has been sent to guide me home.

So here I stand, certain of my direction and my goal, and would like to share with others the truth and principles that helped to set me free. Many paths will lead to what I have found within this Course, but I have chosen to help make clear its truths and teachings simply because of what they have done for me. (Note that it is _A_ Course in Miracles and not The _Course in Miracles_.) But the compulsion to know must draw you willingly, for if it were by any other means, it would no longer be a gift, and a gift it is intended to be.

You will find within this book a selection of readings and quotes all taken from the pages of the Course itself, which I have organized thematically across seven chapters. This book can be read from cover to cover, or can be opened on any page to read selected teachings. There is no wrong way to read this book. The teachings are complemented by my photographs to inspire and offer reflection. My greatest honor to date is simply this opportunity: to have been able to place my creative art next to these most loving truths. May

they be a place of contemplation and letting go for all. This is their sole intent.

Allow me to offer you a brief overview of the contents of _A Course in Miracles_—how it came to be, what it is, and what it says. The first edition of _A Course in Miracles_ was published by the Foundation for Inner Peace in 1975. The Course fast became a global healing path, now accessible to over 93 percent of the world's population, and translated into over 90 percent of the world's languages. Over 3 million copies are in print, and the masses of devoted students throughout every country of the world are simply uncountable. The Course uses traditional Christian language and symbols, but often redefines these terms in nontraditional ways. The Course deals mostly with universal spiritual themes and is said to be more related to Buddhism than Christianity, due to its teaching on metaphysics and Oneness.

How _A Course in Miracles_ came into being is a fascinating story. Helen Schucman and William Thetford, both career-minded psychologists and professors at Columbia University's College of Physicians and Surgeons in New York City, experienced a challenging partnership in their work environment. Together, they agreed to find a "better way" to resolve tensions that existed between the two of them. Shortly after making such an agreement, Helen, who described herself as being conservative in theory and atheistic in belief, started having very vivid and disturbing dreams that were filled with heightened imagery and visions. This entire experience began to feel more religious to her as the figure of Jesus began to appear to her in her dreams. This eventually came to be an inner dictation that told her, "This is _A Course in Miracles_—Please take note." This development started in

October 1965 and became a daily scribing through Helen, and a collaborative effort with Bill transcribing. Their work together continued for a period of seven years. At this period's end, they had completed what is now *A Course in Miracles,* which consists of a 669-page *Text,* a 488-page *Workbook for Students,* and a 92-page *Manual for Teachers.* "It emphasizes application rather than theory and experience rather than theology." It specifically states that "a universal theology is impossible, but a universal experience is not only possible but necessary."

Some years later, due to a student/teacher request to have further clarification on "how to pray," and on "understanding the therapeutic process and Course terms," Helen received and scribed two additional pamphlets that are extensions of Course principles. They are "Psychology" (1975) and the "Song of Prayer" (1977). In addition, she has scribed in 1975 a section that provides the Course's definition of and use of specific words, called the "Clarification of Terms." This also was added to the Course.

I too experienced "heightened imagery" and dreams prior to starting the process of writing this book. I went through my own period of feeling electrified and energized, being gifted with phrasing and page numbers (just on a much smaller level.) The questioning of all of this was made clear to me once I noticed the similarities of what was being given to me and what was to be placed within the pages of this book. Sequencing, page numbers, and corresponding teachings permeated my thoughts. After having completed this work, I stand bewildered at how this was accomplished at all. My faith has been enriched knowing that guiding forces have gifted to me what I was unable to achieve on my own!

Here is how the Introduction to *A Course in Miracles* begins:

This is a course in miracles. It is a required course. Only the time you take it is voluntary. Free will does not mean that you can establish the curriculum. It means only that you can elect what you want to take at a given time. The course does not aim at teaching the meaning of love, for that is beyond what can be taught. It does aim, however, at removing the blocks to the awareness of Love's presence, which is your natural inheritance. The opposite of love is fear, but what is all-encompassing can have no opposite. This Course can be summed up very simply in this way:

Nothing real can be threatened.
Nothing unreal exists.
Herein lies the peace of God.

(God/Love/Spirit, cannot be changed or threatened. Only God and His extensions exists; everything else is an illusion. For you to know this is for you to have the Peace of God.)

It makes a fundamental distinction between the real and the unreal; between knowledge and perception. Knowledge is truth and under one law; the law of Love or God. Truth is unalterable, eternal and unambiguous. It can be unrecognized, but it cannot be changed. The world of perception, on the other hand, is the world of time, of change, of beginnings and endings. It is based on interpretation, not on facts. It is the world of birth and death, founded on the belief in scarcity, loss, separation and death. It is learned rather than given, selective in its perceptual emphases, unstable in its functioning, and inaccurate in its interpretations. From knowledge and perception respectively, two distinct thought systems arise which are opposite in every respect.

Living now in the world of perception, we are being asked to choose again and turn to our Inner Guide to show us a new path that will lead us out of the belief in separation and back into the reality of Truth and Unity. This is what is being referred to when it states: "It is a required Course." It is not referring to *A Course in Miracles* itself. The requirement is simply a conscious choice, inspired by our own free will, to become willing to have all the blocks to the awareness of Love's presence removed for us through the practice of forgiveness under the guidance of the One Who knows.

Our minds are removed from our natural state of being (which is to be at peace in God) when we identify with a personal self/body and this world. It is our perception of separation that requires correction—the shifting of our minds over to the awareness of God's Oneness. *A Course in Miracles* is merely one of the many paths which offer this curriculum for correction. Until this decision has been made, and it must be made in order for us to regain the awareness of truth, we remain asleep and unaware of the love and peace that lies within.

With this understanding, I would like to prepare for you an explanation of the contents of this book so that you are clear on what is to come in the following pages. Chapter titles have all been taken from the Course, with subsection titles of my own wording. Much of the book consists of combined teachings taken from different sections throughout the Course. I have combined "like teachings" to present a thorough and condensed teaching aid for the Course. Although the teachings in the Course and in this book are the same, the order of teachings have different placement. My goal was to uncover and touch on as many teachings as possible, just in much fewer words.

As you start your journey into these pages, please take note of these few cues that will help lead you to a clearer understanding of who is speaking and to whom the message is directed. The entire Course, as well as most of this book, is written in first person, being a direct inner dictation from our brother and teacher Jesus. However, numerous writings and quotations in first person are directed toward you the reader, and you will come to know the difference simply through your practice. In helping you to understand this process, Uppercase *Him* always refers to God, Jesus, or the Holy Spirit, while lowercase *him* refers to our brothers and sisters. Uppercase *Mind* always refers to God's Mind or Spirit, while lowercase *mind* refers to the split mind. And uppercase *Son* always refers to our true Self as we were created in the likeness of our Creator. All *italicized* wording that is included within phrases is meant to be emphasized.

Please note that the contents of the book are not meant to take the place of *A Course in Miracles* itself. The Course can and should stand on its own. This book, which consists of favorite readings and core principles, is nothing more that a teaching aid or condensed guide to bring clarity to the Course's 1, 279-page structure and its seeming complexity. Please take note that errors of any kind that have occurred—in spelling, placement, or otherwise—are due to my own interpretations and do not reflect on the Course itself.

With its many teachings—from forgiveness to prayer, from Atonement to miracles—the Course has as its primary goal to help fan the divine spark of awareness into a strong flame, making us mindful of both wrong-minded perception and our union in God our Father. This leads us toward love without conditions. May it usher you toward truth and inner peace.

In this world of perception, where fear has come

to rule, life seems to be a painful kind of progress. But progress we shall make with the single decision to choose again—longing for what we had, and dreaming ahead to know again. And as we journey into the following pages, let us become aware of the only thing that is being asked of us—our willingness to see everything differently. Jesus tells us in the introduction to the Workbook:

Remember only this; you need not believe the ideas, you need
not accept them, and you need not even welcome them.
Some of them you may actively resist. None of this
will matter, or decrease their efficacy. But do not
allow yourself to make exceptions in applying the
ideas, and whatever your reactions to the ideas may
be, use them. Nothing more than that is required.

So we begin. I have chosen a passage from the Course that I believe sets a lovely tone for what follows. May you come to know that in truth our union with God/Love is never lost, but only forgotten.

Simply be willing to perceive all things differently, allowing these teachings to guide you, for it is by practicing them that you will ferret out the evidence needed to witness their truth. And know that this Course was not given to teach us truth, for truth cannot be learned. You are one with truth. You only need be reminded of what you are and what has always been. I pray that what you are about to read touches you as it has touched me. Godspeed on your journey. With love—Brad

We recognize we are preparing for another phase of understanding. We would take this step completely, that

we may go on again more certain, more sincere, with faith upheld more surely. Our footsteps have not been unwavering, and doubts have made us walk uncertainly and slowly on the road this course sets forth. But now we hasten on, for we approach a greater certainty, a firmer purpose and a surer goal.

So do we bring our practicing to You. And if we
stumble, You will raise us up. If we forget the way,
we count upon Your sure remembering. We wander
off, but You will not forget to call us back.
Quicken our footsteps now, that we may walk more
certainly and quickly unto You. And we accept
the Word You offer us to unify our practicing, as
we review the thoughts that You have given us:

God is but Love, and therefore so am I.

This Self alone knows Love. This Self alone is perfectly consistent in its thoughts; knows its Creator, understands itself, is perfect in its knowledge and its love, and never changes from its constant state of union with its Father and itself. And it is this that waits to meet us at the journey's ending. Every step we take brings us a little nearer. Let us raise our hearts from dust to life, as we remember this is promised us, and that this course was sent to open up the path of light to us, and teach us, step by step, how to return to the eternal Self we thought we lost.

I take the journey with you. For I share your doubts and fears a little while, that You may come to me who recognize the road by which all fears and doubts are overcome. We walk together. I must understand uncertainty and pain, although I know they have no meaning. Yet a savior must remain with those he teaches, seeing what they see, but still retaining in his mind the way that led him out, and now will lead you out with him. God's Son is crucified until you walk along the road with me. My resurrection comes again each time I lead a brother safely to the place at which the journey ends and is forgot. I am renewed each time a brother learns there is a way from misery and pain. I am reborn each time a brother's mind turns to the light in him and looks for me. **I have forgotten no one.** Help me now to lead you back to where the journey was begun, to make another choice with me.

God would not have Heaven incomplete. It waits for you, as I do. I am incomplete without your part in me. And as I am made whole we go together to our ancient home, prepared for us before time was and kept unchanged by time, immaculate and safe, as it will be at last when time is done. The Self from which I call to you is but your own. To Him we go together. Take your brother's hand, for this is not a way we walk alone. In him I walk with you, and you with me. Our Father wills His Son be one with Him. What lives but must not then be one with you?

Hallowed your Name. Your glory undefiled forever. And your wholeness now complete, as God established it.

You are His Son, completing his extension in your own. We practice but an ancient truth we knew before illusion seems to claim the world. And we remind the world that it is free of all illusions every time we say:

God is but Love, and therefore so am I.

THE MIRACLE OF JOINING

To see me is to see me in everyone, and offer everyone the gift you offer me . . . For in our union you will accept all of our brothers.

The gift of union is the only gift that I was born to give.

Each miracle of joining is a mighty herald of eternity.

Jesus the Christ

SIMPLY DO THIS:

Be still, and lay aside all thoughts of what you are and what God is; all concepts you have learned about the world; all images you hold about yourself. Empty your mind of everything it thinks is either true or false, or good or bad, of every thought it judges worthy, and all the ideas of which it is ashamed. Hold onto nothing!

Do not bring with you one thought the past has taught, nor one belief you ever learned before from anything. Forget this world, forget this course, and come with wholly empty hands unto your God.

Heaven itself is reached with empty hands and open minds,
which come with nothing to find
everything and claim it as their own.

Heaven itself is reached with empty hands and open minds,
which come with nothing to find
everything and claim it as their own.

CHAPTER I

The Lessons of Love

Miracles honor you because you are lovable.
They dispel illusions about yourself and perceive
the light in you. They thus atone for your errors by
freeing you from your nightmares. By releasing
your mind from the imprisonment of your
illusions, they restore your sanity.

THE GREATEST GIFT

Prayer is the greatest gift with which God blessed His Son at his creation. It was then what it is to become; the single voice Creator and creation share; the song the Son sings to the Father, Who returns the thanks it offers Him unto the Son. Endless the harmony, and endless, too, the joyous concord of the love they give forever to each other. And in this, creation is extended. God gives thanks to his extension in His Son. His Son gives thanks for his creation, in the song of his creating in his Father's Name. The love they share is what all prayer will be throughout eternity, when time is done. For such it was before time seemed to be.

To you who are in time a little while, prayer takes the form that best will suit your need. You have but one. What God created one must recognize its oneness, and rejoice that what illusions seemed to separate is one forever in the Mind of God. Prayer now must be the means by which God's Son leaves separate goals and separate interests by, and turns in holy gladness to the truth of union in his Father and himself.

Prayer is a way offered by the Holy Spirit to reach God. It is not merely a question or an entreaty. It cannot succeed until you realize that it asks for nothing. How else could it serve its purpose? It is impossible to pray for idols and hope to reach God. True prayer must avoid the pitfall of asking to entreat. Ask, rather, to receive what is already given; to accept what is already there.

The secret of true prayer is to forget the things you think you need. In prayer you overlook your specific needs as you see them, and let them go into God's Hands. There they become your gifts to Him, for they tell Him that you would have no gods before Him; no love but His. What could His answer be but your remembrance of Him? Can this be traded for a bit of trifling advice about a problem of an instant's duration? God answers only for eternity. But still all little answers are contained in this.

Prayer for specifics always asks to have the past repeated in some way. What was enjoyed before, or seemed to be; what was another's and he seemed to love— all these are but illusions from the past. The aim of prayer is to release the present from its chains of past illusions; to let it be a freely chosen remedy from every choice that stood for a mistake. What prayer can offer now so far exceeds all that you asked before that it is pitiful to be content with less.

Prayer is stepping aside; a letting go, a quiet time of listening and loving. It should not be confused with supplication of any kind, because it is a way of remembering your holiness. Why should holiness entreat, being fully entitled to everything Love has to offer? And it is to Love you go in prayer. Prayer is an offering; a giving up of yourself to be at one with Love. There is nothing to ask because there is nothing left to want. That nothingness becomes the altar of God. It disappears in Him.

You have sought first the Kingdom of Heaven,
and all else has indeed been given you.

Herein lies the power of prayer. It asks nothing and receives everything.

The only meaningful prayer is for forgiveness,
because those who have been forgiven have everything.

Miracles mirror
God's eternal Love.

WHAT IS A MIRACLE?

A miracle is a correction. It does not create, nor really change at all. It merely looks on devastation, and reminds the mind that what it sees is false. It undoes error, but does not attempt to go beyond perception, nor exceed the function of forgiveness. Thus it stays within time's limits. Yet it paves the way for the return of timelessness and love's awakening, for fear must slip away under the gentle remedy it brings.

The miracle is useless if you learn but
that the body can be healed,
for that is not the lesson it was sent to teach.
The lesson is the "mind" was sick
that thought the body could be sick; projecting out
its guilt caused nothing; and had no effects.

A miracle contains the gift of grace, for it is given and received as one. And thus it illustrates the law of truth the world does not obey, because it fails entirely to understand its ways. A miracle inverts perception which was upside down before, and thus it ends the strange distortions that were manifest. Now is perception open to the truth. Now is forgiveness seen as justified.

Forgiveness is the home of miracles. The eyes of Christ deliver them to all they look upon in mercy and in love. Perception stands corrected in His sight, and what was meant to curse has come to bless. Each lily of forgiveness offers all the world the silent miracle of love.

Miracle-minded forgiveness is "only" correction.
It has no element of judgment at all.
The statement "Father forgive them for they know not
what they do" in no way evaluates "what" they do.

It is an appeal to God to heal their minds. There is no
reference to the outcome of the error. That does not matter.

The miracle is taken first on faith, because to ask for it implies the mind has been made ready to conceive of what it cannot see and does not understand. Yet faith will bring its witnesses to show that what it rested on is really there. And thus the miracle will justify your faith in it, and show it rested on a world more real that what you saw before; a world redeemed from what you thought was there.

Miracles demonstrate that learning has occurred under the right guidance, for learning is invisible and what has been learned can be recognized only by its results. Its generalization is demonstrated as you use it in more and more situations. You will recognize that you have learned there is no order of difficulty in miracles when you apply them to all situations. There is no situation to which miracles do not apply, and by applying them to all situations you will gain the real world.

Miracles fall like drops of healing rain from Heaven on a dry and dusty world, where starved and thirsty creatures come to die. Now they have water. Now the world is green. And everywhere the signs of life spring up, to show that what is born can never die, for what has life has immortality.

Author's Note: A miracle, as seen by worldly standards, is an event that takes place outside of us and is completely absent of our touch upon it. However, in truth, a miracle originates from a decision for change and healing *within* the mind. Its effects will often seem to show up on the outside, but there is nothing outside of us. It is only a world of perception. The change of mind translates into a change of perception. Each miracle we experience leads us toward our complete awareness of God.

YOUR WORTH

Your worth is not established by teaching or learning. Your worth is established by God. As long as you dispute this everything you do will be fearful, particularly any situation that lends itself to the belief in superiority and inferiority. Teachers must be patient and repeat their lessons until they are learned. I am willing to do this, because I have no right to set your learning limits for you. Again, nothing you do or think or wish or make is necessary to establish your worth. This point is not debatable except in delusions.

Your ego is never at stake because God did not create it. Your spirit is never at stake because He did. Any confusion on this point is delusional, and no form of devotion is possible as long as this delusion lasts.

The Holy Spirit is your strength because He knows nothing but the spirit as you. He is perfectly aware that you do not know yourself, and perfectly aware of how to teach you to remember what you are. Because He loves you, He will gladly teach you what He loves, for He wills to share it. Remembering you always, He cannot let you forget your worth. For the Father never ceases to remind Him of His Son, and He never ceases to remind His Son of the Father. God is in your memory because of Him. You chose to forget your Father but you do not really want to do so, and therefore you can decide otherwise. As it was my decision, so is it yours.

Spirit need not be taught, but the ego must be. Learning is ultimately perceived as frightening because it leads to the relinquishment, not the destruction, of the ego to the light of Spirit. This is the change the ego must fear, because it does not share my charity. My lesson was like yours, and because I learned it I can teach it. I will never attack your ego, but I am trying to teach you how its thought system arose. When I remind you of your true creation, your ego cannot but respond with fear.

If you are willing to renounce the role of guardian of your thought system and open it to me, I will correct it very gently and lead you back to God.

The Kingdom of Heaven is the spirit's right, whose beauty and dignity are far beyond doubt, beyond perception, and stand forever as the mark of the Love of God for His creations, who are wholly worthy of Him and only of Him. Nothing else is sufficiently worthy to be a gift for a creation of God Himself.

You whose mind is darkened by doubt and guilt, remember this: God gave the Holy Spirit to you, and gave Him the mission to remove all doubt and every trace of guilt that his dear Son has laid upon himself. It is impossible that this mission fail. Nothing can prevent what God would have accomplished from accomplishment. Whatever your reactions to the Holy Spirit's Voice may be, whatever voice you choose to listen to, whatever strange thoughts may occur to you, God's will "is" done.

Have faith in only this one thing, and it will be sufficient: God wills you be in Heaven, and nothing can keep you from it, or it from you. Your wildest misperceptions, your weird imaginings, your blackest nightmares all mean nothing. They will not prevail against the peace God wills for you.

THE MOTIVATION FOR PEACE

Forget not that the motivation for this course is the attainment and the keeping of the state of peace. Given this state the mind is quiet, and the condition in which God is remembered is attained. It is not necessary to tell Him what to do. He will not fail. Where He can enter, there He is already. And can it be He cannot enter where He wills to be? Peace will be yours *because* it is His Will. Can you believe a shadow can hold back the Will that holds the universe secure? God does not wait upon illusions to let Him be Himself. Nor more His Son. They *are*. And what illusion that idly seems to drift between Them has the power to defeat what is Their Will?

To learn this course requires willingness to question every value that you hold. Not one can be kept hidden and obscure but it will jeopardize your learning. No belief is neutral.

Every thought you have contributes to truth or to illusions;
either it extends the truth or it multiplies illusions.
You can indeed multiply nothing, but
you will not extend it by doing so.
Besides your recognizing that thoughts are never
idle, salvation requires that you also recognize that
every thought you have brings either
peace or war; either love or fear.
A neutral result is impossible because a
neutral thought is impossible.

Everyone has the power to dictate each decision you make. For a decision is a conclusion based on everything that you believe. It is the outcome of belief, and follows it as surely as does suffering follow guilt and freedom sinlessness. **There is no substitute for peace. What God** creates has no alternative. The truth arises from what He knows. And your decisions come from your beliefs as certainly as all creation rose in His Mind *because* of what He knows.

Peace is an attribute in you. You cannot find it outside.
Illness is some form of external searching.
Health is inner peace.

Knowledge is not the motivation for learning this course. Peace is. This is the prerequisite for knowledge only because those who are in conflict are not peaceful, and peace is the condition of knowledge because it is the condition of the Kingdom. Knowledge can be restored only when you meet its conditions. This is not a bargain made by God, who makes no bargains. It is merely the result of your misuse of His laws on behalf of an imaginary will that is not His. Knowledge is His Will. If you are opposing His Will, how can you have Knowledge?

The great peace of the Kingdom shines in your mind forever,
but it must shine outward to make you aware of it.

Author's Note: As mentioned, obtaining knowledge should not be our motivation for learning, but rather to obtain peace of mind. For knowledge cannot be found where there is no peace. Peace is the condition we must have, prior to having knowledge, restored to us. So our practicing must take precedence over seeking knowledge and intellectually understanding. A peaceful mind is knowing.

WHAT AM I?

I am God's Son, complete and healed and whole, shining in the reflection of His Love. In me is His creation sanctified and guaranteed eternal life. In me is love perfected, fear impossible, and joy established without opposite. I am the holy home of God Himself. I am the Heaven where His Love resides. I am His holy Sinlessness Itself, for in my purity abides His Own.

I am forever an effect of God.

Father, I was created in Your Mind, a holy Thought that never left its home. I am forever Your Effect, and You forever and forever are my Cause. As You created me I have remained. Where You established me I still abide. And all Your attributes abide in me, because it is Your Will to have a son so like his Cause that Cause and Its Effect are indistinguishable. Let me know that I am an Effect of God, and so I have the power to create like You. And as it is in Heaven, so on earth. Your plan I follow here, and at the end I know that You will gather Your Effects into the tranquil Heaven of Your Love, where earth will vanish, and all separate thoughts unite in glory as the Son of God.

The statement "God created man in his own image and likeness" needs reinterpretation. "Image" can be understood as "thought," and "likeness" as "of a like quality." God did create spirit in His Own Thought and of a quality like to His Own. There *is* nothing else.

Spirit am I, a holy Son of God, Free of all limits, safe and healed and whole, free to forgive, and free to save the world.

I am as God created me! This single thought, held firmly in the mind, would save the world. These words are sacred, for they are the words God gave in answer to the world you made. By them it disappears, and all things seen within its misty clouds and vaporous illusions vanish as these words are spoken. For they come from God.

Here is the Word by which the Son became his Father's happiness, His Love and His completion. Here creation is proclaimed, and honored as it is. There is no dream these words will not dispel; no thought of sin and no illusion which the dream contains that will not fade away before their might. They are the trumpet of awakening that sounds around the world. The dead awake in answer to its call. And those who live and hear this sound will never look on death.

You are as God created you. These words dispel the night, and darkness is no more. The light is come today to bless the world.
For you have recognized the Son of God, and
in that recognition is the world's.

Author's Note: We are light, God's holy divine Light. We have forgotten this; therefore, it is the task of the Holy Spirit to reinterpret and remind us on behalf of God.

HOLY ENCOUNTERS

When you meet anyone, remember it is a holy encounter. As you see him you will see yourself. As you treat him you will treat yourself. As you think of him you will think of yourself. Never forget this, for in him you will find yourself or lose yourself. Whenever two Sons of God meet, they are given another chance at salvation. Do not leave anyone without giving salvation to him and receiving it yourself. For I am always there with you, in remembrance of *you*.

The goal of the curriculum, regardless of the teacher you choose, is "Know thyself." There is nothing else to seek. Everyone is looking for himself and for the power and glory he thinks he has lost. Whenever you are with anyone, you have another opportunity to find them. Your power and glory are in him because they are yours. The ego tries to find them in yourself alone, because it does not know where to look. The Holy Spirit teaches you that if you look only at yourself you cannot find yourself, because that is not what you are. Whenever you are with a brother, you are learning what you are because you are teaching what you are. He will respond either with pain or with joy, depending on which teacher you are following. He will be imprisoned or released according to your decision, and so will you. Never forget your responsibility to him, because it is your responsibility to yourself. Give him his place in the Kingdom and you will have yours.

The Kingdom cannot be found alone, and you who are the Kingdom cannot find yourself alone. You can encounter only part of yourself because you are part of God, Who is everything. His power and glory are everywhere, and you cannot be excluded from them. **The ego teaches that your strength is in you alone. The Holy Spirit teaches that all strength is in God and *therefore* in you.** God wills no one suffer. He does not will anyone to suffer for a wrong decision, including you. That is why He has given you the means for undoing it. Through His power and glory all your wrong decisions are undone completely, releasing you and your brother from every imprisoning thought any part of the Sonship holds. Wrong decisions have no power, because they are not true. The imprisonment they seem to produce is no more true than they are.

Power and glory belong to God alone. So do you. God gives whatever belongs to Him because He gives of Himself, and everything belongs to Him. Giving of yourself is the function He gave you. Fulfilling it perfectly will let you remember what you *have* of Him, and by this you will remember also what you *are* in Him. You cannot be powerless to do this, because this is your power. Glory is God's gift to you, because that is what He is. See this glory everywhere to remember what you are.

*Father, You gave me all Your Sons, to be my saviors
and my counselors in sight; the bearers of Your holy
Voice to me. In them are You reflected, and in
them does Christ look back upon me from my Self.
Let not Your Son forget Your holy Name.
Let not Your Son forget his holy Source.
Let not Your Son forget his Name is Yours.*

Author's Note: Jesus told to us: *"On these two Commandments hang all the law and the prophets. Love the Lord your God, with all your heart and all your mind. And love your neighbor as you love yourself."* He was teaching this same truth found here with *A Course in Miracles*: "As you see your brother you will see yourself." Jesus overlooked all other commandments and taught only love.

PEACE AND UNDERSTANDING

Those who remember always that they know nothing, and who have become willing to learn everything, will learn it. But whenever they trust themselves, they will not learn. They have destroyed their motivation for learning by thinking they already know. **Think not you understand anything until you pass the test of perfect peace, for peace and understanding go together and never can be found alone.** Each brings the other with it, for it is the law of God they be not separate. They are cause and effect, each to the other, so where one is absent the other cannot be.

Only those who recognize they cannot know unless the effects of understanding are with them, can really learn at all. For this it must be peace they want, and nothing else. Whenever you think you know, peace will depart from you, because you have abandoned the Teacher of peace. Whenever you fully realize that you know not, peace will return, for you will have invited Him to do so by abandoning the ego on behalf of Him. Call not upon the ego for anything; it is only this that you need do. The Holy Spirit will, of Himself, fill every mind that so makes room for Him.

Leave room for Him, and you will find yourself so filled with power that nothing will prevail against your peace. And this will be the test by which you recognize that you have understood.

You have one test, as sure as God, by which to recognize if what you learned is true. If you are wholly free of fear of any kind, and if all those who meet or even think of you share in your perfect peace, then you can be sure that you have learned God's lesson, and not your own. Unless all this is true, there are dark lessons in your mind that hurt and hinder you, and everyone around you. The absence of perfect peace means but one thing: You think you do not will for God's Son what his Father wills for him.

Make way for peace, and it will come. For understanding is in you, and from it peace will come.

Your task is not to seek for love, but merely to seek and find all of the barriers within yourself that you have built against it. It is not necessary to seek for what is true, but it is necessary to seek for what is false. Every illusion is one of fear, whatever form it takes. And the attempt to escape from one illusion into another must fail. If you seek love outside yourself you can be certain that you perceive hatred within, and are afraid of it. Yet peace will never come from the illusion of love, but only from its reality.

Author's Note: What we think we know—our beliefs and our opinions, and the judgments that stem from them—are the blocks that we have placed before the presence of God's Love. They are the factors that cancel out our peace, and offer suffering in their place. It is in our willingness to change our minds—to forgive and let our beliefs and opinions be replaced by truth—that we finally are able to escape suffering and welcome the return of peace. It is this shift that is the miracle!

WHAT ALWAYS WAS

This world you seem to live in is not home to you. And somewhere in your mind you know that this is true. A memory of home keeps haunting you, as if there were a place that called you to return, although you do not recognize the voice, nor what it is the voice reminds you of. Yet still you feel an alien here, from somewhere all unknown. Nothing so definite that you could say with certainty you are an exile here. Just a persistent feeling, sometimes not more than a tiny throb, at other times hardly remembered, actively dismissed, but surely to return to mind again.

When you are still an instant, when the world recedes from you, when valueless ideas cease to have value in your restless mind, then will you hear His Voice. So poignantly He calls to you that you will not resist Him longer. In that instant He will take you to His Home, and you will stay with Him in perfect stillness, silent and at peace, beyond all words, untouched by fear and doubt, sublimely certain that you are at home.

You have not lost your innocence. It is for this you yearn. This is your heart's desire. This is the voice you hear, and this the call which cannot be denied. Be still an instant and go home with Him, and be at peace a while.

God in His knowledge is not waiting, but His Kingdom is bereft while *you* wait. All the Sons of God are waiting for your return, just as you are waiting for theirs. Delay does not matter in eternity, but it is tragic in time. You have elected to be in time rather than eternity, and therefore believe you *are* in time. Yet your election is both free and alterable. You do not belong in time. Your place is only in eternity, where God Himself placed you forever.

In time, we exist for and with each other. In timelessness, we coexist with God.

Be quiet in your faith in Him Who loves you, and would lead you out of insanity. Madness may be your choice, but not your reality. Never forget the Love of God, Who has remembered you. For it is quite impossible that He could ever let His Son drop from the loving Mind wherein he was created, and where his abode was fixed in perfect peace forever.

Love waits on welcome, not on time, and the real world is but your welcome of what always was. Therefore the call of joy is in it, and your glad response is your awakening to what you have not lost.

Eternity is an idea of God, so the Holy Spirit understands it perfectly. Time is a belief of the ego, so the lower mind, which is the ego's domain, accepts it without question. The only aspect of time that is eternal is *now*.

Author's Note: When will we awaken to our true reality? How long will it take to recognize our true Self? When will we remember "What Always Was"? We are as close as the choice to teach only Love.

TO BE TRULY HELPFUL

You can do much on behalf of your own healing and that of others if, in a situation calling for help, you think of it this way:

I am here only to be truly helpful.
I am here to represent Him Who sent me.
I do not have to worry about what to say or what to do,
because He Who sent me will direct me.
I am content to be wherever He wishes,
knowing He goes there with me.
I will be healed as I let Him teach me to heal.

God is praised whenever any mind learns to be wholly helpful. This is impossible without being wholly harmless, because the two beliefs must coexist. The truly helpful are invulnerable, because they are not protecting their egos and so nothing can hurt them. Their helpfulness is their praise of God, and He will return their praise of Him because they are like Him, and they can rejoice together. God goes out to them and through them, and there is great joy throughout the Kingdom. Every mind that is changed adds to this joy with its individual willingness to share in it. The truly helpful are God's miracle workers, whom I direct until we are all united in the joy of the Kingdom. I will direct you to wherever you can be truly helpful, and to whoever can follow my guidance through you.

Step back in faith and let truth lead
the way. You know not where you go.
But One who knows goes with you.
Let Him lead you with the rest.

As God sent me to you so will I send you to others. And I will go to them with you, so we can teach them peace and union.

Author's Note: To be truly helpful is to be free of all judgment and condemnation, thus becoming a conduit for the Holy Spirit. To join in union is to praise God. To extend His Love is to praise God. Praise in the usual sense is meaningless, for God does not possess an ego. His only desire is for His Love to be shared and to reign.

LOVE WISHES TO BE KNOWN

The meaning of the Son of God lies solely in his relationship with his Creator. If it were elsewhere it would rest on contingency, but there *is* nothing else. And this is wholly loving and forever. Yet has the Son of God invented an unholy relationship between him and his Father. His real relationship is one of perfect union and unbroken continuity. The one he made is partial, self-centered, broken into fragments and full of fear. The one created by his Father is wholly Self-encompassing and Self-extending. The one he made is wholly self-destructive and self-limiting.

Nothing can show the contrast better than the experience of both a holy and an unholy relationship. The first is based on love, and rests on it serene and undisturbed. The body does not intrude upon it. Any relationship in which the body enters is based not on love, but on idolatry.

*Love wishes to be known, completely understood and shared.
It has no secrets; nothing that it would keep apart and hide.
It walks in sunlight, open-eyed and calm, in
smiling welcome and in sincerity so simple and
so obvious it cannot be misunderstood.*

But idols do not share. Idols accept, but never make return. They can be loved, but cannot love. They do not understand what they are offered, and any relationship in which they enter has lost its meaning. The love of them has made love meaningless. They live in secrecy, hating the sunlight and happy in the body's darkness, where they can hide and keep their secrets hidden along with them. And they have no relationships, for no one else is welcome there. They smile on no one, and those who smile on them they do not see.

Love has no darkened temples where mysteries are kept obscure and hidden from the sun. It does not seek for power, but for relationships. The body is the ego's chosen weapon for seeking power through relationships. And its relationships must be unholy, for what they are it does not even see. It wants them solely for the offerings on which its idols thrive. The rest it merely throws away, for all that it could offer is seen as valueless. Homeless, the ego seeks as many bodies as it can collect to place its idols in, and so establish them as temples to itself.

The Holy Spirit's temple is not a body, but a relationship.

Love's Arms are open to receive you, and give you peace forever.

Author's Note: This teaching is trying to help us see past all form as being the source of all our happiness, joy, and peace of mind. Bodies cannot join, and thus cannot share, and thus cannot offer joy. It is only through relationships of the mind/spirit where all joy and happiness and peace of mind are found. To join in mind and spirit is to share. Inward relationships are the only grounds for freedom.

THE SOLE CRITERION

The emphasis of this course always remains the same; it is at this moment that complete salvation is offered you, and it is at this moment that you can accept it. This is still your one responsibility. Atonement might be equated with total escape from the past and total lack of interest in the future. Heaven is here. There is nowhere else. Heaven is now. There is no other time. No teaching that does not lead to this is of concern to God's teachers. All beliefs will point to this if properly interpreted. In this sense, it can be said that their truth lies in their usefulness. All beliefs that lead to progress should be honored. This is the sole criterion this course requires. No more than this is necessary.

Heaven is your home, and being in God it must also be in you.

Heaven is chosen consciously. The choice cannot be made until alternatives are accurately seen and understood. All that is veiled in shadows must be raised to understanding, to be judged again, this time with Heaven's help. And all mistakes in judgment that the mind had made before are open to correction, as the truth dismisses them as causeless. Now are they without effects. They cannot be concealed, because their nothingness is recognized.

What is Heaven but a song of gratitude and love and praise by everything created to the Source of its creation?

The Bible repeatedly states that you should praise God. This hardly means that you should tell Him how wonderful He is. He has no ego with which to accept such praise, and no perception with which to judge it. But unless you take your part in the creation, His joy is not complete because yours is incomplete. And this He does know. He knows it in His Own Being and its experience of His Son's experience. The constant going out of His Love is blocked when His channels are closed, and He is lonely when the minds He created do not communicate fully with Him.

God has kept your Kingdom for you, but He cannot share His joy with you until you know it with your whole mind.

To be in the Kingdom is merely to focus your full attention on it.

Author's Note: The statement: "Heaven is chosen, Heaven is here, Heaven is now," is what Jesus was teaching in Scripture when he said: "The Kingdom of Heaven is at hand." Jesus knew that Heaven was obtainable here and now in this present moment, this "holy instant." Being timeless, Heaven is nowhere but here and now. We are capable of experiencing heaven now, consciously choosing to extend God's Love. You could even say that our relationship with Truth/God is vertical rather than horizontal. Both past and future are nonexistent. Eternity has nothing to do with life after death or the hereafter, as we call it. This is it! Here and now! Eternity *is* timelessness. We must learn to find our peace in God—in the here and now because it cannot be found anywhere else. This is our function here—to find Heaven; to live in eternity here and now because there is no other time or space. We awaken to this only through true forgiveness.

GOD'S ONLY TREASURE

We are the joint will of the Sonship, whose Wholeness is for all. We begin the journey back by setting out together, and gather in our brothers as we continue together. **Every gain in our strength is offered for all, so they too can lay aside their weakness and add their strength to us. God's welcome waits for us all, and He will welcome us as I am welcoming you.** Forget not the Kingdom of God for anything the world has to offer.

> *The world can add nothing to the power and the*
> *glory of God and His holy Sons, but it can blind*
> *the Sons to the Father if they behold it. You cannot*
> *behold the world and know God. Only one is true.*
> *I am come to tell you that the choice of*
> *which is true is not yours to make. If it were,*
> *you would have destroyed yourself.*
> *Yet God did not will the destruction of His creations,*
> *having created them for eternity. His Will saved you,*
> *not from yourself but from your illusion of*
> *yourself. He has saved you "for" yourself.*

Let us glorify Him Whom the world denies, for over His Kingdom the world has no power. No one created by God can find joy in anything except the eternal; not because he is deprived of anything else, but because nothing else is worthy of him. What God and His Sons create is eternal, and in this and this only is Their joy.

Listen to the story of the prodigal son, and learn what God's treasure is and yours: This son of a loving father left his home and thought he had squandered everything for nothing of any value, although he had not understood its worthlessness at the time. He was ashamed to return to his father, because he thought he had hurt him. Yet when he came home the father welcomed him with joy, because the son himself *was* his father's treasure. He wanted nothing else.

God wants only His Son because His Son is His only treasure. You want your creations as He wants His. Can the creations of God Himself take joy in what is not real? And what is real except the creations of God and those that are created like His? Your creations love you as you love your Father for the gift of creation. There is no other gift that is eternal, and therefore there is no other gift that is true. How, then can you accept anything else or give anything else, and expect joy in return? And what else but joy would you want? **You made neither yourself nor your function. You made only the decision to be unworthy of both.** Yet you cannot make yourself unworthy because you are the treasure of God, and what He values is valuable. There can be no question of its worth, because its value lies in God's sharing Himself with it and establishing its value forever.

Your function is to add to God's treasure by creating yours. His Will *to* you is His Will *for* you. He would not withhold creation from you because His joy is in it. You cannot find joy except as God does. His joy lay in creating you, and he extends His Fatherhood to you so that you can extend yourself as he did. You do not understand this because you do not understand Him. No one who does not accept his function can understand what it is, and no one can accept his function unless he knows what *he* is. Creation is the Will of God. His Will created you to create. Your will was not created separate from His, so you must will as He wills.

An "unwilling will" does not mean anything, being a contradiction in terms that actually means nothing. When you think you are unwilling to will with God, you are not thinking. God's Will *is* thought. It cannot be contradicted *by* thought. God does not contradict Himself, and His Sons, who are like Him, cannot contradict themselves or Him. Yet their thought is so powerful that they can even imprison the mind of God's Son, if they so choose. This choice does make the Son's function unknown to him, but never to his Creator. And because it is not unknown to his Creator, it is forever knowable to him.

There is no question but one you should ever ask of yourself: "Do I want to know my Father's Will for me?" He will not hide it. He has revealed it to me because I asked it of Him, and learned of what He had already given. Our function is to work together, because apart from each other we cannot function at all. The whole power of God's Son lies in all of us, but not in any of us alone. God would not have us be alone because *He* does not will to be alone. That is why He created His Son, and gave him the power to create with Him. Our creations are as holy as we are, and we are the Sons of God Himself, as holy as He is. Through our creations we extend our love, and thus increase the joy of the Holy Trinity (Creator, His Voice for Love, and our brother Jesus—all of which we are part of). You do not understand this, because you who are God's Own treasure do not regard yourself as valuable. Given this belief, you cannot understand anything.

I share with God the knowledge of the value He puts upon you. My devotion to you is of Him, being born of my knowledge of myself and Him. We cannot be separated. Whom God has joined cannot be separated, and God has joined all His Sons with Himself. Can you be separated from your life and your being?

The journey to God is merely the reawakening of the knowledge of
where you are always, and what you are forever.
It is a journey without distance to a
goal that has never changed.

Truth can only be experienced. It cannot be described and it cannot be explained. I can make you aware of the conditions of truth, but the experience is of God. Together we can meet its conditions, but truth will dawn upon you of itself.

What God has willed for you *is* yours. He has given His Will to His treasure, whose treasure it is. Your heart lies where your treasure is, as His does. You who are beloved of God are wholly blessed. Learn this of me, and free the holy will of all those who are as blessed as you are.

As you perceive the holy companions who travel with you,
you will realize that there is no journey,
but only an awakening.

Author's Note: It is a *"journey without distance"* because the journey is within our minds. We have never left our place on high. We are only dreaming otherwise.

THE PURPOSE OF YOUR LEARNING
This is a course in mind training.

This is a course in how to know yourself. You have taught
what you are, but have not let what you are teach you.
Come therefore unto me, and learn of the truth in you.

The purpose of your learning is to enable you
to bring the quiet with you, and to heal distress and
turmoil. This is not done by avoiding them and seeking
a haven of isolation for yourself. You will yet learn that
peace is part of you, and requires only that you be there
to embrace any situation in which you are. And finally
you will learn that there is no limit to where you are, so
that your peace is everywhere, as you are.

Yet your willingness to learn of Him depends on
your willingness to question everything you learned of
yourself, for you who learned amiss should not be your
own teacher.

The Holy Spirit needs a happy learner, in whom
His mission can be happily accomplished. You who are
steadfastly devoted to misery must first recognize that
you are miserable and not happy. The Holy Spirit cannot
teach without this contrast, for you believe that misery *is*
happiness.

Contrast and differences are necessary teaching aids, for
by them you learn what to avoid and what to seek.

The Holy Spirit, seeing where you are but knowing
you are elsewhere, begins His lesson in simplicity with the
fundamental teaching that *truth* is true. This is the hardest
lesson you will ever learn, and in the end the only one.
Simplicity is very difficult for twisted minds.

The truth is true. Nothing else matters, nothing else
is real, and everything beside it is not there.
Let Me make the one distinction for you that
you cannot make, but need to learn.
Offer your faith to Me, and I will place it
gently in the holy place where it belongs.
You will not find deception there,
but only the simple truth. And you will love
it because you will understand it.

When you teach anyone that truth is true, you learn
it with him. And so you learn that what seemed hardest
was the easiest. Learn to be a happy learner. You will never
learn how to make nothing everything. Yet see that this
has been your goal, and recognize how foolish it has been.
Be glad it is undone, for when you look at it in simple
honesty, it *is* undone. I said before, "Be not content with
nothing," for you have believed that nothing could content
you. *It is not so.*

If you would be a happy learner, you must give
everything you have learned to the Holy Spirit, to be
unlearned for you. And then begin to learn the joyous
lessons that come quickly on the firm foundation that
truth is true. For what is builded there is true, and built on
truth. The universe of learning will open up before you in
all its gracious simplicity. With truth before you, you will
not look back.

Author's Note: True forgiveness is just that: to give
everything to the Holy Spirit. To For—Give is to Give Up.
To relinquish control is to be given understanding.

Healing must be as complete as fear,
for love cannot enter where there
is one spot of fear to mar its welcome.

THE WORLD'S ONLY PURPOSE

Forget not that the healing of God's Son is all the world is for. That is the only purpose the Holy Spirit sees in it, and thus the only one it has. Until you see the healing of the Son as all you wish to be accomplished by the world, by time and all appearances, you will not know the Father nor yourself. For you will use the world for what is not its purpose, and will not escape its laws of violence and death. Yet it is given you to be beyond its laws in all respects, in every way and every circumstance, in all temptation to perceive what is not there, and all belief God's Son can suffer pain because he sees himself as he is not.

You cannot understand yourself alone. This is because you have no meaning apart from your rightful place in the Sonship, and the rightful place of the Sonship is God. This is your life, your eternity and your Self. It is of this that the Holy Spirit reminds you. It is this that the Holy Spirit sees.

Can you imagine what it means to have no cares, no worries, no anxieties, but merely to be perfectly calm and quiet all the time? Yet this is what time is for; to learn just that and nothing more.

Father, we would return our minds to You. We have betrayed them, held them in a vise of bitterness, and frightened them with thoughts of violence and death. Now would we rest again in You, as You created us.

All healing is release from the past. That is why the Holy Spirit is the only Healer. He teaches that the past does not exist, a fact which belongs to the sphere of knowledge, and which therefore no one in the world can know.

My mind is preoccupied with past thoughts. This idea is, of course, the reason you see only the past. It is the reason why nothing that you see means anything. It is the reason why you have given everything you see all the meaning that it has for you. It is the reason why you do not understand anything you see. It is the reason why your thoughts do not mean anything, and why they are like the things you see. It is the reason why you are never upset for the reason you think. It is the reason why you are upset because you see something that is not there.

Give the past to Him who can change
your mind about it for you.
But first, be sure you fully realize what you
have made the past to represent, and why.

Unless the past is over in my mind, the real world must escape my sight. For I am really looking nowhere, seeing but what is not there. How can I then perceive the world forgiveness offers? This the past was made to hide, for this the world that can be looked on only now. It has no past. For what can be forgiven but the past, and if it is forgiven it is gone.

Take this very instant, now, and think of it as all there
is of time. Nothing can reach you here out of the past,
and it is here that you are completely absolved,
completely free and wholly without condemnation.

THE MESSAGE OF THE CRUCIFIXION AND THE RESURRECTION

There is a positive interpretation of the crucifixion that is wholly devoid of fear, and therefore wholly benign in what it teaches, if it is properly understood.

The crucifixion is nothing more than an extreme example.

Its value, like the value of any teaching device, lies solely in the kind of learning it facilitates. It can be, and has been, misunderstood. This is only because the fearful are apt to perceive fearfully. I have already told you that you can always call on me to share my decision, and thus make it stronger. I have also told you that the crucifixion was the last useless journey the Sonship need take, and that it represents release from fear to anyone who understands it. While I emphasized only the resurrection before, the purpose of the crucifixion and how it actually led to the resurrection was not clarified then. Nevertheless, it has a definite contribution to make to your own life, and if you will consider it without fear, it will help you understand your own role as a teacher.

You have probably reacted for years as if you were being crucified. This is a marked tendency of the separated, who always refuse to consider what they have done to themselves. Projection means anger, anger fosters assault, and assault promotes fear. The real meaning of the crucifixion lies in the *apparent* intensity of the assault of some of the Sons of God upon another. This, of course, is impossible, and must be fully understood *as* impossible. Otherwise, I cannot serve as a model for learning.

*The ultimate purpose of projections
is always to get rid of guilt.*

The crucifixion did not establish the Atonement; the resurrection did. Many sincere Christians have misunderstood this. No one who is free of the belief in scarcity could possibly make this mistake. If the crucifixion is seen from an upside-down point of view, it does appear as if God permitted and even encouraged one of His Sons to suffer because he was good. This particularly unfortunate interpretation, which arose out of projection, has led many people to be bitterly afraid of God. Such anti-religious concepts enter into many religions. Yet the real Christian should pause and ask, "How could this be?" Is it likely that God Himself would be capable of the kind of thinking which His Own words have clearly stated is unworthy of His Son?

Persecution frequently results in an attempt to "justify" the terrible misperception that God Himself persecuted His Own Son on behalf of salvation. The very words are meaningless. Can you believe our Father really thinks this way? It is so essential that all such thinking be dispelled that we must be sure that nothing of this kind remains in your mind. I was not "punished" because you were bad. The wholly benign lesson the Atonement teaches is lost if it is tainted with this kind of distortion in any way.

Assault can ultimately be made only on the body. There is little doubt that one body can assault another, and can even destroy it. Yet if destruction itself is impossible, anything that is destructible cannot be real. Its destruction, therefore, does not justify anger. To the extent to which you believe that it does, you are accepting false premises and teaching them to others. **The message the crucifixion was intended to teach was that it is not necessary to perceive any form of assault in persecution, because you cannot *be* persecuted. If you respond with anger, you must be equating yourself with the destructible, and are therefore regarding yourself insanely.**

I have made it perfectly clear that I am like you and you are like me, but our fundamental equality can be demonstrated only through joint decision. You are free to perceive yourself as persecuted if you choose. When you do choose to react that way, however, you might remember that I was persecuted as the world judges, and did not share this evaluation for myself. And because I did not share it, I did not strengthen it. I therefore offered a different interpretation of attack, and one which I want to share with you. If you will believe it, you will help me teach it.

As I have said before, "As you teach so shall you learn." **If you react as if you are persecuted, you are teaching persecution. This is not a lesson a Son of God should want to teach if he is to realize his own salvation. Rather teach your own perfect immunity, which is the truth in you, and realize that it cannot be assailed.** Do not try to protect it yourself, or you are believing that it is assailable. You are not asked to be crucified, which was part of my own teaching contribution. You are merely asked to follow my example in the face of much less extreme temptations to misperceive, and not to accept them as false justifications for anger. There can be no justification for the unjustifiable. Do not believe there is, and do not teach that there is. Remember always that what you believe you will teach. Believe with me, and we will become equal as teachers.

Your resurrection is your reawakening. I am the model for rebirth, but rebirth itself is merely the dawning on your mind of what is already in it. God placed it there Himself, and so it is true forever. I believed in it, and therefore accepted it as true for me. Help me to teach it to our brothers in the name of the Kingdom of God, but first believe that it is true for you, or you will teach amiss.

Very simply, the resurrection is the overcoming or surmounting of death. It is a reawakening or a rebirth; a change of mind about the meaning of the world. It is the acceptance of the Holy Spirit's interpretation of the world's purpose; the acceptance of the Atonement for oneself. It is the end of dreams of misery, and the glad awareness of the Holy Spirit's final dream. The resurrection is the denial of death, being the assertion of life. Thus is all the thinking of the world reversed entirely. Life is now recognized as salvation, and pain and misery of any kind perceived as hell. Love is no longer feared, but gladly welcomed. Idols have disappeared, and the remembrance of God shines unimpeded across the world.

The crucifixion cannot be shared because it is the symbol of projection, but the resurrection is the symbol of sharing because the reawakening of every Son of God is necessary to enable the Sonship to know its wholeness. Only this is knowledge.

The message of the crucifixion is perfectly clear: *Teach only love, for that is what you are.*

If you interpret the crucifixion in any other way, you are using it as a weapon for assault rather than as the call for peace for which it was intended.

Each day, each hour and minute, even each second, you are deciding between the crucifixion and the resurrection; between the ego and the Holy Spirit. The ego is the choice for guilt; the Holy Spirit the choice for guiltlessness. The power of decision is all that is yours. What you can decide between is fixed, because there are no alternatives except truth and illusion. And there is no overlap between them, because they are opposites which cannot be reconciled and cannot both be true. You are guilty or guiltless, bound or free, unhappy or happy.

THE DWELLING PLACE

There is nothing outside you. That is what you must ultimately learn, for it is the realization that the Kingdom of Heaven is restored to you. For God created only this, and He did not depart from it nor leave it separate from Himself. The Kingdom of Heaven is the dwelling place of the Son of God, who left not his Father and dwells not apart from Him. Heaven is not a place nor a condition. It is merely an awareness of perfect Oneness, and the knowledge that there is nothing else; nothing outside this Oneness, and nothing else within.

What could God give but knowledge of Himself? What else is there to give? The belief that you could give and get something else, something outside yourself, has cost you the awareness of Heaven and of your identity. And you have done a stranger thing than you yet realize. You have displaced your guilt to your body from your mind. Yet a body cannot be guilty, for it can do nothing of itself.

Minds are joined; bodies are not—the mind cannot attack, but it can deceive itself. And this is all it does when it believes it has attacked the body. It can project its guilt, but it will not lose it through projection.

The body is outside you, and but seems to surround you, shutting you off from others and keeping you apart from them, and them from you. It is not there. There is no barrier between God and His Son, nor can His Son be separated from himself except in illusions. This is not his reality, though he believes it is. Yet this could only be if God were wrong. God would have had to create differently, and to have separated Himself from His Son to make this possible. He would have had to create different things, and to establish different orders of reality, only some of which were love. Yet love must be forever like itself, changeless forever, and forever without alternative. And so it is. You cannot put a barrier around yourself, because God placed none between Himself and you.

Everyone has experienced what he would call a sense of being transported beyond himself. This feeling of liberation far exceeds the dream of freedom sometimes hoped for in special relationships. It is a sense of actual escape from limitations. If you will consider what this "transportation" really entails, you will realize that it is a sudden unawareness of the body, and a joining of yourself and something else in which your mind enlarges to encompass it. It becomes part of you, as you unite with it. And both become whole, as neither is perceived as separate. What really happens is that you have given up the illusion of limited awareness, and lost your fear of union. And while this lasts you are not uncertain of your identity, and would not limit it. You have escaped from fear to peace, asking no questions of reality, but merely accepting it.

Come to this place of refuge, where you can be yourself in peace. Not through destruction, not through a breaking out, but merely a quiet melting in. For peace will join you there, simply because you have been willing to let go the limits you have placed upon love, and joined it where it is and where it led you, in answer to its gentle call to be at peace.

Inward is sanity; insanity is outside you.

Author's Note: We can deny that we are one with God, but there is nothing that can alter this fact. It is only through the experience of miracles that we are reminded of this truth. Once revelation has been given us, all fear and doubt are completely and temporarily suspended, and the remembrance of this truth become obvious and can no longer be denied.

Healing is the effect of minds that join,
as sickness comes from minds
that separate.

MANY PATHS/ONE TRUTH

There is a course for every teacher of God. The form of the course varies greatly. So do the particular teaching aids involved. But the content of the course never changes. Its central theme is always:

God's Son is guiltless, and in his innocence is his salvation.

It can be taught by actions or thoughts; in words or soundlessly; in any language or in no language; in any place or time or manner. It does not matter who the teacher was before he heard the Call. He has become a savior by his answering. He has seen someone else as himself. He has therefore found his own salvation and the salvation of the world. In his rebirth is the world reborn.

They come from all over the world. They come from all religions and from no religion. They are the ones who have answered. The Call is universal. It goes on all the time everywhere. It calls for teachers to speak for It and redeem the world. Many hear It, but few will answer. Yet it is all a matter of time. Everyone will answer in the end, but the end can be a long, long way off. It is because of this that the plan of the teachers was established. Their function is to save time. Each one begins as a single light, but with the Call at its center it is a light that cannot be limited. And each one saves a thousand years of time as the world judges it. To the Call Itself time has no meaning.

God's guiltless Son is only light. There is no darkness in him anywhere, for he is whole.

Call all your brothers to witness to his wholeness, as I am calling you to join with me. Each voice has a part in the song of redemption, the hymn of gladness and thanksgiving for the light to the Creator of light. The holy light that shines forth from God's Son is the witness that his light is of his Father.

Ask for light and learn that you *are* light. If you want understanding and enlightenment you will learn it, because your decision to learn it is the decision to listen to the Teacher who knows of light, and can therefore teach it to you. There is no limit on your learning because there is no limit on your mind. There is no limit on His teaching because He was created to teach. Understanding His function perfectly He fulfills it perfectly, because that is His joy and yours.

Can you offer guilt to God? You cannot, then, offer it to His son. For they are not apart, and gifts to one are offered to the other. You know not God because you know not this. And yet you do know God and also this.

Author's Note: We block our remembrance of God when we project guilt upon another, for in doing so we veil the truth from our awareness. It is only by forgiveness that the light returns to our minds, where Love comes to take its place. Remember, light *is* understanding! To accuse and to blame is to *not* understand.

"*In our struggle for freedom, truth is the only weapon we possess.*"

Dalai Lama

CHAPTER II

Forgiveness
and the
Holy
Relationship

Miracles transcend the body.
They are sudden shifts into invisibility,
away from the bodily level.
That is why they heal.

WHAT IS FORGIVENESS?

Forgiveness recognizes what you thought your brother did to you has not occurred. It does not pardon sins and make them real. It sees there was no sin. And in that view are all your sins forgiven. What is sin, except a false idea about God's Son? Forgiveness merely sees its falsity, and therefore lets it go. What then is free to take its place is now the Will of God.

An unforgiving thought is one which makes a judgment that it will not raise to doubt, although it is not true. The mind is closed, and will not be released. The thought protects projection, tightening its chains, so that distortions are more veiled and more obscure; less easily accessible to doubt, and further kept from reason.

An unforgiving thought does many things. In frantic action it pursues its goal, twisting and overturning what it sees as interfering with its chosen path. Distortion is its purpose, and the means by which it would accomplish it as well. It sets about its furious attempts to smash reality, without concern for anything that would appear to pose a contradiction to its point of view.

Forgiveness, on the other hand, is still, and quietly does nothing. It offends no aspect of reality, nor seeks to twist it to appearances it likes. It merely looks, and waits, and judges not.

> *He who would not forgive must judge, for*
> *he must justify his failure to forgive.*
> *But he who would forgive himself must learn*
> *to welcome truth exactly as it is.*

The unforgiving are sick, believing they are unforgiven. The hanging-on to guilt, its hugging-close and sheltering, its loving protection and alert defense—all this is but the grim refusal to forgive. "God may not enter here" the sick repeat, over and over, while they mourn their loss and yet rejoice in it. Healing occurs as a patient begins to hear the dirge he sings, and questions its validity. Until he hears it, he cannot understand that it is he who sings it to himself. To hear it is the first step in recovery. To question it must then become his choice.

Forgiveness is unknown in Heaven, where the need for it would be inconceivable. However, in this world, forgiveness is a necessary correction for all the mistakes that we have made. To offer forgiveness is the only way for us to have it, for it reflects the law of Heaven that giving and receiving are the same. Heaven is the natural state of all the Sons of God as He created them. Such is their reality forever. It has not changed because it has been forgotten.

Forgiveness is the means by which we will remember. Through forgiveness the thinking of the world is reversed. The forgiven world becomes the gate of Heaven, because by its mercy we can at last forgive ourselves. Holding no one prisoner to guilt, we become free. Acknowledging Christ in all our brothers, we recognize His presence in ourselves. Forgetting all our misperceptions, and with nothing from the past to hold us back, we can remember God. Beyond this, Learning cannot go. When we are ready, God Himself will take the final step in our return to Him.

> *Once forgiveness has been accepted, prayer in the*
> *usual sense becomes utterly meaningless.*
> *The prayer for forgiveness is nothing more than a request*
> *that you may be able to recognize what you already have.*

As prayer is always for yourself, so is forgiveness always given you. It is impossible to forgive another, for it is only your sins you see in him. You want to see them there, and not in you. That is why forgiveness of another is an illusion. Yet it is the only happy dream in all the world; the only one that does not lead to death. Only in someone else can you forgive yourself, for you have called him guilty of your sins, and in him must your innocence now be found. Who but the sinful need to be forgiven? And do not even think you can see sin in anyone except yourself.

Forgiveness is not pity, which but seeks to
pardon what it thinks to be the truth.
Good cannot "be" returned for evil, for forgiveness
does not first establish sin and then forgive it.

Author's Note: Let us pause a minute and reflect on what true forgiveness is and what it offers us and others. Forgiveness is not pardon, nor is it a favor to bestow upon another. Forgiveness can only be true if it sets both giver and receiver free. Does sin free? Does pardon free? Do hateful favors free? No, they do not. Then it must be that true forgiveness means something we do not understand. Sin, pardon, and hateful favors are judgments and "evil" transgressions; all our attack thoughts and mistakes—these are what we give up. We lay these forms of fear that burden our minds at the altar of Truth within, and in return we are graced with peace of mind. Now has the window been opened for understanding.

WHAT IS SIN?

Sin is insanity. It is the means by which the mind is driven mad, and seeks to let illusions take the place of truth. And being mad, it sees illusions where the truth

should be, and where it really is. Sin gave the body eyes, for what is there the sinless would behold? What need have they of sights or sounds or touch? What would they hear to reach to grasp? What would they sense at all? To sense is not to know. And truth can be but filled with knowledge, and with nothing else.

Sin is the home of all illusions, which but stand for things
imagined, issuing from thoughts that are untrue.

Sin is the symbol of attack. Behold it anywhere, and I will suffer. For forgiveness is the only means whereby Christ's vision comes to me. Let me accept what His sight shows me as the simple truth, and I am healed completely. Brother, come and let me look on you. Your loveliness reflects my own. Your sinlessness is mine. You stand forgiven, and I stand with you.

So would I look on everyone today. My brothers are Your Sons. Your Fatherhood created them, and gave them all to me as part of You, and my own Self as well. Today I honor You through them, and thus I hope this day to recognize my Self.

How long, O Son of God, will you maintain the game of sin? Shall we not put away these sharp-edged children's toys? How soon will you be ready to come home? Perhaps today? There is no sin. Creation is unchanged. Would you still hold return to Heaven back? How long, O holy Son of God, how long?

Forgive your brother, and you cannot separate
yourself from him nor from his Father.
You need no forgiveness, for the wholly pure have never sinned.

TO FORGET WHO YOU ARE

You who were created by love like itself can hold no grievances and know your Self. To hold a grievance is to forget who you are. To hold a grievance is to see yourself as a body. To hold a grievance is to let the ego rule your mind and to condemn the body to death. Perhaps you do not yet fully realize just what holding grievances does to your mind. It seems to split you off from your Source and make you unlike Him. It makes you believe that He is like what you think you have become, for no one can conceive of his Creator as unlike himself.

Shut off from your Self, which remains aware of Its likeness to Its Creator, your Self seems to sleep, while the part of your mind that weaves illusions in its sleep appears to be awake. Can all this arise from holding grievances? Oh, yes! For he who holds grievances denies he was created by love, and his Creator has become fearful to him in his dream of hate. Who can dream of hatred and not fear God?

It is as sure that those who hold grievances will redefine God in their own image, as it is certain that God created them like Himself, and defined them as part of Him. It is as sure that those who hold grievances will suffer guilt, as it is certain that those who forgive will find peace. It is as sure that those who hold grievances will forget who they are, as it is certain that those who forgive will remember.

Forgiveness opens up the way to truth, which has been blocked by dreams of guilt. Now are you free to follow in the way your true forgiveness opens up to you.

For if one brother has received this gift of you, the door is open to yourself.

Would you not be willing to relinquish your grievances if you believed all this were so? Perhaps you do not think you can let your grievances go. That, however, is simply a matter of motivation. Today we will try to find out how you would feel without them. If you succeed even by ever so little, there will never be a problem in motivation ever again.

Love holds no grievances. I would wake to my Self by laying all my grievances aside and wakening in Him.

Judgment was made to be a weapon used against the truth. It separates what it is being used against, and sets it off as if it were a thing apart. And then it makes of it what you would have it be. It judges what it cannot understand, because it cannot see totality and therefore judges falsely. Let us not use it today, but make a gift of it to Him Who has a different use for it. He will relieve us of the agony of all the judgments we have made against ourselves, and re-establish peace of mind by giving us God's Judgment of His Son.

Author's Note: God's Judgment is always "for" us and never "against" us. His Judgment is always healing; a correction of our faulty choices. It reminds us of our wholeness in Him—forever pure, forever innocent, and free of all condemnation. Forgiveness releases all grievances and worldly judgments, thus allowing God's loving judgment to take their place.

OUR INTERFERENCE: WHAT NEEDS TO BE UNDONE

Where learning ends there God begins, for learning ends before Him Who is complete where He begins, and where there *is* no end. It is not for us to dwell on what cannot be attained. There is too much to learn. The readiness for knowledge still must be attained.

Love is not learned. Its meaning lies within itself. And learning ends when you have recognized all it is "not."

That is the interference; that is what needs to be undone. **Love is not learned, because there never was a time in which you knew it not. Learning is useless in the Presence of your Creator, Whose acknowledgment of you and yours of Him so far transcend all learning that everything you learned is meaningless, replaced forever by the knowledge of love and its one meaning.**

Your relationship with your brother has been uprooted from the world of shadows, and its unholy purpose has been safely brought through the barriers of guilt, washed with forgiveness, and set shining and firmly rooted in the world of light. From there it calls to you to follow the course it took, lifted high above the darkness and gently placed before the gates of Heaven. The holy instant in which you and your brother were united is but the messenger of love, sent from beyond forgiveness to remind you of all that lies beyond. Yet it is through forgiveness that it will be remembered.

And when the memory of God has come to you in the holy place of forgiveness you will remember nothing else, and memory will be as useless as learning, for your only purpose will be creating. Yet this you cannot know until every perception has been cleansed and purified, and finally removed forever. **Forgiveness removes only the untrue, lifting the shadows from the world and carrying it, safe and sure within its gentleness, to the bright world of new and clean perception. There is your purpose *now*. And it is there that peace awaits you.**

Forgiveness is the means appointed for perception's ending. Knowledge is restored after perception first is changed, and then gives way entirely to what remains forever past its highest reach. For sights and sounds, at best, can serve but to recall the memory that lies beyond them all. Forgiveness sweeps away distortions, and opens the hidden altar to the truth. Its lilies shine into the mind, and call it to return and look within, to find what it has vainly sought without. For here, and only here, is peace of mind restored, for this the dwelling place of God Himself!

In quiet may forgiveness wipe away my dreams of separation and of sin. Then let me, Father, look within, and find Your promise of my sinlessness is kept; Your Word remains unchanged within my mind, Your Love is still abiding in my heart.

WHAT IS CHRIST?

Christ is God's Son as He created Him. He is the Self we share, uniting us with one another, and with God as well. He is the Thought which still abides within the Mind that is His Source. He has not left His holy home, nor lost the innocence in which He was created. He abides unchanged forever in the Mind of God.

Christ is the link that keeps you one with God, and guarantees that separation is no more than an illusion of despair, for hope forever will abide in Him. Your mind is part of His, and His of yours. He is the part in which God's Answer lies; where all decisions are already made, and dreams are over. He remains untouched by anything the body's eyes perceive. For though in Him His Father placed the means for your salvation, yet does He remain the Self Who, like His Father, knows no sin.

Home of the Holy Spirit, and at home in God alone, does Christ remain at peace within the Heaven of your holy mind. This is the only part of you that has reality in truth. The rest is dreams. Yet will these dreams be given unto Christ, to fade before His glory and reveal your holy Self, the Christ, to you at last.

The Holy Spirit is the idea of healing. Being thought, the idea gains as it is shared. Being the Call "for" God, it is also the idea "of" God.

The Holy Spirit reaches from the Christ in you to all your dreams, and bid them come to Him, to be translated into truth. He will exchange them for the final dream which God appointed as the end of dreams. For when forgiveness rests upon the world and peace has come to every Son of God, what could there be to keep things separate, for what remains to see except Christ's face?

Christ waits for your acceptance of Him as yourself, and of His Wholeness as yours. Christ is the extension of the Love and the loveliness of God, as perfect as His Creator and at peace with Him.

There is no need for help to enter Heaven for you have never left. But there is need for help beyond yourself as you are circumscribed by false beliefs of your identity, which God alone established in reality. Helpers are given you in many forms, although upon the altar they are one. Beyond each one there is a Thought of God, and this will never change. But they have names which differ for a time, for time needs symbols, being itself unreal. Their names are legion, but we will not go beyond the names the course itself employs. God does not help because He knows no need. But He creates all Helpers of His Son while he believes his fantasies are true. Thank God for them for they will lead you home.

The name of *Jesus* is the name of one who was a man but saw the face of Christ in all his brothers and remembered God. So he became identified with *Christ*, a man no longer, but at one with God. The man was an illusion, for he seemed to be a separate being, walking by himself, within a body that appeared to hold his self from Self, as all illusions do. Yet who can save unless he sees illusions and then identifies them as what they are? Jesus remains a savior because he saw the false without accepting it as true. And Christ needed his form that He might appear to men and save them from their own illusions.

*The sight of Christ is all there is to see. The
song of Christ is all there is to hear.
The hand of Christ is all there is to hold. There
is no journey but to walk with Him.*

*Come unto me who holds it open for you, for while
I live it cannot be shut, and I live forever.
God is my life and yours, and nothing
is denied by God to His Son.*

Is he God's only helper? No, indeed. For Christ takes many forms with different names until their oneness can be recognized. But Jesus is for you the bearer of Christ's single message of the Love of God.

Christ is at God's altar, waiting to welcome His Son. But come wholly without condemnation, for otherwise you will believe that the door is barred and you cannot enter. The door is not barred, and it is impossible that you cannot enter the place where God would have you be. But love yourself with the Love of Christ, for so does your Father love you. You can refuse to enter, but you cannot bar the door that Christ holds open.

Not one does Christ forget. But you will remember Him until you look on all as He does.

Author's Note: What is Christ? It is God's greatness— His Truth, which He placed within our minds. It is the extension of the Love of God. Jesus, our brother and teacher, modeled perfectly the Christ Mind. He is due our respect and love simply because he remains a model for our complete awareness of God!

*Christ is Mind—it is the thought without limitation,
forever expanding into the formlessness of God.*

Paul Ferrini

WHAT PERCEPTION SEES

From knowledge and perception respectively, two distinct thought systems arise which are opposite in every respect. In the realm of knowledge no thoughts exist apart from God, because God and His Creation share one Will. The world of perception, however, is made by the belief in opposites and separate wills, in perpetual conflict with each other and with God. What perception sees and hears appears to be real because it permits into awareness only what conforms to the wishes of the perceiver. This leads to a world of illusions, a world which needs constant defense precisely because it is not real.

When you have been caught in the world of perception you are caught in a dream. You cannot escape without help, because everything your senses show merely witnesses to the reality of the dream. God has provided the Answer, the only Way out, the true Helper. It is the function of His Voice, His Holy Spirit, to mediate between the two worlds. He can do this because, while on the one hand He knows the truth, on the other He also recognizes our illusions, but without believing in them. **It is the Holy Spirit's goal to help us escape from the dream world by teaching us how to reverse our thinking and unlearn our mistakes. Forgiveness is the Holy Spirit's great learning aid in bringing this thought reversal about. However, the Course has its own definition of what forgiveness really is just as it defines the world in its own way.**

The world we see merely reflects our own internal frame of reference—the dominate ideas, wishes and emotions in our minds. "Projection makes perception." We look inside first, decide the kind of world we want to see and then project that world outside, making it the truth *as we see it*. We make it true by our interpretations of what it is we are seeing. If we are using perception to justify our own mistakes—our anger, our impulses to attack, our lack of love in whatever form it may take—we will see a world of evil, destruction, malice, envy and despair. All this we must learn to forgive, not because we are being "good" and "charitable," but because what we are seeing is not true. We have distorted the world by our twisted defenses, and are therefore seeing what is not there. As we learn to recognize our perceptual errors, we also learn to look past them or "forgive." At the same time we are forgiving ourselves, looking past our distorted self-concepts to the Self That God created in us and as us.

Forgiveness is the healing of perception of separation.

*This is the shift that true perception brings:
What was projected out is seen within, and
there forgiveness lets it disappear.*

Author's Note: Our beliefs and our concepts are not truth, they are simply our point of view; that is, our perceptions. By recognizing that our beliefs and concepts are simply perceptions, we open ourselves up to the opportunity to change our minds. And by becoming willing to see things differently, we are free to invite the Holy Spirit to choose for us, where healing is always given.

THE LIGHTHOUSE OF MIRACLES

Christ's vision is the Holy Spirit's gift, God's alternative to the illusion of separation and to the belief in the reality of sin, guilt and death. It is the one correction for all errors of perception; the reconciliation of the seeming opposites on which this world is based. Its kindly light shows all things from another point of view, reflecting the thought system that arises from knowledge and making return to God not only possible but inevitable. What was regarded as injustice done to one by someone else now becomes a call for help and for union. Sin, sickness and attack are seen as misperceptions calling for remedy through gentleness and love. Defenses are laid down because where there is no attack there is no need for them. Our brother's needs become our own, because they are taking the journey with us as we go to God.

Without us they would lose their way. Without them we could never find our own.

The opposite of seeing through the body's eyes is the vision of Christ, which reflects strength rather than weakness, unity rather than separation, and love rather than fear. The opposite of hearing through the body's ears is communication through the Voice for God, the Holy Spirit, which abides in each of us.

Christ's vision is the holy ground in which the lilies of forgiveness set their roots. This is their home. They can be brought from here back to the world, but they can never grow in its unnourishing and shallow soil. They need the light and warmth and kindly care Christ's charity provides. They need the love with which He looks on them. And they become His messengers, who give as they received.

Take from His storehouse, that its treasures may increase. His lilies do not leave their home when they are carried back into the world. Their roots remain. They do not leave their Source, but carry its beneficence with them, and turn the world into a garden like the one they came from, and to which they go again with added fragrance. Now are they twice blessed. The messages they brought from Christ have been delivered, and returned to them. And they return them gladly unto Him.

Christ has dreamed the dream of a forgiven world. It is His gift, whereby a sweet transition can be made from death to life; from hopelessness to hope. Let us an instant dream with Him. His dream awakens us to truth. His vision gives the means for a return to our unlost and everlasting sanctity in God.

Author's Note: To look on the world with Christ's vision is to look on the world with complete innocence.

THE SPECIAL LOVE RELATIONSHIP

Comparison must be an ego device, for love makes none. Specialness always makes comparisons. It is established by a lack seen in another, and maintained by searching for, and keeping clear in sight, all lacks it can perceive. Against the littleness you see in him you stand as tall and stately, clean and honest, pure and unsullied, by comparison with what you see. Nor do you understand it is yourself that you diminish thus.

You are not special. If you think you are, and would defend your specialness against the truth of what you really are, how can you know the truth? What answer that the Holy Spirit gives can reach you, when it is your specialness to which you listen, and which asks and answers? Its tiny answer, soundless in the melody that pours from God to you eternally in loving praise of what you are, is all you listen to. And that vast song of honor and of love for what you are seems silent and unheard before its "mightiness." You strain your ears to hear its soundless voice, and yet the Call of God Himself is soundless to you.

You can defend your specialness, but never will you hear the Voice for God beside it. They speak a different language and they fall on different ears. To every special one a different message, and one with different meaning, is the truth. Yet how can truth be different to each one?

The special love relationship is the ego's chief weapon for keeping you from Heaven. It does not appear to be a weapon, but if you consider how you value it and why, you will realize what it must be.

Specialness is a lack of trust in anyone except yourself. Faith is invested in yourself alone. Everything else becomes your enemy; feared and attacked, deadly and dangerous, hated and worthy only of destruction. Whatever gentleness it offers is but deception, but its hate is real.

What could the purpose of the body be but specialness? And it is this that makes it frail and helpless in its own defense. It was conceived to make *you* frail and helpless. The goal of separation is its curse. Yet bodies have no goal. Purpose is of the mind. And minds can change as they desire. What they are, and all their attributes, they cannot change. But what they hold as purpose can be changed, and body states must shift accordingly. Of itself the body can do nothing. See it as means to hurt, and it is hurt. See it as means to heal, and it is healed.

The special ones are all asleep, surrounded by a world of loveliness they do not see. Freedom and peace and joy stand there, beside the bier on which they sleep, and call them forth and waken from their dream of death. Yet they hear nothing. They are lost in dreams of specialness. Open your eyes a little; see the savior God gave to you that you might look on him, and give him back his birthright. It is yours.

Forgiveness is the end of specialness. Only illusions can be forgiven, and then they disappear. Forgiveness is release from all illusions, and that is why it is impossible but partly to forgive.

You cannot enter into real relationships with any of God's Sons unless you love them equally. Love is not special. You can love only as God loves. Seek not to love unlike Him, for there is no love apart from His. Until you recognize that this is true, you will have no idea what love is like.

THE ONLY RELATIONSHIP

In the Holy Spirit alone lies the awareness of what God cannot know, and what you do not understand. It is His holy function to accept them both, and by removing every element of disagreement, to join them into one. He will do this because it is His function. Leave, then, what seems to you to be impossible, to Him Who knows it must be possible because it is the Will of God. And let Him Whose teaching is only of God teach you the only meaning of relationships.

For God created the only relationship that has meaning,
and that is His relationship with you.

The Voice of the Holy Spirit does not command, because it is incapable of arrogance. It does not demand, because it does not seek control. It does not overcome, because it does not attack. It merely reminds. It is compelling only because of what it reminds you of.

Do as God's Voice directs. And if it asks a thing of you which seems impossible, remember Who it is that asks, and who would make denial. Then consider this; which is more likely to be right? The Voice that speaks for the Creator of all things, Who knows all things exactly as they are, or a distorted image of yourself, confused, bewildered, inconsistent and unsure of everything? Let not its voice direct you. Hear instead a certain Voice, which tells you of a function given you by your Creator Who remembers you, and urges that you now remember Him.

His gentle Voice is calling from the known to the unknowing. He would comfort you, although He knows no sorrow. He would make a restitution, though He is complete; a gift to you, although He knows that you have everything already. He has Thoughts which answer every need His Son perceives, although He sees them not. For Love must give, and what is given in His Name takes on the form most useful in a world of form.

These are the forms which never can deceive, because they come from Formlessness Itself. Forgiveness is an earthly form of love, which as it is in Heaven has no form. Yet what is needed here is given here as it is needed. In this form you can fulfill your function even here, although what love will mean to you when formlessness has been restored to you is greater still. **Salvation of the world depends on you who can forgive. Such is your function here.**

You will never rest until you know your function and fulfill it,
for only in this can your will and your
Father's be wholly joined.

Author's Note: Allow me to bring your attention once more to the beginning paragraph. This teaching is trying to help bring our awareness to the truth that God is unaware of us being lost in dreams in a body—in a world. He knows us only as we were created and therefore has no idea of all the suffering and madness that is taking place here within our dreams. But His Holy Spirit is aware of all this, and understands perfectly how to resolve all conflict. The Holy Spirit is the link that joins God's Truth to us, for this is His one mission. However, our Father is completely aware that His constant flow of love is blocked by the barriers we have placed before Him.

THE FORGIVEN WORLD/
THE RETURN OF REASON

Can you imagine how beautiful those you forgive will look to you? In no fantasy have you ever seen anything so lovely. Nothing you see here, sleeping or waking, comes near to such loveliness. And nothing will you value like unto this, nor hold so dear. Nothing that you remember that made your heart sing with joy has ever brought you even a little part of the happiness this sight will bring you. For you will see the Son of God. You will behold the beauty the Holy Spirit loves to look upon, and which He thanks the Father for. He was created to see this for you, until you learned to see it for yourself. And all His teaching leads to seeing it and giving thanks with Him.

This loveliness is not a fantasy. It is the real world, bright and clean and new, with everything sparkling under the open sun. Nothing is hidden here, for everything has been forgiven and there are no fantasies to hide the truth. The bridge between that world and this is so little and so easy to cross, that you could not believe it is the meeting place of worlds so different. Yet this little bridge is the strongest thing that touches on this world at all. This little step, so small it has escaped your notice, is a stride through time into eternity, beyond all ugliness into beauty that will enchant you, and will never cease to cause you wonderment at its perfection.

This step, the smallest ever taken, is still the greatest accomplishment of all in God's plan of Atonement. All else is learned, but this is given, complete and wholly perfect. No one but Him Who planned salvation could complete it thus. The real world, in its loveliness, you learn to reach. Fantasies are all undone, and no-one and nothing remain still bound by them, and by your own forgiveness you are free to see. Yet what you see is only what you made, with the blessing of your forgiveness on it. And with this final blessing of God's Son upon himself, the real perception, born of the new perspective he has learned, has served its purpose.

The stars will disappear in light, and the sun that opened up the world to beauty will vanish. Perception will be meaningless when it has been perfected, for everything that has been used for learning will have no function. Nothing will ever change; no shifts nor shadings, no differences, no variations that made perception possible will still occur. The perception of the real world will be so short you will barely have time to thank God for it. For God will take the last step swiftly, when you have reached the real world and have been made ready for Him.

The real world is attained simply by the complete forgiveness of the old, the world you see without forgiveness. The great Transformer of perception will undertake with you the careful searching of the mind that made this world, and uncover to you the seeming reasons for your making it. In the light of the real reason that He brings, as you follow Him, He will show you that there is no reason here at all. Each spot His reason touches grows alive with beauty, and what seemed ugly in the darkness of your lack of reason is suddenly released to loveliness. Not even what the Son of God made in insanity could be without a hidden spark of beauty that gentleness could release.

All this beauty will rise to bless your sight as you look upon the world with forgiving eyes. For forgiveness literally transforms vision, and lets you see the real world reaching quietly and gently across chaos, removing all illusions that had twisted your perception and fixed it on the past. The smallest leaf becomes a thing of wonder, and a blade of grass a sign of God's perfection.

From the forgiven world the Son of God is lifted easily into his home. And there he knows that he has always rested there in peace. Even salvation will become a dream, and vanish from his mind. **For salvation is the end of dreams,** and with the closing of the dream will have no meaning. Who, awake in Heaven, could dream that there could ever be a need of salvation?

How much do you want salvation? It will give you the real world, trembling with readiness to be given you. The eagerness of the Holy Spirit to give you this is so intense He would not wait, although He waits in patience. Meet His patience with your impatience at delay in meeting Him. Go out in gladness to meet with your Redeemer, and walk with Him in trust out of this world, and into the real world of beauty and forgiveness.

I ask Your blessing on my sight today. It is the means
which You have chosen to become the way
to show me my mistakes, and look beyond
them. It is given me to find a new perception
through the Guide You gave to me,
and through His lessons to surpass perception
and return to truth. I ask for the illusion

which transcends all those I made.
Today I choose to see a world forgiven, in which
everyone shows me the face of Christ, and teaches me
what I look upon belongs to me; that
nothing is, except Your holy Son.

Ask not to be forgiven, for this has already been accomplished. Ask, rather, to learn how to forgive, and to restore what always was to your unforgiving mind.

Author's Note: This last prayer is a plea to see through Christ eye's—to see the world with innocence and Love. It is a request to be given "the illusion which transcends all those I made"—forgiveness. For forgiveness is also an illusion, being the means of healing in a world that needs to be healed. What need is there for forgiveness in the real world? You could say that forgiveness is the one illusion that undoes all illusions.

Forgiveness is the return of reason. All reason is of the Holy Spirit. There is no reason here at all. To reason is to understand that "Nothing real can be threatened and Nothing unreal exists." Reason reminds us that only God's Love is real.

Forgiveness is the fragrance the violet sheds
on the heel that has crushed it.

Mark Twain

YOU ARE THE LIGHT OF THE WORLD!

Who is the light of the world except God's Son? This, then, is merely a statement of the truth about yourself. It is the opposite of a statement of pride, of arrogance, or of self-deception. It does not describe the self-concept you have made. It does not refer to any of the characteristics with which you have endowed your idols. It refers to you as you were created by God. It simply states the truth.

In this world you can become a spotless mirror,
in which the Holiness of your Creator
shines forth from you to all around you.
You can reflect Heaven here.
You need but leave the mirror clean and clear of all the
images of hidden darkness you have drawn upon it.
God will shine upon it of Himself.

It is your forgiveness that will bring the world of darkness to the light. It is your forgiveness that lets you recognize the light in which you see. Forgiveness is the demonstration that you are the light of the world. Through your forgiveness does the truth about yourself return to your memory. Therefore, in your forgiveness lies your salvation.

Illusions about yourself and the world are one. That is why all forgiveness is a gift to yourself. Your goal is to find out who you are, having denied your Identity by attacking creation and its Creator. Now you are learning how to remember the truth. For this attack must be replaced by forgiveness, so that thoughts of life may replace thoughts of death.

Remember that in every attack you call upon your own weakness, while each time you forgive you call upon the strength of Christ in you. Do you not then begin to understand what forgiveness will do for you? It will remove all sense of weakness, strain and fatigue from your mind. It will take away all fear and guilt and pain. It will restore the invulnerability and power God gave His Son to your awareness. Say to yourself today:

Forgiveness is my function as the light of the world.
I would fulfill my function that I may be happy.

Forgiveness has a Teacher Who will fail in nothing. Rest a while in this; do not attempt to judge forgiveness, nor to set it in an earthly frame. Let it arise to Christ, Who welcomes it as gift to Him. He will not leave you comfortless, nor fail to send His angels down to answer you in His Own Name. He stands beside the door to which forgiveness is the only key. Give it to Him to use instead of you, and you will see the door swing silently open upon the shining face of Christ. Behold your brother there beyond the door; the Son of God as He created him.

Do you believe that I would leave you in the
darkness that you agreed to leave with me?

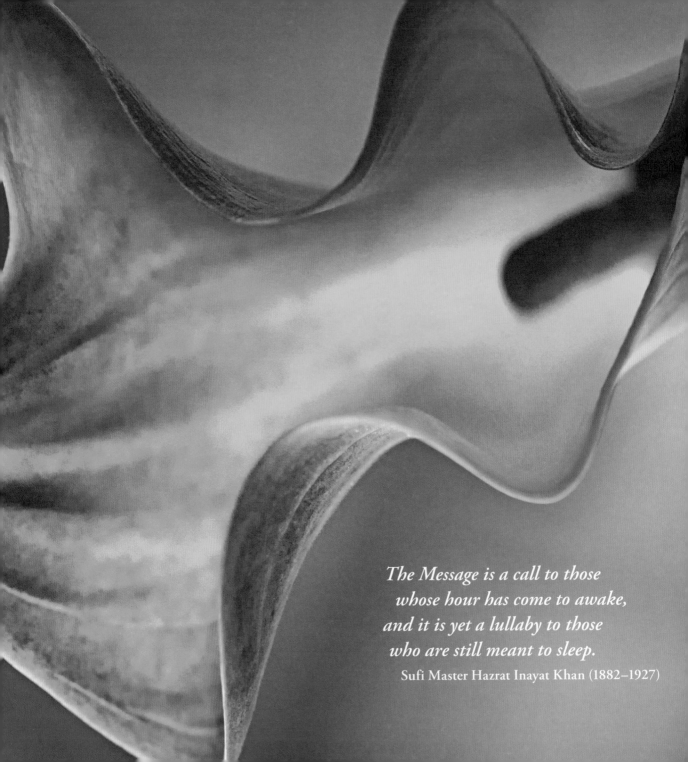

The Message is a call to those
whose hour has come to awake,
and it is yet a lullaby to those
who are still meant to sleep.
Sufi Master Hazrat Inayat Khan (1882–1927)

GOD IS THE LOVE IN WHICH I FORGIVE

God does not forgive because he has never condemned. And there must be condemnation before forgiveness is necessary. Forgiveness is the great need of this world, but that is because it is a world of illusions. Those who forgive are thus releasing themselves from illusions, while those who withhold forgiveness are binding themselves to them. As you condemn only yourself, so do you forgive only yourself.

Yet although God does not forgive, His Love is nevertheless the basis of forgiveness. Fear condemns and love forgives. Forgiveness thus undoes what fear has produced, returning the mind to the awareness of God. For this reason, forgiveness can truly be called salvation. It is the means by which illusions disappear.

Close your eyes . . . and spend a minute or two in searching your mind for those whom you have not forgiven. It does not matter "how much" you have not forgiven them. You have forgiven them entirely or not at all. After you have applied the idea to all those who have come to mind, tell yourself:

God is the Love in which I forgive myself.

God does not forgive because He has never condemned. The blameless cannot blame, and those who have accepted their innocence see nothing to forgive. Yet forgiveness is the means by which I will recognize my innocence. It is the reflection of God's Love on earth. It will bring me near enough to Heaven that the Love of God can reach down to me and raise me up to Him.

Innocence is not a partial attribute. It is not real "until" it is total.

Here is the answer! Do not turn away in aimless wandering again. Accept salvation now. It is the gift of God, and not the world. The world can give no gifts of any value to a mind that has received what God has given as its own. God wills salvation be received today, and that the intricacies of your dreams no longer hide their nothingness from you.

Open your eyes today and look upon a happy world of safety and of peace. Forgiveness is the means by which it comes to take the place of hell. In quietness it rises up to greet your open eyes, and fill your heart with deep tranquility as ancient truths, forever newly born, arise in your awareness. What you will remember then can never be described. Yet your forgiveness offers it to you.

Those who would see "will" see. And they will join with me in carrying their light into the darkness, when the darkness in them is offered to the light, and is removed forever.

HIS COMPLETION

Ask and He will answer. The responsibility is His, and He alone is fit to assume it. To do so is His function. To refer the questions to Him is yours. Would you want to be responsible for decisions about which you understand so little? Be glad you have a Teacher Who cannot make a mistake. His answers are always right. Would you say that of yours?

Do not, then, think that following the Holy Spirit's guidance is necessary merely because of your own inadequacies. It is the way out of hell for you.

Here again is the paradox often referred to in the course. To say, "Of myself I can do nothing" is to gain all power. And yet it is but a seeming paradox. As God created you, you *have* all power. The image you made of yourself has none. The Holy Spirit knows the truth about you. The image you made does not. To ask the Holy Spirit to decide for you is simply to accept your true inheritance. Does this mean that you cannot say anything without consulting Him? No, indeed! That would hardly be practical, and it is the practical with which this course is most concerned. If you have made it a habit to ask for help when and where you can, you can be confident that wisdom will be given you when you need it. Prepare for this each morning, remember God when you can throughout the day, ask the Holy Spirit's help when it is feasible to do so, and thank Him for His guidance at night. And your confidence will be well founded indeed.

Never forget that the Holy Spirit does not depend on your words. He understands the requests of your heart, and answers them. For God has given Him the power to translate your prayers of the heart into His language. He understands that an attack is a call for help. And He responds with help accordingly. God would be cruel if He let your words replace His Own.

Remember you are His completion and His Love. Remember your weakness is His strength. But do not read this hastily or wrongly. If His strength is in you, what you perceive as your weakness is but illusion. And He has given you the means to prove it so. Ask all things of His Teacher, and all things are given you. Not in the future but immediately; now. God does not wait, for waiting implies time and He is timeless. Forget your foolish images, your sense of frailty and your fear of harm, your dreams of danger and selected "wrongs." God knows but His Son, and as he was created so he is. In confidence I place you in His Hands, and I give thanks for you that this is so.

Have faith in Him Who is your Father. Trust all things to Him. Let Him reveal all things to you, and be you undismayed because you are His Son.

Author's Note: In the language of Aramaic, which was Jesus's native tongue, *to ask* meant *to claim*. By asking the Holy Spirit for guidance, we are claiming what has already been given us—our true inheritance.

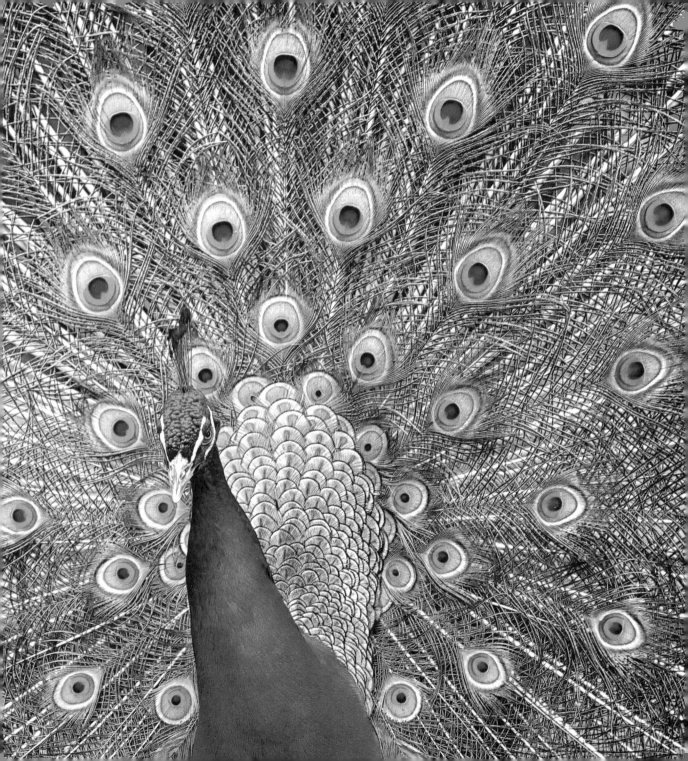

UNION BROUGHT CLOSER

The ego seeks to "resolve" its problems, not at their Source, but where they were not made. And thus it seeks to guarantee there will be no solution. The Holy Spirit wants only to make His resolutions complete and perfect, and so He seeks and finds the source of problems where it is, and there undoes it. And with each step in His undoing is the separation more and more undone, and union brought closer. He is not at all confused by any "reasons" for separation. All He perceives in separation is that it must be undone. Let Him uncover the hidden spark of beauty in your relationships, and show it to you. Its loveliness will so attract you that you will be unwilling ever to lose the sight of it again. And you will let this spark transform the relationship so you can see it more and more. For you will want it more and more, and become increasingly unwilling to let it be hidden from you. And you will learn to seek for and establish the conditions in which this beauty can be seen.

All this you will do gladly, if you but let Him hold the spark before you, to light your way and make it clear to you. **God's Son is One. Whom God has joined as one, the ego cannot put asunder.** The spark of holiness must be safe, however hidden it may be, in every relationship. For the Creator of the one relationship has left no part of it without Himself. This is the only part of the relationship the Holy Spirit sees, because He knows that only this is true. You have made the relationship unreal, and therefore unholy, by seeing it where it is not and as it is not.

The past becomes the justification for entering into a continuing, unholy alliance with the ego against the present. For the present *is* forgiveness. Therefore, the relationships the unholy alliance dictates are not perceived nor felt as *now*. Yet the frame of reference to which the present is referred for meaning is an *illusion* of the past, in which those elements that fit the purpose of the unholy alliance are retained, and all the rest let go. And what is thus let go is all the truth the past could ever offer to the present as witnesses for its reality. What is kept but witnesses to the reality of dreams.

The past that you remember never was, and represents only the denial of what always was.

The way to God is through forgiveness. There is no other way. If sin had not been cherished by the mind, what need would there have been to find the way to where you are? Who would still be uncertain? Who could be unsure of who he is? And who would yet remain asleep, in heavy clouds of doubt about the holiness of him whom God created sinless? Here we can but dream. But we can dream we have forgiven him in whom all sin remains impossible, and it is this we choose to dream today.

God is our goal; forgiveness is the means by which our minds return to Him at last.

ALL THAT I GIVE IS GIVEN TO MYSELF

Today's idea, completely alien to the ego and the thinking of the world, is crucial to the thought reversal that this course will bring about. If you believed this statement, there would be no problem in complete forgiveness, certainty of goal, and sure direction. You would understand the means by which salvation comes to you, and would not hesitate to use it now.

Let us consider what you do believe, in place of this idea. It seems to you that other people are apart from you, and able to behave in ways which have no bearing on your thoughts, nor yours on theirs. Therefore, your attitudes have no effect on them, and their appeals for help are not in any way related to your own. You further think that they can sin without affecting your perception of yourself, while you can judge their sin, and yet remain apart from condemnation and at peace.

When you "forgive" a sin, there is no gain to you directly. You give charity to one unworthy, merely to point out that you are better, on a higher plane than he whom you forgive. He has not earned your charitable tolerance, which you bestow on one unworthy of the gift, because his sins have lowered him beneath a true equality with you. He has no claim on your forgiveness. It holds out a gift to him, but hardly to yourself.

Thus is forgiveness basically unsound; a charitable whim benevolent yet underserved, a gift bestowed at times, at other times withheld. Unmerited, withholding it is just, nor is it fair that you should suffer when it is withheld. The sin that you forgive is not your own. Someone apart from you committed it. And if you then are gracious unto him by giving him what he does not deserve, the gift is no more yours than was his sin.

If this be true, forgiveness has no grounds on which to rest dependably and sure. It is an eccentricity, in which you sometimes choose to give indulgently an undeserved reprieve. Yet it remains your right to let the sinner not escape the justified repayment for his sin. Think you the Lord of Heaven would allow the world's salvation to depend on this? Would not His care for you be small indeed, if your salvation rested on a whim?

You do not understand forgiveness. As you see it, it is but a check upon overt attack, without requiring correction in your mind. It cannot give you peace as you perceive it. It is not a means for your release from what you see in someone other than yourself. It has no power to restore your unity with him to your awareness. It is not what God intended it to be for you.

Not having given Him the gift He asks of you, you cannot recognize His gifts, and think He has not given them to you. Yet would He ask you for a gift unless it was for you? Could He be satisfied with empty gestures, and evaluate such petty gifts as worthy of His Son? Salvation is a better gift than this. And true forgiveness, as the means by which it is attained, must heal the mind that gives, for giving is receiving. What remains as unreceived has not been given, but what has been given must have been received.

Today we try to understand the truth that giver and receiver are the same. You will need help to make this meaningful, because it is so alien to the thoughts to which you are accustomed. But the Help you need is there. Give Him your faith today, and ask Him that He share your practicing in truth today. And if you only catch a tiny glimpse of the release that lies in the idea we practice for today, this is a day of glory for the world.

Give (time) today to the attempt to understand today's idea. It is the thought that will release your mind from every bar to what forgiveness means, and let you realize its worth to you.

In silence, close your eyes upon the world that does not understand forgiveness, and seek sanctuary in the quiet place where thoughts are changed and false beliefs laid by. Repeat today's idea, and ask for help in understanding what it really means. Be willing to be taught. Be glad to hear the Voice of truth and healing speak to you, and you will understand the words He speaks, and recognize He speaks your words to you.

All that I give is given to myself.
The Help I need to learn that this
is true is with me now.
And I will trust in Him.

The cost of giving is receiving. Either it is a penalty from which you suffer, or the happy purchase of a treasure to hold dear.

Author's Note: True forgiveness teaches us to look at our brothers with the spiritual *knowledge* of their innocence, rather than the physical *perception* of their guilt! All guilt, conflict, and suffering lie within our own minds and nowhere else. Therefore, we must direct forgiveness toward ourselves rather than toward others. We alone can set ourselves free because we along hold the thoughts that bind us. We forgive ourselves our own illusions and thus offer ourselves peace of mind. Hence: "All that I give is given to myself."

We make a living by what we "get."
We make a life by what we "give."
Winston Churchill

THE GUIDE TO CORRECTION

Atonement is for all, because it is the way to undo the belief that anything is for you alone. To forgive is to overlook. Look, then, beyond error and do not let your perception rest upon it, for you will believe what your perception holds. Accept as true only what your brother is, if you would know yourself. Perceive what he is not and you cannot know what you are, because you see him falsely. Remember always that your Identity is shared, and that Its sharing is Its reality.

You have a part to play in the Atonement, but the plan of the Atonement is beyond you. You do not understand how to overlook errors, or you would not make them. It would merely be further error to believe either that you do not make them, or that you can correct them without a Guide to correction. And if you do not follow this Guide, your errors will not be corrected. The plan is not yours because of your limited ideas about what you are. This sense of limitation is where all errors arise. The way to undo them, therefore, is not *of* you but *for* you.

You cannot be your guide to miracles, for
it is you who made them necessary.

The ego, too, has a plan of forgiveness because you are asking for one, though not of the right teacher. The ego's plan, of course, makes no sense and will not work. By following its plan you will merely place yourself in an impossible situation, to which the ego always leads you. The ego's plan is to have you see error clearly first, and then overlook it. Yet how can you overlook what you have made real? By seeing it clearly, you have made it real and *cannot* overlook it.

Forgiveness that is learned of me does not use fear to undo fear. Nor does it make real the unreal and then destroy it. Forgiveness through the Holy Spirit lies simply in looking beyond error from the beginning, and thus keeping it unreal for you. Do not let any belief in its realness enter your mind, or you will also believe that you must undo what you have made in order to be forgiven. What has no effect does not exist, and to the Holy Spirit the effects of error are nonexistent. By steadily and consistently canceling out all its effects, everywhere and in all respects, He teaches that the ego does not exist and proves it.

Follow the Holy Spirit's teaching in forgiveness, then, because forgiveness is His function and He knows how to fulfill it perfectly. His work is not your function, and unless you accept this you cannot learn what your function is.

If all but loving thoughts have been
forgotten, what remains is eternal.

My trust in you is greater than yours in me at the moment, but it will not always be that way. Your mission is very simple. You are asked to live so as to demonstrate that you are not an ego, and I do not choose God's channels wrongly. The Holy One shares my trust, and accepts my atonement decisions because my will is never out of accord with His. I have said before that I am in charge of the Atonement. This is only because I completed my part in it as a man, and can now complete it through others. My chosen channels cannot fail, because I will lend them my strength as long as theirs is wanting.

CHAPTER III

The Attainment *of* Peace

*A miracle is a service. It is the maximal service
you can render to another. It is a way of loving
your neighbor as yourself. You recognize your own
and your neighbor's worth simultaneously.*

I AM RESPONSIBLE

We have repeated how little is asked of you to learn this course. It is the same small willingness you need to have your whole relationship transformed to joy; the little gift you offer to the Holy Spirit for which He gives you everything; the very little on which salvation rests; the tiny change of mind by which the crucifixion is changed to resurrection. And being true, it is so simple that it cannot fail to be completely understood. Rejected yes, but not ambiguous. And if you choose against it now it will not be because it is obscure, but rather that this little cost seemed, in your judgment, to be too much to pay for peace.

This is the only thing that you need do for vision, happiness, release from pain and the complete escape from sin, all to be given you. Say only this, but mean it with no reservations, for here the power of salvation lies:

I "am" responsible for what I see.
I choose the feelings I experience, and I
decide upon the goal I would achieve.
And everything that seems to happen to me
I ask for, and receive as I have asked.

Deceive yourself no longer that you are helpless in the face of what is done to you. Acknowledge but that you have been mistaken, and all effects of your mistakes will disappear.

It is impossible the Son of God be merely driven by events outside of him. It is impossible that happenings that come to him were not his choice. His power of decision is the determiner of every situation in which he seems to find himself by chance or accident. **No accident nor chance is possible within the universe as God created it, outside of which is nothing. Suffer, and you decided sin was your**

goal. Be happy, and you gave the power of decision to Him who must decide for God for you. **This is the little gift you offer to the Holy Spirit, and even this He gives to you to give yourself. For by this gift is given you the power to release your savior, that he may give salvation unto you.**

The power of decision, which you made in place of the power of creation, He would teach you how to use on your behalf. You who made it to crucify yourself must learn of Him how to apply it to the holy cause of restoration.

Be willing, for an instant, to leave your altars free of what you placed upon them, and what is really there you cannot fail to see. Then is it possible to look within and see what must be there, plainly in sight, and wholly independent of inference and judgment. **Undoing is not your task, but it *is* up to you to welcome it or not.** Faith and desire go hand in hand, for everyone believes in what he wants.

We have already said that wishful thinking is how the ego deals with what it wants, to make it so. There is no better demonstration of the power of wanting, and therefore of faith, to make its goals seem real and possible. **Faith in the unreal leads to adjustments of reality to make it fit the goal of madness. The goal of sin induces the perception of a fearful world to justify its purpose. What you desire, you will see. And if its reality is false, you will uphold it by not realizing all the adjustments you have introduced to make it so.**

When vision is denied, confusion of cause and effect becomes inevitable. The purpose now becomes to keep obscure the cause of the effect, and make effect appear to be a cause. This seeming independence of effect enables it to be regarded as standing by itself, and capable of serving as a cause of the events and feelings its maker thinks it causes. Nothing can have effects without a cause, and to confuse the two is merely to fail to understand them both.

It is as needful that you recognize you made the world you see, as that you recognize that you did not create yourself. *They are the same mistake.* **Nothing created not by your Creator has any influence over you. And if you think what you have made can tell you what you see and feel, and place your faith in its ability to do so, you are denying your Creator and believing that you made yourself. For if you think the world you made has power to make you what it wills, you are confusing Son and Father; effect and Source.**

God is the only Cause. Teach no one he has hurt you, for if you do, you teach yourself that what is not of God has power over you. "The causeless cannot be."

Each day, each hour, every instant, I am choosing what I want to look upon, the sounds I want to hear, the witnesses to what I want to be the truth for me. Today I choose to look upon what Christ would have me see, to listen to God's Voice, and seek the witnesses to what is true in God's creation. In Christ's sight, the world and God's creations meet, and as they come together all perception disappears. His kindly sight redeems the world from death, for nothing that He looks on but must live, remembering the Father and the Son; Creator and creation unified.

Author's Note: God's Love is the only cause, and God's peace is its only effect, along with all the other attributes that derive from it. Fear of any kind, as well as everything unlike to love, has no cause, and therefore has no effects and is only a matter of mind. Hence: "Nothing real can be threatened. Nothing unreal exists."

The ego (personal thought system) has no cause, being an invention of our own split minds. And without a cause, there can be no effects. What stands in opposition to Truth has no power over you, but rather is given power by you. Only in Truth (Cause) are we able to tap into the resources of our own true power.

If not us, then who?
If not now, then when?
John E. Lewis

THE AUTHORITY PROBLEM

To extend is a fundamental aspect of God which He gave to His Son. In the creation, God extended Himself to His creations and imbued them with the same loving Will to create. You have not only been fully created, but have also been created perfect. There is no emptiness in you. Because of your likeness to your Creator you are creative. No child of God can lose this ability because it is inherent in what he is, but he can use it inappropriately by projecting. The inappropriate use of extension, or projection, occurs when you believe that some emptiness or lack exist in you, and that you can fill it with your own ideas instead of truth. This process involves the following steps:

- First, you believe that what God created can be changed by your own mind.
- Second, you believe that what is perfect can be rendered imperfect or lacking.
- Third, you believe that you can distort the creations of God, including yourself.
- Fourth, you believe that you can create yourself, and that the direction of your own creation is up to you.

These related distortions represent a picture of what actually occurred in the separation, or the "detour into fear." None of this existed before the separation, nor does it actually exist now . . . All fear is ultimately reducible to the basic misperception that you have the ability to usurp the power of God. Of course, you neither can nor have been able to do this.

Correction has one answer to all this, and to the world that rest on this:

You but mistake interpretation for the truth. And you are wrong. But a mistake is not a sin, nor has reality been taken from its throne by your mistakes. God reigns forever, and His laws alone prevail upon you and upon this world. His Love remains the only thing there is. Fear is illusion, for you are like Him.

The issue of authority is really a question of authorship. When you have an authority problem, it is always because you believe you are the author of yourself and project your delusion onto others. You then perceive the situation as one in which others are literally fighting you for your authorship. This is the fundamental error of all those who believe they have usurped the power of God. This belief is very frightening to them, but hardly troubles God. He is, however, eager to undo it, not to punish His children, but only because He knows that it makes them unhappy. God's creations are given their true Authorship, but you prefer to be anonymous when you choose to separate yourself from your Author. Being uncertain of your true Authorship, you believe that your creation was anonymous. This leaves you in a position where it sounds meaningful to believe that you created yourself. The dispute over authorship has left such uncertainty in your mind that it may even doubt whether you really exist at all.

Only those who give over all desire to reject can know that their own rejection is impossible. You have not usurped the power of God, but you have lost it. Fortunately, to lose something does not mean that it has gone. It merely means that you do not remember where it is.

I WILL ACCEPT ATONEMENT
FOR MYSELF

Here is the end of choice. For here we come to a decision to accept ourselves as God created us. And what is choice except uncertainty of what we are? There is no doubt that is not rooted here. There is no question but reflects this one. There is no conflict that does not entail the single, simple question, "What am I?"

Yet who could ask this question except one who has refused to recognize himself? Only refusal to accept yourself could make the question seem to be sincere. The only thing that can be surely known by any living thing is what it is. From this one point of certainty, it looks on other things as certain as itself.

Atonement remedies the strange idea that it is possible to
doubt yourself, and be unsure of what you really are.
This is the depth of madness. Yet it is the
universal question of the world. What does
this mean except the world is mad?
Why share its madness in the sad belief
that what is universal here is true?

Nothing the world believes is true. It is a place whose purpose is to be a home where those who claim they do not know themselves can come to question what it is they are. And they will come again until the time Atonement is accepted, and they learn it is impossible to doubt yourself, and not to be aware of what you are.

Only acceptance can be asked of you, for what you are is certain. It is set forever in the holy Mind of God, and in your own. It is so far beyond all doubt and question that to ask what it must be is all the proof you need to show that you believe the contradiction that you know not what you

cannot fail to know. Is this a question, or a statement which denies itself in statement? Let us not allow our holy minds to occupy themselves with senseless musing such as this.

We have a mission here. We did not come to reinforce the madness that we once believed in. Let us not forget the goal that we accepted. It is more than just our happiness alone we came to gain. What we accept as what we are proclaims what everyone must be, along with us. **Fail not your brothers, or you fail yourself. Look lovingly on them, that they may know that they are part of you, and you of them.**

This does Atonement teach, and demonstrates the oneness of God's Son is unassailed by his belief he knows not what he is. Today accept Atonement, not to change reality, but merely to accept the truth about yourself, and go your way rejoicing in the endless Love of God. It is but this that we are asked to do. It is but this that we will do today.

We have not lost the knowledge that God gave to us when He created us like Him. We can remember it for everyone, for in creation are all minds as one. And in our memory is the recall how dear our brothers are to us in truth, how much a part of us is every mind, how faithful they have really been to us, and how our Father's Love contains them all. Let your mind be cleared of all the foolish cobwebs which the world would weave around the holy Son of God. And learn the fragile nature of the chains that seem to keep the knowledge of yourself apart from your awareness, as you say:

I will accept Atonement for myself, For
I remain as God created me.

*If the sole responsibility of the miracle worker is to accept the Atonement for himself,
and I assure you that it is, then the responsibility for what is atoned for cannot be yours.
The dilemma cannot be resolved except by accepting the solution of undoing.*

IDEAS LEAVE NOT THEIR SOURCE

What keeps the world in chains but your beliefs? And what can save the world except your Self? Belief is powerful indeed. The thoughts you hold are mighty, and illusions are as strong in their effects as is the truth. A madman thinks the world he sees is real, and does not doubt it. Nor can he be swayed by questioning his thoughts' effects. It is but when their source is raised to question that the hope of freedom comes to him at last.

Yet is salvation easily achieved, for anyone is free to change his mind, and all his thoughts change with it. Now the Source of thought has shifted, for to change your mind means you have changed the Source of all ideas you think or ever thought or yet will think. You free the past from what you thought before. You free the future from all ancient thoughts of seeking what you do not want to find.

The present now remains the only time. Here in the present is the world set free. For as you let the past be lifted and release the future from your ancient fears, you find escape and give it to the world. You have enslaved the world with all your fears, your doubts and miseries, your pain and tears; and all your sorrows press on it, and keep the world a prisoner to your beliefs. Death strikes it everywhere because you hold the bitter thoughts of death within your mind.

The world is nothing in itself. Your mind must give it meaning. And what you behold upon it are your wishes, acted out so you can look on them and think them real. Perhaps you think you did not make the world, but came unwillingly to what was made already, hardly waiting for your thoughts to give it meaning. Yet in truth you found exactly what you looked for when you came.

There is no world apart from what you wish, and herein lies your ultimate release. Change but your mind on what you want to see, and all the world must change accordingly. Ideas leave not their Source. This central theme is often stated in the text, and must be borne in mind if you would understand. It is not pride which tells you that you made the world you see, and that it changes as you change your mind . . . but it is pride that argues you have come into a world quite separate from yourself, impervious to what you think and quite apart from what you chance to think it is. **There is no world! This is the central thought the course attempts to teach.**

What is the World? The world is false perception. It is born of error, and it has not left its Source. It will remain no longer than the thought that gave it birth is cherished. When the thought of separation has been changed to one of true forgiveness, will the world be seen in quite another light; and one which leads to truth, where all the world must disappear and all its errors vanish. Now its source has gone, and its effects are gone as well.

The world was made as an attack on God. It symbolizes fear. And what is fear except love's absence? Thus the world was meant to be a place where God could enter not, and where His Son could be apart from Him. Here was perception born, for knowledge could not cause such insane thoughts. But eyes deceive, and ears hear falsely. Now mistakes become quite possible, for certainty has gone.

A lesson earlier repeated once must now be stressed again, for it contains the firm foundation for today's idea. **You are as God created you. There is no place where you can suffer, and no time that can bring change to your eternal state. How can a world of time and place exist, if you remain as God created you?**

What is the lesson except another way of saying that to know your Self is the salvation of the world? To free the world from every kind of pain is but to change your mind about yourself.

There is no world because it is a thought apart from God, and made to separate the Father and the Son, and break away a part of God Himself and thus destroy His Wholeness. Can a world which comes from this idea be real? Can it be anywhere? Deny illusions, but accept the truth. Deny you are a shadow briefly laid upon a dying world. Release your mind, and you will look upon a world released.

You need not realize that healing comes to many brothers far across the world, as well as to the ones you see nearby, as you send out these thoughts to bless the world. But you will sense your own release, although you may not fully understand as yet that you could never be released alone.

You cannot give yourself your innocence, for you are too confused about yourself. But should *one* brother dawn upon your sight as wholly worthy of forgiveness, then your concept of yourself is wholly changed.

By focusing upon the good in him, the body grows decreasingly persistent in your sight, and will at length be seen as little more than just a shadow circling round the good. And this will be your concept of yourself, when you have reached the world beyond the sight your eyes alone can offer you to see. For you will not interpret what you see without the Aid that God has given you. And in His sight there *is* another world.

Hold out your hand, that you may have the gift
of kind forgiveness which you offer one whose
need for it is just the same as yours.
And let the cruel concept of yourself be changed
to one that brings the peace of God.

Author's Note: We are an idea, a *thought*, an extension of God's holy Mind—just as this world is an idea, an erroneous *perception* that was projected outward from our split mind—an experience due to the unconscious guilt that we feel from our belief in having separated ourselves from our Source. And as the Course teaches: "Projection makes perception." In both cases, ideas leave not their Source. We have never left the Mind of God, just as our ideas/erroneous perceptions have never left our split minds. Our perceptions are returned to truth by forgiveness. In truth, we have never left the Mind of God—"Ideas leave not their Source." We are only perceiving that we have.

MY SALVATION COMES FROM ME

All temptation is nothing more than some form of the basic temptation not to believe the idea for today. Salvation seems to come from anywhere except from you. So, too, does the source of guilt. You see neither guilt nor salvation as in your own mind and nowhere else. **When you realize that all guilt is solely an invention of your mind, you also realize that guilt and salvation must be in the same place. In understanding this you are saved.**

The enemy is you, as is the Christ.

The seeming cost of accepting today's idea is this: It means that nothing outside yourself can save you; nothing outside yourself can give you peace. But it also means that nothing outside yourself can hurt you, or disturb your peace or upset you in any way. Today's idea places you in charge of the universe, where you belong because of what you are. This is not a role that can be partially accepted. And you must surely begin to see that accepting it is salvation.

It may not, however, be clear to you why the recognition that guilt is in your own mind entails the realization that salvation is there as well. God would not have put the remedy for the sickness where it cannot help. That is the way your mind has worked, but hardly His. He wants you to be healed, so He has kept the Source of healing where the need for healing lies.

The secret of salvation is but this: that you are doing this unto yourself. No matter what the form of the attack, this still is true. Whoever takes the role of enemy and of attacker, still is this the truth. Whatever seems to be the cause of any pain and suffering you feel, this is still true. For you would not react at all to figures in a dream you knew that you were dreaming. Let them be as hateful and as vicious as they may, they could have no effect on you unless you failed to recognize it is your dream.

This single lesson learned will set you free from suffering, whatever form it takes. The Holy Spirit will repeat this one inclusive lesson of deliverance until it has been learned, regardless of the form of suffering that brings you pain. Whatever hurt you bring to Him He will make answer with this very simple truth. For this one answer takes away the cause of every form of sorrow and of pain. The form affects His answer not at all, for He would teach you but the single cause of all of them, no matter what their form. And you will understand that miracles reflect the simple statement, "*I* have done this thing, and it is this I would undo."

How differently will you perceive the world when this is recognized! When you forgive the world your guilt, you will be free of it.

Author's Note: All guilt, being an ingenuity of the split mind, stems from our fear of having seemingly separated ourselves from Truth/God. Guilt is a false belief the ego used to keep our thoughts on the personal self, preventing us from turning inward to unite with Truth/God as One. It is the source of all our troubles in life, and can show up in the most pervasive and inconceivable ways. They include: the fear of God; self judgment; unworthiness; defensiveness; self-medicating addiction; worry and anxiety about the future; the need to be right; self-punishment; an inability to be alone or sit quietly; phobias and nightmares and fearing death. To experience any of these, whether unconsciously or consciously, is to believe in guilt.

TRANSCENDING TIME

The ego, like the Holy Spirit, uses time to convince you of the inevitability of the goal and end of teaching.

> *To the ego the goal is death, which "is" its end.*
> *But to the Holy Spirit the goal is life, which "has" no end.*

Out of (the ego's) unwillingness for you to find peace even in death, it offers you immortality in hell. It speaks to you of Heaven, but assures you that Heaven is not for you. How can the guilty hope for Heaven?

The belief in hell is inescapable to those who identify with the ego. Their nightmares and their fears are all associated with it. The ego teaches that hell is in the future, for this is what all its teaching is directed to. Hell is its goal. For although the ego aims at death and dissolution as an end, it does not believe it. The goal of death, which it craves for you, leaves it unsatisfied. No one who follows the ego's teaching is without the fear of death. Yet if death were thought of merely as an end of pain, would it be feared? The ego teaches thus: Death is the end as far as home of Heaven goes. Yet because you and the ego cannot be separated, and because it cannot conceive of its own death, it will pursue you still, because guilt is eternal. Such is the ego's version of immortality. And it is this the ego's version of time supports . . . How bleak and despairing is the ego's use of time! And how terrifying!

The Holy Spirit teaches thus: There is no hell. Hell is only what the ego has made of the present. The belief in hell is what prevents you from understanding the present, because you are afraid of it. The Holy Spirit leads as steadily to Heaven as the ego drives to hell. For the Holy Spirit, Who knows only the present, uses it to undo the fear by which the ego would make the present useless. There is no escape from fear in the ego's use of time. For time, according to its teaching, is nothing but a teaching device for compounding guilt until it becomes all-encompassing, demanding vengeance forever.

The Holy Spirit would undo all of this *now*. **Fear is not of the present, but only of the past and future, which do not exist. There is no fear in the present when each instant stands clear and separated from the past, without its shadow reaching out into the future. Each instant is a clean, untarnished birth, in which the Son of God emerges from the past into the present. And the present extends forever. It is so beautiful and so clean and free of guilt that nothing but happiness is there. No darkness is remembered, and immortality and joy are now.**

How long is an instant? As long as it takes to re-establish perfect sanity, perfect peace and perfect love for everyone, for God and for yourself. As long as it takes to remember immortality, and your immortal creations who share it with you. As long as it takes to exchange hell for Heaven. Long enough to transcend all of the ego's making, and ascend unto your Father.

Time is your friend, if you leave it to the Holy Spirit to use. He needs but very little to restore God's whole power to you. He Who transcends time for you understands what time is for. Holiness lies not in time, but in eternity. There never was an instant in which God's Son could lose his purity. His changeless state is beyond time, for his purity remains forever beyond attack and without variability. Time stands still in his holiness, and changes not. And so it is no longer time at all. For caught in the single instant of the eternal sanctity of God's creation, it is transformed into forever. Give the eternal instant, that eternity may be remembered for you, in that shining instant of perfect release.

*Offer the miracle of the holy instant
through the Holy Spirit, and leave
His giving it to you to Him.*

THE KINGDOM IS YOU

It is hard to understand what "The Kingdom of Heaven is within you" really means. This is because it is not understandable to the ego, which interprets it as if something outside is inside, and this does not mean anything. The word "within" is unnecessary. **The Kingdom of Heaven *is* you. What else *but* you did the Creator create, and what else *but* you is His Kingdom?** Your ego and your spirit will never be co-creators, but your spirit and your Creator will always be.

You *are* the Kingdom of Heaven, but you have let the belief in darkness enter your mind and so you need a new light. The Holy Spirit is the radiance that you must let banish the idea of darkness. His is the glory before which dissociation falls away, and the Kingdom of Heaven breaks through into its own. Before the separation you did not need guidance. You knew as you will know again, but as you do not know now.

Any split in mind must involve a rejection of part of it, and this is the belief in separation.

> *The wholeness of the Kingdom does not*
> *depend on your perception,*
> *but your awareness of its wholeness does.*

It is only your awareness that needs protection, since being cannot be assailed. Yet a real sense of being cannot be yours while you are doubtful of what you are. This is why vigilance is essential. Doubts about being must not enter your mind, or you cannot know what you are with certainty. Certainty is of God for you. Vigilance is not necessary for truth, but it is necessary against illusions.

Truth is without illusions and therefore within the Kingdom. Everything outside the Kingdom is illusion. When you threw truth away, you saw yourself as if you were without it. By making another kingdom that you valued, you did not keep *only* the Kingdom of God in your mind, and thus placed part of your mind outside it. **What you made has imprisoned your will, and given you a sick mind that must be healed. Your vigilance against this sickness is the way to heal it.**

> *You will find Heaven. Everything you seek but this will*
> *fall away. Why wait for Heaven? It is here today.*
> *Time is the great illusion; it is past or in the future. Yet*
> *this cannot be, if it is where God wills His Son to be.*
> *How could the Will of God be in the past,*
> *or yet to happen? What He wills is now,*
> *without a past and wholly futureless.*
> *It is as far removed from time as is a tiny*
> *candle from a distant star, or what you*
> *chose from what you really want.*

The way is not in the sky—the way is in the heart.

Buddha

87

THE CONDITION FOR HIS WILL

It has been said that there is a kind of peace that is not of this world. How is it recognized? How is it found? And being found, how can it be retained? Let us consider each of these questions separately, for each reflects a different step along the way.

First, how can the peace of God be recognized? God's peace is recognized at first by just one thing; in every way it is totally unlike all previous experiences. It calls to mind nothing that went before. It brings with it no past associations. It is a new thing entirely. There is a contrast, yes, between this thing and all the past. But strangely, it is not a contrast of true differences. The past just slips away, and in its place is everlasting quiet. Only that.

How is the quiet found? No one can fail to find it who but seeks out its conditions. **God's peace can never come where anger is, for anger must deny that peace exists. Who sees anger as justified in any way or any circumstance proclaims that peace is meaningless, and must believe that it cannot exist. In this condition, peace cannot be found. Therefore, forgiveness is the necessary condition for finding the peace of God. More than this, given forgiveness there** *must* **be peace. For what except attack will lead to war? And what but peace is opposite to war? Here the initial contrast stands out clear and apparent. Yet when peace is found, the war is meaningless. And it is conflict now that is perceived as nonexistent and unreal.**

How is the peace of God retained, once it is found? Returning anger, in whatever form, will drop the heavy curtain once again, and the belief that peace cannot exist will certainly return. War is again accepted as the one reality. Now must you once again lay down your sword, although you do not recognize that you have picked it up again. But you will learn, as you remember even faintly now what happiness was yours without it, that you must have taken it again as your defense. Stop for a moment now and think of this: Is conflict what you want, or is God's peace the better choice? Which gives you more? A tranquil mind is not a little gift. Would you rather live than choose to die?

Living is joy, but death can only weep. You see in death escape from what you made. But this you do not see; that you made death, and it is but illusion of an end. Death cannot be escape, because it is not life in which the problem lies. Life has no opposite, for it is God. Life and death seem to be opposites because you have decided death ends life. *Forgive the world, and you will understand that everything that God created cannot have an end, and nothing He did not create is real. In this one sentence is our course explained. In this one sentence is our practicing given its one direction. And in this one sentence is the Holy Spirit's whole curriculum specified exactly as it is.*

What is the peace of God? No more than this; the simple understanding that His Will is wholly without opposite. The Will of God is One and all there is. This is your heritage. The universe beyond the sun and stars, and all the thoughts of which you can conceive, belongs to you.

Author's Note: The entire curriculum of the Holy Spirit has but one purpose: to remove the obstacles to Love's presence. But we must follow the teachings of the Holy Spirit in order for this to be accomplished, for He alone knows knowledge and what we are. The ego has no idea of either. Its teaching can only lead to confusion being confused itself. Learn from the Teacher Who knows your reality, and peace of mind is guaranteed.

God's peace is the condition for His Will.
Attain His peace, and you remember him.

TO DECIDE OTHERWISE

God Himself gave you the perfect Correction for everything you made that is not in accord with His holy Will. I am making His plan perfectly explicit to you, and will also tell you of your part in it, and how urgent it is to fulfill it. God weeps at the "sacrifice" of His children who believe they are lost to Him.

Whenever you are not wholly joyous, it is because you have reacted with a lack of love to one of God's creations [this includes ourselves]. Perceiving this as "sin" you become defensive because you expect attack. The decision to react in this way is yours, and can therefore be undone. It cannot be undone by repentance in the usual sense, because this implies guilt. If you allow yourself to feel guilty, you will reinforce the error rather than allow it to be undone for you.

Decision cannot be difficult. This is obvious, if you realize that you must already have decided not to be wholly joyous if that is how you feel. Therefore, the first step in the undoing is to recognize that you actively decided wrongly, but can as actively decide otherwise. Be very firm with yourself in this, and keep yourself fully aware that the undoing process, which does not come from you, is nevertheless within you because God placed it there. Your part is merely to return your thinking to the point at which the error was made, and give it over to the Atonement in peace. Say this to yourself as sincerely as you can, remembering that the Holy Spirit will respond fully to your slightest invitation:

I must have decided wrongly, because I am not at peace. I made the decision myself, but I can also decide otherwise. I want to decide otherwise, because I want to be at peace. I do not feel guilty, because the Holy Spirit will undo all the consequences of my wrong decision if I will let Him. I choose to let Him, by allowing Him to decide for God for me.

The ego tries to persuade you that it is up to you to decide which voice is true, but the Holy Spirit teaches you that truth was created by God, and your decision cannot change it. As you begin to realize the quiet power of the Holy Spirit's Voice, and its perfect consistency, it must dawn on your mind that you are trying to undo a decision that was irrevocably made for you. That is why I suggested before that you remind yourself to allow the Holy Spirit to decide for God for you.

. . . nothing is difficult that is wholly desired. To desire wholly is to create, and creating cannot be difficult if God Himself created you as a creator.

The Holy Spirit's Voice is as loud as your willingness to listen. It cannot be louder without violating your freedom of choice, which the Holy Spirit seeks to restore, never to undermine.

SLAVE TO NOTHING

Faith is the acknowledgment of union.
It is the gracious acknowledgment of everyone
as a Son of your most loving Father,
loved by Him like you, and therefore loved by you as
yourself. It is His Love that joins you and your brothers,
and for His Love you would keep no one separate from yours.

Faith is the gift of God, through Him Whom God has given you. Faithlessness looks upon the Son of God, and judges him unworthy of forgiveness. But through the eyes of faith, the Son of God is seen already forgiven, free of all the guilt he laid upon himself. Faith sees him only *now* because it looks not to the past to judge him, but would see in him only what it would see in you. It sees not through the body's eyes, nor looks to bodies for its justification. It is the messenger of the new perception, sent forth to gather witnesses unto its coming, and to return their messages to you.

As faithlessness will keep your little kingdom barren and separate, so will faith help the Holy Spirit prepare the ground for the most holy garden that He would make of it.

For faith brings peace, and so it calls on truth to enter and make lovely what has already been prepared for loveliness. Truth follows faith and peace, completing the process of making lovely that they begin. For faith is still a learning goal, no longer needed when the lesson has been learned. Yet truth will stay forever.

Let, then, your dedication be to the eternal, and learn how not to interfere with it and make it slave to time. For what you think you do to the eternal you do to *you*. **Whom God created as His Son is slave to nothing, being lord of all, along with his Creator. You can enslave a body, but an idea is free, incapable of being kept in prison or limited in any way except by the mind that thought it. For it remains joined to its source, which is its jailer or its liberator, according to which it chooses as its purpose for itself.**

Author's Note: Faith was not given us to be used for conquering and overcoming obstacles. It is for experiencing them all the way through—trusting not in ourselves, but in the power of God within. The struggle or the conflict to awaken is the very obstacle to its accomplishment.

The only real success is faithfulness.
Mother Teresa

GOD'S WILL

*God does not know of learning. Yet His Will
extends to what He does not understand,
in that He wills the happiness
His Son inherited of Him be undisturbed; eternal
and forever gaining scope, eternally expanding
in the joy of full creation, and eternally open
and wholly limitless in Him. That is His Will.
And thus His Will provides the means
to guarantee that it is done.*

God sees no contradictions. Yet His Son believes he sees them. Thus he has a need for One Who can correct his erring sight, and give him vision that will lead him back to where perceptions cease. God does not perceive at all. Yet it is He Who gives the means by which perception is made true and beautiful enough to let the light of Heaven shine upon it. It is He Who answers what His Son would contradict, and keeps his sinlessness forever safe.

These are the lessons God would have you learn. His will reflects them all, and they reflect His loving kindness to the Son He loves. Each lesson has a central thought, the same in all of them. The form alone is changed, with different circumstances and events; with different characters and different themes, apparent but not real. They are the same in fundamental content. It is this:

Forgive, and you will see this differently.

These are the words the Holy Spirit speaks in all your tribulations, all your pain, all suffering regardless of its form. These are the words with which temptation ends, and guilt, abandoned, is revered no more. These are the words which end the dream of sin, and rid the mind of fear. These are the words by which salvation comes to all the world.

Shall we not learn to say these words when we are tempted to believe that pain is real, and death becomes our choice instead of life? Shall we not learn to say these words when we have understood their power to release all minds from bondage? These are words which give you power over all events that seem to have been given power over you. You see them rightly when you hold these words in full awareness, and do not forget these words apply to everything you see or any brother looks upon amiss.

This is the lesson God would have you learn: There is a way to look on everything that lets it be to you another step to Him, and to salvation of the world. To all that speaks of terror, answer thus: I will forgive, and this will disappear. To every apprehension, every care and every form of suffering, repeat these selfsame words. And then you hold the key that opens Heaven's gate, and brings the Love of God the Father down to earth at last, to raise it up to Heaven.

*Have no fear that He will fail in what He wills. Nor
that you be excluded from the Will that is for you.*

Heaven itself is union with all of creation, and with its one Creator. And Heaven remains the Will of God for you.

Author's Note: Look close to see the hidden message within the image paired with this teaching. It is a small practice in seeking and finding. Blessings.

LOVE MAKES NO COMPARISONS

Gratitude is a lesson hard to learn for those who look upon the world amiss. The most that they can do is see themselves as better off than others. And they try to be content because another seems to suffer more than they. How pitiful and deprecating are such thoughts! For who has cause for thanks while others have less cause? And who could suffer less because he sees another suffer more? Your gratitude is due to Him alone Who made all cause of sorrow disappear throughout the world.

It is insane to offer thanks because of suffering. But it is equally insane to fail in gratitude to One Who offers you the certain means whereby all pain is healed, and suffering replaced with laughter and with happiness. Nor could the even partly sane refuse to take the steps which He directs, and follow in the way He sets before them, to escape a prison that they thought contained no door to the deliverance they now perceive.

Love makes no comparisons. And gratitude can only be sincere if it be joined to love. We offer thanks to God our Father that in us all things will find their freedom. It will never be that some are loosed while others still are bound. For who can bargain in the name of love.

Therefore give thanks, but in sincerity. And let your gratitude make room for all who will escape with you; the sick, the weak, the needy and afraid, and those who mourn a seeming loss or feel apparent pain, who suffer cold or hunger, or who walk the way of hatred and the path of death. All these go with you. Let us not compare ourselves with them, for thus we split them off from our awareness of the unity we share with them, as they must share with us.

We thank our Father for one thing alone; that we are separate from no living thing, and therefore one with Him. And we rejoice that no exceptions ever can be made which would reduce our wholeness, nor impair or change our function to complete the One Who is Himself completion. We give thanks for every living thing, for otherwise we offer thanks for nothing, and we fail to recognize the gifts of God to us.

Walk, then, in gratitude the way of love. For hatred is forgotten when we lay comparisons aside. What more remains as obstacles to peace? The fear of God is now undone at last, and we forgive without comparing. Thus we cannot choose to overlook some things, and yet retain some other things still locked away as "sins." When your forgiveness is complete you will have total gratitude, for you will see that everything has earned the right to love by being loving, even as your Self.

Gratitude goes hand in hand with love, and
where one is the other must be found.
For gratitude is but an aspect of the Love
which is the Source of all creation.

Author's Note: To behold separation anywhere, regardless of the form, is to sleep, being consciously unaware of Reality. To join (in mind and spirit) is to wake. Duality can only be found in dreams, for Oneness is our true Reality.

YOU WHO MADE FEAR

You who want peace can find it only by complete forgiveness. No learning is acquired by anyone unless he wants to learn it and believes in some way that he needs it. While lack does not exist in the creation of God, it is very apparent in what you have made. It is, in fact, the essential difference between them. Lack implies that you would be better off in a state somehow different from the one you are in. Until the "separation," which is the meaning of the "fall," nothing was lacking. There were no needs at all. Needs arise only when you deprive yourself. You act according to the particular order of needs you establish. This, in turn, depends on your perception of what you are.

*A sense of separation from God is the
only lack you really need correct.*

This sense of separation would never have arisen if you had not distorted your perception of truth, and had thus perceived yourself as lacking. The idea of order of needs arose because, having made this fundamental error, you had already fragmented yourself into levels with different needs.

The real purpose of this world is to use it to correct your unbelief. You can never control the effects of fear yourself, because you made fear, and you believe in what you made. In attitude, then, though not in content, you resemble your Creator, Who has perfect faith in His creations *because* He created them. Belief produces the acceptance of existence. That is why you can believe what no one else thinks is true. It is true for you because it was made by you.

All aspects of fear are untrue because they do not exist at the creative level, and therefore do not exist at all. To whatever extent you are willing to submit your beliefs to this test, to that extent are your perceptions corrected. In sorting out the false from the true, the miracle proceeds along these lines:

*Perfect love cast out fear. If fear exist,
Then there is not perfect love.
But:
Only perfect love exists. If there is fear,
It produces a state that does not exist.*

Believe this and you will be free. Only God can establish this solution, and this faith *is His gift*.

Author's Note: Perfect love is all-encompassing, and "What is all encompassing can have no opposite." If we are not practicing an all-encompassing love, we give rise to what is not real. God knows nothing of a "special" love.

YOUR APPOINTED FRIEND

Anything in this world that you believe is good and valuable and worth striving for can hurt you, and will do so. Not because it has the power to hurt, but just because you have denied it is but an illusion, and made it real. And it is real to you. It is not nothing, and through its perceived reality has entered all the world of sick illusions. All belief in sin, in power of attack, in hurt and harm, in sacrifice and death, has come to you. For no one can make one illusion real, and still escape the rest. For no one can choose to keep the ones that he prefers, and find the safety that the truth alone can give. Who can believe illusions are the same, and still maintain that even one is best?

Brother, take not one step in the descent to hell. For having taken one, you will not recognize the rest for what they are. And they *will* follow. Attack in any form has placed your foot upon the twisted stairway that leads from Heaven. Yet any instant it is possible to have all this undone. How can you know whether you chose the stairs to Heaven or the way to hell? Quite easily. How do you feel? Is peace in your awareness? Are you certain which way you go? And are you sure the goal of Heaven can be reached? If not, you walk alone. Ask, then, your Friend to join with you, and give you certainty of where you go.

Lead not your little life in solitude, with one illusion as your only friend. This is no friendship worthy of God's Son, nor one with which he could remain content. Yet God has given him a better Friend, in Whom all power in earth and Heaven rests. The one illusion that you think is a friend obscures His grace and majesty from you, and keeps His friendship and forgiveness from your welcoming embrace. Without Him you are friendless. Seek not another friend to take His place. There *is* no other friend.

What God appointed has no substitute, for what illusions can replace the truth?

Who dwells with shadows is alone indeed, and loneliness is not the Will of God. Would you allow one shadow to usurp the throne that God appointed for your Friend, if you but realized its emptiness has left yours empty and unoccupied? Make no illusion friend, for if you do, it can but take the place of Him Whom God has called your Friend. And it is He Who is your only friend in truth. He brings you gifts that are not of this world, and only He to Whom they have been given can make sure that you receive them. He will place them on your throne, when you make room for Him on His.

Let your mind wander not through darkened corridors, away from light's center. You and your brother may choose to lead yourselves astray, but you can be brought together only by the Guide appointed for you.

We gather at the throne of God today, the quiet place within the mind where He abides forever, in the holiness that He created and will never leave.

He has not waited until you return your mind to Him to give His Word to you. He has not hid Himself from you, while you have wandered off a little while from Him. He does not cherish the illusions which you hold about yourself. He knows His Son, and wills that he remain as part of Him regardless of his dreams; regardless of his madness that his will is not his own.

Author's Note: Our appointed friend is God's Holy Spirit, and His one mission is to heal our belief in separation from God.

ONLY GOD'S PLAN FOR SALVATION WILL WORK

You may not realize that the ego has set up a plan for salvation in opposition to God's. It is the plan in which you believe. Since it is the opposite of God's, you also believe that to accept God's plan in place of the ego's is to be damned. This sounds preposterous, of course. Yet after we have considered just what the ego's plan is, perhaps you will realize that, however preposterous it may be, you do believe in it.

The ego's plan for salvation centers around holding grievances. It maintains that, if someone else spoke or acted differently, if some external circumstance or event were changed, you would be saved. Thus, the source of salvation is constantly perceived as outside yourself. Each grievance you hold is a declaration, and an assertion in which you believe, that says, "If this were different, I would be saved." The change of mind necessary for salvation is thus demanded of everyone and everything except yourself.

The role assigned to your own mind in this plan, then, is simply to determine what, other than itself, must change if you are to be saved. According to this insane plan, any perceived source of salvation is acceptable, provided that it will not work. This ensures that the fruitless search will continue, for the illusion persists that, although this hope has always failed, there is still grounds for hope in other places and in other things. Another person will yet serve better; another situation will yet offer success.

Such is the ego's plan for salvation. Surely you can see how it is in strict accord with the ego's basic doctrine, "Seek but do not find." For what could more surely guarantee

that you will not find salvation than to channelize all your efforts in searching for it where it is not?

God's plan for salvation works simply because, by following His direction, you seek for salvation where it is. But if you are to succeed, as God promises you will, you must be willing to seek there only. Otherwise, your purpose is divided and you will attempt to follow two plans for salvation that are diametrically opposed in all ways. The result can only bring confusion, misery and a deep sense of failure and despair.

How can you escape all this? Very simply, the idea for today is the answer. Only God's plan for salvation will work. There can be no real conflict about this, because there is no possible alternative to God's plan that will save you. His is the only plan that is certain in its outcome. His is the only plan that must succeed.

Let us rejoice that there is an answer to what seems to be a conflict with no resolution possible. All things are possible to God. Salvation must be yours because of His plan, which cannot fail.

Give Him full charge, and let Him tell you what needs to be done by you in His plan for your salvation. He will answer in proportion to your willingness to hear His Voice. Refuse not to hear. The very fact that you are doing the exercises proves that you have some willingness to listen. This is enough to establish your claim to God's answer.

Author's Note: And what is God's plan for salvation other than to follow His Guide to correction. His Guide alone can heal our minds of all past thoughts, all fear and guilt, and free us to experience the present moment and the perfect happiness He wills for us. This alone is salvation!

I MERELY FOLLOW

Father, You are the One Who gave the plan for my salvation to me. You have set the way I am to go, the role to take, and every step in my appointed path. **I cannot lose the way. I can but choose to wander off a while, and then return.** Your loving Voice will always call me back, and guide my feet aright. My brothers all can follow in the way I lead them. Yet I merely follow in the way to You, as You direct me and would have me go.

So let us follow One Who knows the way. We need not tarry, and we cannot stray except an instant from His loving hand. We walk together, for we follow Him. And it is He Who makes the ending sure, and guarantees a safe returning home.

I will use the power of my will today. **It is not my will to grope about in darkness, fearful of shadows and afraid of things unseen and unreal. Light shall be my guide today. I will follow it where it leads me, and I will look only on what it shows me.** This day I will experience the peace of true perception.

I will there be light. Darkness is not my will.

Understanding is light, and light leads to knowledge. The Holy Spirit is in light because He is in you who are light, but you yourself do not know this. It is therefore the task of the Holy Spirit to reinterpret you on behalf of God.

Nothing will change unless it is understood, since light *is* understanding.

Only be quiet.
You will need no rule but this, to let your practicing
today lift you above the thinking of the world,
and free your vision from the body's eyes.
Only be still and listen. You will hear
the Word in which the Will of God
the Son joins in His Father's Will, at one
with it, with no illusions interposed between
the wholly indivisible and true.
. . . be still a moment and remind yourself you have a special
purpose for this day; in quiet to receive the Word of God.

Author's Note: One of the best known stories in the Gospels is that of Jesus calming the storm on the lake, in which he instructed his disciples, "Peace, be still." From this simple teaching came the greatest instruction given to us to be filled with God's Peace—although it is the most overlooked.

GOD IS

Grace is an aspect of the Love of God which is most like the state prevailing in the unity of truth. It is the world's most lofty aspiration, for it leads beyond the world entirely. It is past learning, yet the goal of learning, for grace cannot come until the mind prepares itself for true acceptance. Grace becomes inevitable instantly in those who have prepared a table where it can be gently laid and willingly received; an altar clean and holy for the gift.

Grace is acceptance of the Love of God within a world of seeming hate and fear. By grace alone the hate and fear are gone, for grace presents a state so opposite to everything the world contains, that those whose minds are lighted by the gift of grace cannot believe the world of fear is real.

Grace is not learned. The final step must go beyond all learning. Grace is not the goal this course aspires to attain. Yet we prepare for grace in that an open mind can hear the Call to waken. It is not shut tight against God's Voice. It has become aware that there are things it does not know, and thus is ready to accept a state completely different from experience with which it is familiarly at home.

Oneness is simply the idea God is. And in His Being, He encompasses all things. No mind holds anything but Him. We say, "God is," and then we cease to speak, for in that knowledge words are meaningless. There are no lips to speak them, and no part of mind sufficiently distinct to feel that it is now aware of something not itself. It has united with its Source. And like its Source Itself, it merely is.

God is, and in Him all created things must be eternal.
Do you not see that otherwise He has an opposite,
and fear would be as real as love?

We cannot speak nor write nor even think of this at all. It comes to every mind when total recognition that its will is God's has been completely given and received completely. It returns the mind into the endless present, where the past and future cannot be conceived. It lies beyond salvation; past all thought of time, forgiveness and the holy face of Christ. The Son of God has merely disappeared into his Father, as his Father has in him. The world has never been at all. Eternity remains a constant state.

There is no need to further clarify what no one in the world can understand. When revelation of your oneness comes, it will be known and fully understood. Now we have work to do, for those in time can speak of things beyond, and listen to words which explain what is to come is past already. Yet what meaning can the words convey to those who count the hours still, and rise and work and go to sleep by them?

Suffice it, then, that you have work to do to play your part. The ending must remain obscure to you until your part is done. It does not matter. For your part is still what all the rest depends on. As you take the role assigned to you, salvation comes a little nearer each uncertain heart that does not beat as yet in tune with God.

Forgiveness is the central theme that runs throughout salvation, holding all its parts in meaningful relationships, the course it runs directed and its outcome sure. And now we ask for grace, the final gift salvation can bestow. Experience that grace provides will end in time, for grace forever shadows Heaven, yet does not replace the thought of time but for a little while.

The interval suffices. It is here that miracles are laid; to be returned by you from holy instants you received, through grace in your experience, to all who see the light that lingers in your face.

What is the face of Christ but his who
went a moment into timelessness,
and brought a clear reflection of the unity he
felt an instant back to bless the world?

How could you finally attain to it forever, while a part of you remains outside, unknowing, unawakened, and in need of you as witness to the truth? Be grateful to return, as you were glad to go an instant, and accept the gifts that grace provided you. You carry them back to yourself.

By grace I live. By grace I am released.
By grace I give. By grace I will release.

Author's Note: Raising our awareness to the presence of Love/God is the most fundamental, yet greatest, lesson we can learn. It is this lesson alone that will bring about the greatest shifts and blessings toward inner peace and joy. "God is." And in these words we are reminded of the simplest of teachings. It is this: "Nothing real can be threatened. Nothing unreal exists. Herein lies the peace of God." Only God is real. All the rest need be forgotten.

CHAPTER IV

The Justice of God

There is no order of difficulty in miracles.
One is not "harder" or "bigger" than another.
They are all the same. All expressions of love are maximal.

CAN THIS BE JUSTICE?

There is a kind of justice in salvation of which the world knows nothing. To the world, justice and vengeance are the same, for sinners see justice only as their punishment, perhaps sustained by someone else, but not escaped. The laws of sin demand a victim. Who it may be makes little difference. But death must be the cost and must be paid. This is not justice, but insanity. Yet how could justice be defined without insanity where love means hate, and death is seen as victory and triumph over eternity and timelessness and life?

Can this be justice? God knows not of this. But justice does He know, and knows it well. For He is wholly fair to everyone. Vengeance is alien to God's Mind because He knows of justice. To be just is to be fair, and not be vengeful. Fairness and vengeance are impossible, for each one contradicts the other and denies that it is real. It is impossible for you to share the Holy Spirit's justice with a mind that can conceive of specialness at all.

You have the right to all the universe; to perfect peace, complete deliverance from all effects of sin, and to the life eternal, joyous and complete in every way, as God appointed for His Holy Son. This is the only justice Heaven knows, and all the Holy Spirit brings to earth. Your special function shows you nothing else but perfect justice can prevail for you. And you are safe from vengeance in all forms. The world deceives, but it cannot replace God's justice with a version of its own. For only love is just, and can perceive what justice must accord the Son of God. Let love decide, and never fear that you, in your unfairness, will deprive yourself of what God's justice has allotted you.

What could you not accept, if you but knew that everything that happens, all events, past, present and to come, are gently planned by One Whose only purpose is your good? Perhaps you have misunderstood His plan, for He would never offer pain to you. But your defenses did not let you see His loving blessing shine in every step you ever took. While you made plans for death, He led you gently to eternal life.

Heaven asks nothing.
It is hell that makes extravagant demands for sacrifice.

"Vengeance is mine, sayeth the Lord" is easily reinterpreted if you remember that ideas increase only by being shared. The statement emphasizes that vengeance cannot be shared. Give it therefore to the Holy Spirit, Who will undo it in you because it does not belong in your mind, which is part of God.

Author's Note: Sacrifice is a concept completely foreign to the Holy Spirit. In the statement "Vengeance is mine, sayeth the Lord," Jesus is asking us to forgo or to surrender all of our fears and judgments and all our guilt and vengeance over to His loving care. And in His hands it is undone. This is the only "act of giving up" we are being asked to do. All other demands for sacrifice are of the ego. Vengeance is not of God.

Once this is understood, the scripture "God giveth and taketh away" takes on new meaning. For God gives only life, for that is what God is. And He takes away our fears. Nothing more.

YOU WHO ARE SO HOLY

What fear has hidden still is part of you. Joining the Atonement is the way out of fear. The Holy Spirit will help you reinterpret everything that you perceive as fearful, and teach you that only what is loving it true. **Truth is beyond your ability to destroy, but entirely within your ability to accept.** It belongs to you because, as an extension of God, you created it with Him. It is yours because it is part of you, just as you are part of God because He created you. Nothing that is good can be lost because it comes from the Holy Spirit, the Voice for creation. Nothing that is not good was ever created, and therefore cannot be protected. **The Atonement is the guarantee of the safety of the Kingdom, and the union of the Sonship is its protection. The ego cannot prevail against the Kingdom because the Sonship is united. In the presence of those who hear the Holy Spirit's Call to be as one, the ego fades away and is undone.**

"The wicked shall perish" becomes a statement of Atonement, if the word "perish" is understood as "be undone." Every loveless thought must be undone, a word the ego cannot even understand.

Every loving thought held in any part of the Sonship belongs to every part. It is shared *because* it is loving. Sharing is God's way of creating, and also yours. The ego can keep you in exile from the Kingdom, but in the Kingdom itself it has no power. Ideas of the spirit do not leave the mind that thinks them, nor can they conflict with each other. However, ideas of the ego can conflict because they occur at different levels and also include opposite thoughts at the same level. It is impossible to share opposing thoughts. You can share only the thoughts that are of God and that He keeps for you. And of such is the Kingdom of Heaven. The rest remains with you until the Holy Spirit has reinterpreted them in the light of the Kingdom, making them, too, worthy of being shared. When they have been sufficiently purified He lets you give them away. The decision to share them *is* their purification.

*Miracles are everyone's right,
but purification is necessary first.*

How can you who are so holy suffer? All your past except its beauty is gone, and nothing is left but a blessing. I have saved all your kindnesses and every loving thought you ever had. I have purified them of the errors that hid their light, and kept them for you in their own perfect radiance. They are beyond destruction and beyond guilt. They came from the Holy Spirit with you, and we know what God creates is eternal. You can indeed depart in peace because I have loved you as I loved myself.

You go with my blessing and for my blessing. Hold it and share it, that it may always be ours. I place the peace of God in your heart and in your hands, to hold and share. The heart is pure to hold it, and the hands are strong to give it. We cannot lose. My judgment is as strong as the wisdom of God, in Whose Heart and Hands we have our being. His quiet children are His blessed Sons. The Thoughts of God are with you.

Author's Note: Remember, God's judgment is a healing—the undoing of error of everything unlike His Love. It should not be feared but welcomed.

GOD'S ONLY CREATION

Nothing beyond yourself can make you fearful or loving, because nothing *is* beyond you. Time and eternity are both in your mind, and will conflict until you perceive time solely as a means to regain eternity. You cannot do this as long as you believe that anything happening to you is caused by factors outside yourself. You must learn that time is solely at your disposal, and that nothing in the world can take this responsibility from you. You can violate God's laws in your imagination, but you cannot escape from them. They were established for your protection and are as inviolate as your safety.

God created nothing besides you and nothing besides you exists, for you are part of Him. What except Him can exist? Nothing beyond Him can happen, because nothing except Him is real. Your creations add to Him as you do, but nothing is added that is different because everything has always been. What can upset you except the ephemeral, and how can the ephemeral be real if you are God's only creation and He created you eternal? Your holy mind establishes everything that happens to you. Every response you make to everything you perceive is up to you, because your mind determines your perception of it.

You who are part of God are not at home except in His peace.
If peace is eternal, you are at home only in eternity.

God does not change His Mind about you, for He is not uncertain of Himself. And what He knows can be known, because He does not know it only for Himself. He created you for Himself, but He gave you the power to create for yourself so you would be like Him. That is why your mind is holy. Can anything exceed the Love of God? Can anything, then, exceed your will? Nothing can reach you from beyond it because, being in God, you encompass everything. Believe this, and you will realize how much is up to you. When anything threatens your peace of mind, ask yourself, "Has God changed His Mind about me?" Then accept His decision, for it is indeed changeless, and refuse to change your mind about yourself.

God will never decide against you, or He
would be deciding against Himself.

Author's Note: Eternity does not equate itself with time. To think of eternity as past, present, and future is not to understand its meaning. Eternity is timelessness itself. It is the absence of everything in time as we know it.

A dream you dream alone is only a dream.
A dream you dream together, becomes reality.

John Lennon

HALLUCINATIONS REPLACED

Vision will come to you at first in glimpses, but they will be enough to show you what is given you who see your brother sinless. Truth is restored to you through your desire, as it was lost to you through your desire for something else. Open the holy place that you closed off by valuing the "something else," and what was never lost will quietly return. It has been saved for you. Vision would not be necessary had judgment not been made. Desire now its whole undoing, and it is done for you.

Do you not want to know your own Identity? Would you not happily exchange your doubts for certainty? Would you not willingly be free of misery, and learn again of joy? Your holy relationship offers all this to you. As it was given you, so will be its effects. And as its holy purpose was not made by you, the means by which its happy end is yours is also not of you. Rejoice in what is yours but for the asking, and think not that you need make either means or end. All this is given you who would but see your brother sinless. All this is given, waiting on your desire but to receive it. Vision is freely given to those who ask to see.

Everything looked upon with vision falls gently into place,
according to the laws brought to it by
His calm and certain sight.

Vision is the means by which the Holy Spirit translates your nightmares into happy dreams, your wild hallucinations that show you all the fearful outcomes of imagined sin into the calm and reassuring sights with which He would replace them. These gentle sights and sounds are looked on happily, and heard with joy. They are His substitutes for all the terrifying sights and screaming sounds the ego's purpose brought to your horrified awareness. They step away from sin, reminding you that it is not reality which frightens you, and that the errors which you made can be corrected.

When you have looked on what seemed terrifying, and seen it change to sights of loveliness and peace; when you have looked on scenes of violence and death, and watched them change to quiet views of gardens under open skies, with clear, life-giving water running happily beside them in dancing brooks that never waste away; who need persuade you to accept the gift of vision? And after vision, who is there who could refuse what must come after? Think but an instant just on this; you can behold the holiness God gave His Son. And never need you think that there is something else for you to see.

You will first dream of peace, and then awaken to it.
Your first exchange of what you made for
what you want is the exchange of nightmares
for the happy dreams of love.

Child of God, you were created to create the good, the beautiful and the holy. Do not forget this. The Love of God, for a little while, must still be expressed through one body to another, because vision is still so dim. You can use your body best to help you enlarge your perception so you can achieve real vision, of which the physical eye is incapable. Learning to do this is the body's only true usefulness.

Author's Note: Through our bodies' eyes we see only dreams, projected outward. Whereas vision, seen through the light of the Holy Spirit, beholds our true reality.

COUNTLESS BLESSINGS

Here is the only "sacrifice" You ask of Your beloved Son;
You ask him to give up all suffering,
all sense of loss and sadness,
all anxiety and doubt, and freely let Your
Love come streaming into his awareness,
healing him of pain, and giving
him Your Own eternal joy.
Such is the "sacrifice" You ask of me, and
one I gladly make; the only "cost"
of restoration of Your memory to me,
for the salvation of the world.

God wills you Heaven, and will always will you nothing
else. The Holy Spirit knows only of His Will.
There is no chance that Heaven will not be yours,
for God is sure, and what He wills is as sure as He is.

God gives but to unite. To take away is meaningless to Him.
And when it is as meaningless to you, you can
be sure you share one Will with Him,
and He with you.

From Him you cannot wander,
and there is no possibility that the plan the Holy Spirit
offers "to" everyone, for the salvation "of" everyone,
will not be perfectly accomplished.

You are entitled to miracles because of what you are.
You will receive miracles because of what God is.
And you will offer miracles because
you are one with God.
Again, how simple is salvation!
It is merely a statement of your true Identity.
It is this we celebrate today!

Say His Name, and you invite the angels to surround
the ground on which you stand, and sing to you as they
spread out their wings to keep you safe, and shelter you
from every worldly thought that would
intrude upon your holiness.

HEAVEN'S HELP

Everyone here has entered darkness, yet no one has entered it alone. Nor need he stay more than an instant. For he has come with Heaven's help within him, ready to lead him out of darkness (ignorance) into light (understanding) at any time. The time he chooses can be any time, for help is there, awaiting but his choice. And when he chooses to avail himself of what is given him, then will he see each situation that he thought before was means to justify his anger turned into an event which justifies his love. He will hear plainly that the calls to war he heard before are really calls to peace. He will perceive that where he gave attack is but another altar where he can, with equal ease and far more happiness, bestow forgiveness. And he will reinterpret all temptation as just another chance to bring him joy.

How can a misperception be a sin? Let all your brother's errors be to you nothing except a chance for you to see the workings of the Helper given you to see the world He made instead of yours. This world has much to offer to your peace, and many chances to extend your own forgiveness. Such its purpose is, to those who want to see peace and forgiveness descend on them, and offer them the light.

Sin is the fixed belief perception cannot change. What has been damned is damned and damned forever, being forever unforgivable. If, then, it is forgiven, sin's perception must have been wrong. And thus is change made possible. The Holy Spirit, too, sees what He sees as far beyond the chance of change. But on His vision sin cannot encroach, for sin has been corrected by His sight. And thus it must have been an error, not a sin. For what it claimed could never be, has been. Sin is attacked by punishment, and so preserved. But to forgive it is to change its state from error into truth.

The Son of God could never sin, but he can wish for what would hurt him. And he has the power to think he can be hurt. What could this be except a misperception of himself? Is this a sin or a mistake, forgivable or not? Does he need help or condemnation? Is it your purpose that he be saved or damned? Forgetting not that what he is to you will make this choice your future? For you make it *now*, the instant when all time becomes a means to reach a goal. Make, then, your choice. But recognize that in this choice the purpose of the world you see is chosen, and will be justified.

Sin is the only thought that makes the goal of God seem unattainable. What else could blind us to the obvious, and make the strange and the distorted seem more clear? What else but sin engenders our attacks? What else but sin could be the source of guilt, demanding punishment and suffering? And what but sin could be the source of fear, obscuring God's creation; giving love the attributes of fear and of attack?

Father, I would not be insane today. I would not be
afraid of love, nor seek for refuge in its opposite.
For love can have no opposite. You are
the Source of everything there is.
And everything that is remains with You, and You with it.

Author's Note: The belief or the idea that we should be punished for separating ourselves from God fails to acknowledge that our perception of separation from God is only an error of the split mind. Separation is an illusion. The plan of the Atonement was established to correct this error in perception. When the correction of separation from God has been completed, there will be no more use for time.

What I have chosen to see has cost me vision.
Now I would choose again, that I may see.

THE JUSTICE OF HEAVEN

What can it be but arrogance to think your little errors cannot be undone by Heaven's justice? And what could this mean except that they are sins and not mistakes, forever uncorrectable, and to be met with vengeance, not with justice? Are you willing to be released from all effects of sin? You cannot answer this until you see all that the answer must entail. For if you answer "yes" it means you will forgo all values of this world in favor of the peace of Heaven. Not one sin would you retain. And not one doubt that this is possible will you hold dear that sin be kept in place. You mean that truth has greater value now than all illusions. And you recognize that truth must be revealed to you, because you know not what it is.

To give reluctantly is not to gain the gift, because you are reluctant to accept it. It is saved for you until reluctance to receive it disappears, and you are willing it be given you. **God's justice warrants gratitude, not fear. Nothing you give is lost to you or anyone, but cherished and preserved in Heaven, where all of the treasures given to God's Son are kept for him, and offered anyone who but holds out his hand in willingness they be received. Nor is the treasure less as it is given out. Each gift but adds to the supply. For God is fair. He does not fight against His Son's reluctance to perceive salvation as a gift from Him. Yet would His justice not be satisfied until it is received by everyone.**

Be certain any answer to a problem the Holy Spirit
solves will be one in which no one loses.
The Holy Spirit's problem solving is the
way in which the problem ends.

To give a problem to the Holy Spirit to solve for you means that you *want* it solved. To keep it for yourself to solve without His help is to decide it should remain unsettled, unresolved, and lasting in its power of injustice and attack. No one can be unjust to you, unless you have decided first to *be* unjust. And then must problems rise to block your way, and peace be scattered by the winds of hate.

Unless you think that all your brothers have an equal right to miracles with you, you will not claim your right to them because you were unjust to one with equal rights. Seek to deny and you will feel denied. Seek to deprive, and you have been deprived. A miracle can never be received because another could receive it not. Only forgiveness offers miracles. And pardon must be just to everyone.

Everything you think that is not through
the Holy Spirit is lacking.

When a brother behaves insanely, you can heal him only by perceiving the sanity in him. If you perceive his errors and accept them, you are accepting yours. If you want to give yours over to the Holy Spirit, you must do this with his. Unless this becomes the one way in which you handle all errors, you cannot understand how all errors are undone. How is this different from telling you that what you teach you learn? Your brother is as right as you are, and if you think he is wrong you are condemning yourself.

You cannot correct yourself. Is it possible, then,
for you to correct another? Yet you can see
him truly, because it is possible for you
to see yourself truly. It is not up to you to change
your brother, but merely to accept him as he is.

To perceive errors in anyone, and to react to them as if they were real, is to make them real to you. You will not escape paying the price for this, not because you are being punished for it, but because you are following the wrong guide and will therefore lose your way.

The little problems that you keep and hide become your secret sins, because you did not choose to let them be removed for you. And so they gather dust and grow, until they cover everything that you perceive and leave you fair to no one. Not one right do you believe you have. And bitterness, with vengeance justified and mercy lost, condemns you as unworthy of forgiveness. The unforgiven have no mercy to bestow upon another. That is why your sole responsibility must be to take forgiveness for yourself.

The miracle that you receive, you give. Each one becomes an illustration of the law on which salvation rests; that justice must be done to all, if anyone is to be healed. No one can lose, and everyone must benefit. Each miracle is an example of what justice can accomplish when it is offered to everyone alike. It is received and given equally. It is awareness that giving and receiving are the same. Because it does not make the same unlike, it sees no differences where none exist. And thus it is the same for everyone, because it sees no differences in them. Its offering is universal, and it teaches but one message:

What is God's belongs to everyone, and "is" his due.

I will never leave you or forsake you, because to forsake you would be to forsake myself and God Who created me. You forsake yourself and God if you forsake any of your brothers. You must learn to see them as they are, and understand they belong to God as you do.

Injustice anywhere is a peril to justice everywhere.
Martin Luther King, Jr.

THE HOLY INSTANT/YOUR INVITATION TO LOVE

The holy instant is your invitation to love to enter into your bleak and joyless kingdom, and to transform it into a garden of peace and welcome. Love's answer is inevitable. It will come because you came without the body, and interposed no barriers to interfere with its glad coming. In the holy instant, you ask of love only what it offers everyone, neither less nor more. Asking for everything, you will receive it. And your shining Self will lift the tiny aspect that you tried to hide from Heaven straight to Heaven. No part of love calls on the whole in vain. No Son of God remains outside His Fatherhood.

The holy instant is a miniature of eternity. It is a picture of timelessness, set in a frame of time.

What is the holy instant but God's appeal to you to recognize what He has given you? Here is the great appeal to reason; the awareness of what is always there to see, the happiness that could be always yours. Here is the constant peace you could experience forever. Here is what denial has denied revealed to you. For here the final question is already answered, and what you ask for given. Here is the future *now*, for time is powerless because of your desire for what will never change. For you have asked that nothing stand between the holiness of your relationship and your *awareness* of its holiness.

If God's Will for you is complete peace and joy,
unless you experience only this you must
be refusing to acknowledge His Will.
His Will does not vacillate, being changeless forever.
When you are not at peace it can only be because
you do not believe you are in Him.

God's Will for me is perfect happiness. And I can suffer but from the belief there is another will apart from His.

This holy instant would I give to You. Be You in charge.
For I would follow You, Certain that
Your direction gives me peace.

Author's Note: The holy instant is this present moment. It is the decision to choose the Holy Spirit's guidance over the ego's, freeing our minds of all past guilt and fear, all future worry and doubt, thus releasing our minds to return to the present.

THE BROTHER WHO STANDS BESIDE YOU

Forget not that you came this far together, you and your brother. And it was surely not the ego that led you here. No obstacle to peace can be surmounted through its help. It does not open up its secrets, and bid you look on them and go beyond them. It would not have you see its weakness, and learn it has no power to keep you from the truth. The Guide Who brought you here remains with you, and when you raise your eyes you will be ready to look on terror with no fear at all. But first, lift up your eyes and look on your brother in innocence born of complete forgiveness of his illusions, and through the eyes of faith that sees them not.

This brother who stands beside you still seems to be a stranger. You do not know him, and your interpretation of him is very fearful. And you attack him still, to keep what seems to be yourself unharmed. Yet in his hands is your salvation. You see his madness, which you hate because you share it. And all the pity and forgiveness that would heal it gives way to fear. Brother, you need forgiveness of your brother, for you will share in madness or in Heaven together. And you and he will raise your eyes in faith together, or not at all.

Beside you is one who offers you the chalice of Atonement, for the Holy Spirit is in him. Would you hold his sins against him, or accept his gift to you? Is this giver of salvation your friend or enemy? Choose which he is, remembering that you will receive of him according to your choice. He has in him the power to forgive your sin, as you for him. Neither can give it to himself alone. And yet your savior stands beside each one. Let him be what he is, and seek not to make of love an enemy.

*Those you do not forgive you fear. And no
one reaches love with fear beside him.*

To love my Father is to love His Son—let me not think that I can find the way to God, if I have hatred in my heart. Let me not try to hurt God's Son, and think that I can know his Father or my Self. Let me not fail to recognize myself, and still believe that my awareness can contain my Father, or my mind conceive of all the love my Father has for me, and all the love which I return to Him.

Let me forget my brother's past today. This is the thought that leads the way to You, and brings me to my goal. I cannot come to You without my brother. And to know my Source, I first must recognize what You created one with me. My brother's is the hand that leads me on the way to You. His sins are in the past, along with mine, and I am saved because the past is gone. Let me not cherish it within my heart, or I will lose the way to walk to You. My brother is my savior. Let me not attack the savior You have given me. But let me honor him who bears Your Name, and so remember that It is my own.

*What could restore Your memory to me, except to see my
brother's sinlessness?
His holiness reminds me that he was created one with me,
and like myself.
In him I find my Self, and in Your Son I
find the memory of You as well.*

Author's Note: Within this teaching, when it refers to our brothers' sins, remember there is no sin; it is simply an error. Therefore, the word "sin" is used to describe a lack of love. For if it is sin we see in our brother we condemn ourselves, veiling the Truth from both of us. Salvation's door can only be found in our brother, for God resides in him—and the only key to this door is forgiveness!

EQUALITY AND AWE

God, who encompasses all being, created beings who have everything individually, but who want to share it to increase their joy. Nothing real can be increased except by sharing. That is why God created you. Divine Abstraction takes joy in sharing. That is what creation means. "How," "what" and "to whom" are irrelevant, because real creation gives everything, since it can create only like itself.

When I said, "I am with you always," I meant it literally. I am not absent to anyone in any situation. Because I am always with you, *you* are the way, the truth, and the life. You did not make this power, any more than I did. It was created to be shared, and therefore cannot be meaningfully perceived as belonging to anyone at the expense of another. Such a perception makes it meaningless by elimination or overlooking its real and only meaning.

I have said that awe is inappropriate in connection with the Sons of God, because you should not experience awe in the presence of your equals. However, it was also emphasized that awe is proper in the Presence of your Creator. I have stressed that awe is not an appropriate reaction to me because of our inherent equality.

Awe should be reserved for revelation, to which it is perfectly and correctly applicable.

*Revelation induces complete but temporary
suspension of doubt and fear.
It reflects the original form of communication
between God and His creations.*

It is not appropriate for miracles because a state of awe is worshipful, implying that one of lesser order stands before his Creator. You are a perfect creation, and should experience awe only in the Presence of the Creator of perfection. The miracle is therefore a sign of love among equals. Equals should not be in awe of one another because awe implies inequality. It is therefore an inappropriate reaction to me. An elder brother is entitled to respect for his greater experience, and obedience for his greater wisdom. He is also entitled to love because he is a brother, and to devotion if he is devoted. It is only my devotion that entitles me to yours. There is nothing about me that you cannot attain. I have nothing that does not come from God. The difference between us now is that I have nothing else. This leaves me in a state which is only potential in you.

Author's Note: Revelation, which transcends perception, is always intensely personal. It is beyond words and cannot be truly communicated. The experience of revelation that comes to each mind may indeed be unique, but is always of the same Truth. Revelation reminds us that we are One with God, which God has not forgotten, but we have.

"There is nothing about me that you cannot attain. I have nothing that does not come from God." Jesus is stating here within this teaching something that perhaps has become the most overlooked teaching of them all. Religion has taught us to worship Jesus rather than to simply join with Him. His message was an offer of salvation: principles and tools that worked for Him that will work for us as well if we are willing to follow them. Jesus is indeed a master at teaching and a brother to all, but is not our God. God alone holds the only position that deserves our utmost reverence and awe.

I AM UNDER NO LAWS BUT GOD'S

We have observed before how many senseless things have seemed to you to be salvation. Each has imprisoned you with laws as senseless as itself. You are not bound by them. Yet to understand that this is so, you must first realize salvation lies not there. While you would seek for it in things that have no meaning, you bind yourself to laws that make no sense. Thus do you seek to prove salvation is where it is not. Today we will be glad we cannot prove it. For if you could, you would forever seek salvation where it is not, and never find it. This statement tells you once again how simple is salvation. Look for it where it waits for you, and there it will be found. Look nowhere else, for it is nowhere else.

Think of the freedom in the recognition that you are not bound by all the strange and twisted laws you have set up to save you. **You really think that you would starve unless you have stacks of green paper strips and piles of metal discs. You really think a small round pellet or some fluid pushed into your veins through a sharpened needle will ward off disease and death. You really think you are alone unless another body is with you.**

It is insanity that thinks these things. You call them laws, and put them under different names in a long catalogue of rituals that have no use and serve no purpose. You think you must obey the "laws" of medicine, or economics and of health. Protect the body, and you will be saved.

These are not laws, but madness! The body is endangered by the mind that hurts itself. The body suffering is a mask the mind holds up to hide what really suffers. It would not understand it is its own enemy; that it attacks itself and wants to die. It is from this your "laws" would save the body. It is for this you think you are a body.

Perhaps you even think that there are laws which set forth what is God's and what is yours. Many "religions" have been based on this. They would not save but damn in Heaven's name.

There are no laws but God's. Dismiss all foolish magical beliefs, and hold your mind in silent readiness to hear the Voice that speaks the truth to you. You will be listening to One Who says there is no loss under the laws of God. Payment is neither given nor received. Exchange cannot be made; there are no substitutes; and nothing is replaced by something else. God's laws forever give and never take.

There are no laws except the laws of God. It is our statement of freedom from all danger and all tyranny. It is our acknowledgment that God is our Father, and that His Son is saved.

Father, I wake today with miracles correcting
my perception of all things.
And so begins the day I share with You as I will
share eternity, for time has stepped aside today.

I do not seek the things of time, and so I will not look upon them. What I seek today transcends all laws of time and things perceived in time. I would forget all things except Your Love. I would abide in You, and know no laws except Your law of love. And I would find the peace which You created for Your Son, forgetting all the foolish toys I made as I behold Your glory and my own.

Author's Note: Instead of giving truth to illusions outside of us, we are being asked to give our illusions to the truth within.

FACETS OF HUMILITY

Humility is strength in this sense only;
that to recognize and accept the
fact that you do not know
is to recognize and accept that fact that He does know.

Humility will never ask that you
remain content with littleness.
But it does require that you be not content with
less than greatness that comes not of you.

Of your ego you can do nothing to save yourself or others,
but of your spirit you can do everything
for the salvation of both.
Humility is a lesson for the ego, not for the spirit. Spirit
is beyond humility, because it recognizes its radiance
and gladly sheds its light everywhere. The meek shall
inherit the earth because their egos are humble,
and this gives them truer perception.

I am the light of the world.
True humility requires that you accept this idea
because it is God's Voice which tells you it is true.

Be humble before Him, but great in Him.
And value no plan of the ego before the plan of God.
For you leave empty your place in His plan,
which you must fill if you would join with me,
by your decision to join in any plan but His.

Truth is humble in acknowledging its mightiness,
its changelessness and its eternal wholeness,
all-encompassing, God's perfect gift to His
beloved Son. We lay aside the arrogance which
says that we are sinners, guilty and afraid, ashamed
of what we are; and lift our hearts in true humility
instead to Him Who has created us immaculate,
like to Himself in power and love.

In peace there's nothing so becomes a man
as modest stillness and humility.

William Shakespeare

THE MEANING OF THE LAST JUDGMENT/THE DOORWAY TO LIFE

The Last Judgment is one of the most threatening ideas in your thinking. This is because you do not understand it. **Judgment is not an attribute of God.** It was brought into being only after the separation, when it became one of the many learning devices to be built into the overall plan. Just as the separation occurred over millions of years, the Last Judgment will extend over a similarly long period, and perhaps an even longer one. Its length can, however, be greatly shortened by miracles, the device for shortening but not abolishing time. If a sufficient number become truly miracle-minded, this shortening process can be virtually immeasurable. It is essential, however, that you free yourself from fear quickly, because you must emerge from the conflict if you are to bring peace to other minds.

The Last Judgment is generally thought of as a procedure undertaken by God. Actually it will be undertaken by my brothers with my help. It is a final healing rather than a meting out of punishment, however much you may think that punishment is deserved. Punishment is a concept totally opposed to right-mindedness, and the aim of the Last Judgment is to restore right-mindedness to you. The Last Judgment might be called a process of right evaluation. It simply means that everyone will finally come to understand what is worthy and what is not. After this, the ability to choose can be directed rationally. Until this distinction is made, however, the vacillations between free and imprisoned will cannot but continue.

If it is the judgment of the Holy Spirit it will be right, for judgment "is" His function. You share His function only by judging as He does, reserving no judgment at all for yourself. You will judge against yourself, but He will judge for you.

Everyone will ultimately look upon his own creations and choose to preserve only what is good, just as God Himself looked upon what He had created and knew that it was good. At this point, the mind can begin to look with love on its own creations because of their worthiness. At the same time the mind will inevitably disown its miscreations which, without belief, will no longer exist.

The term "Last Judgment" is frightening not only because it has been projected onto God, but also because of the association of last with death. This is an outstanding example of upside-down perception. If the meaning of the Last Judgment is objectively examined, it is quite apparent that it is really the doorway to life. No one who lives in fear is really alive. Your own last judgment cannot be directed toward yourself, because you are not your own creation. You can, however, apply it meaningfully and at any time to everything you have made, and retain in your memory only what is creative and good. This is what your right-mindedness cannot but dictate. The purpose of time is solely to "give you time" to achieve this judgment. It is your own perfect judgment of your own perfect creations. When everything you retain is lovable, there is no reason for fear to remain with you. This is your part in the Atonement.

Is each one to be judged in the end? Indeed, yes! No one can escape God's Final Judgment. Who could flee forever from the truth? But the Final Judgment will not come until it is no longer associated with fear. One day each one will welcome it, and on that very day it will be given him. He will hear his sinlessness proclaimed around and around the world, setting it free as God's Final Judgment on him is received. This is the Judgment in which salvation lies. This is the Judgment that will set him free. This is the Judgment in which all things are freed with him. Time pauses as eternity comes near, and silence lies across the world that everyone may hear this Judgment of the Son of God: *Holy are you, eternal, free and whole, at peace forever in the Heart of God. Where is the world, and where is sorrow now?*

Do you believe that this is wholly true? No; not yet, not yet. But this is still your goal; why you are here. It is your function to prepare yourself to hear this Judgment and to recognize that it is true. One instant of complete belief in this, and you will go beyond belief to Certainty. One instant out of time can bring time's end. Judge not, for you but judge yourself, and thus delay this Final Judgment. What is your judgment of the world, teacher of God? Have you yet learned to stand aside and hear the Voice of Judgment in yourself? Or do you still attempt to take His role from Him? Learn to be quiet, for His Voice is heard in stillness. And His Judgment comes to all who stand aside in quiet listening, and wait for Him.

You who believed that God's Last Judgment would condemn the world to hell along with you, accept this holy truth: God's Judgment is the gift of the correction He bestowed on all your errors, freeing you from them, and all effects they ever seemed to have. To fear God's saving grace is but to fear complete release from suffering, return to peace, security and happiness, and union with your own Identity.

Do not fear the Last Judgment, but welcome it and do not wait, for the ego's time is "borrowed" from your eternity. This is the Second Coming that was made for you as the First was created. The Second Coming is merely the return of sense . . . the Second Coming is the awareness of reality, not its return. Can this be fearful?

Christ's Second Coming, which is as sure as God is, is merely the correction of mistakes, and the return of sanity. It is a part of the condition that restores the never lost, and re-establishes what is forever and forever true. It is the invitation to God's Word to take illusion's place; the willingness to let forgiveness rest upon all things without exception and without reserve.

The Second Coming ends the lessons that the Holy Spirit teaches, making way for the Last Judgment, in which learning ends in one last summary that will extend beyond itself, and reaches up to God . . . for everyone who ever came to die, or yet will come or who is present now, is equally released from what he made. In this equality is Christ restored as one Identity, in which the Sons of God acknowledge that they all are one. And God the Father smiles upon His Son, His one creation and His only joy.

This is God's Final Judgment:

You are still My holy Son, forever innocent, forever loving and forever loved, as limitless as your Creator, and completely changeless and forever pure. Therefore awaken and return to Me. I am your Father and you are My Son.

Author's Note: God/Truth/Love has no need for judgment. Its only need for judgment is to correct illusions within our minds. Love's judgment (healing) is necessary only in the presence of opposites or differences. The ego uses judgment to give meaning to a world of form and duality (beautiful/ugly, right/wrong/, up/down, inward/outward, love/hate, valuable/invaluable). This form of judgment is defensive. However, to use the mind to make judgments for practical reasons, while being aware of one's own innocence rather than guilt, is to use judgment in a way that offers freedom and healing rather than conflict and compounding guilt.

A MEANINGLESS WORLD

I have given what I see all the meaning it has for me. I have judged everything I look upon, and it is this and only this I see. This is not vision. It is merely an illusion of reality, because my judgments have been made quite apart from reality. I am willing to recognize the lack of validity in my judgments, because I want to see. My judgments have hurt me, and I do not want to see according to them.

I do not understand anything I see. How could I understand what I see when I have judged it amiss? What I see is the projection of my own errors of thought. I do not understand what I see because it is not understandable. There is no sense in trying to understand it. But there is every reason to let it go, and make room for what can be seen and understood and loved. I can exchange what I see now for this merely by being willing to do so. Is not this a better choice than the one I made before?

These thoughts do not mean anything. The thoughts of which I am aware do not mean anything because I am trying to think without God. What I call "my" thoughts are not my real thoughts. My real thoughts are the thoughts I think with God. I am not aware of them because I have made my thoughts to take their place. I am willing to recognize that my thoughts do not mean anything, and to let them go. I choose to have them be replaced by what they were intended to replace. My thoughts are meaningless, but all creation lies in the thoughts I think with God.

Since the purpose of the world is not the one I ascribed to it, there must be another way of looking at it. I see everything upside down, and my thoughts are the opposite of truth.

God did not create a meaningless world—How can a meaningless world exist if God did not create it? He is the Source of all meaning, and everything that is real is in His Mind. It is in my mind too, because He created it with me. Why should I continue to suffer from the effects of my own insane thoughts, when the perfection of creation is my home? Let me remember the power of my decision, and recognize where I really abide.

The world you see has nothing to do with reality. It is of your own making, and it does not exist. What God did not create can only be in your own mind apart from His. Therefore, it has no meaning. Your reality is only spirit.

What you made can always be changed because, when you do not think like God, you are not really thinking at all. Delusional ideas are not real thoughts, although you can believe in them. But you are wrong. The function of thought comes from God and is in God. As part of His thought, you *cannot* think apart from Him.

Author's Note: Our thoughts do not mean anything because we have given everything in our lives all the meaning it has for us. And when they no longer serve our greater good, we change their meaning to serve our own purpose. Will is thought. But the only thoughts that are real are the loving thoughts that come from the Mind of God. They do not shift or change, forever remaining as loving as they were when created. To wake in Him is to question every value we hold dear, and accept the new translation God's Love would give to them.

CHAPTER V

The Undoing of Fear

Miracles represent freedom from fear.
"Atoning" means "undoing."
The undoing of fear is an essential part
of the Atonement value of miracles.

I AM ONE SELF, UNITED WITH MY CREATOR

You are one Self, united and secure in light and joy and peace. You are God's Son, one Self, with one Creator and one goal: to bring awareness of this oneness to all minds, that true creation may extend the allness and the unity of God. You are one Self, complete and healed and whole, with power to lift the veil of darkness from the world, and let the light in you come through to teach the world the truth about yourself.

There is no veil the Love of God in us together cannot lift. The way to truth is open.

No one who understands what you have learned, how carefully you learned it, and the pains to which you went to practice and repeat the lessons endlessly, in every form you could conceive of them, could ever doubt the power of your learning skill. There is no greater power in the world. The world was made by it, and even now depends on nothing else. **The lessons you have taught yourself have been so overlearned and fixed they rise like heavy curtains to obscure the simple and the obvious.** Say not you cannot learn them. For your power to learn is strong enough to teach you that your will is not your own, your thoughts do not belong to you, and even you are someone else.

You are one Self, in perfect harmony with all there is, and all that there will be. You are one Self, the holy Son of God, united with your brothers in that Self; united with your Father in His Will. Feel this one Self in you, and let it shine away all your illusions and your doubts. This is your Self, the

Son of God Himself, sinless as Its Creator, with His strength within you and His Love forever yours. You are one Self, and it is given you to feel this Self within you, and to cast all your illusions out of the one Mind that is this Self, the holy truth in you.

Repeat today's idea as frequently as possible, and understand each time you do so, someone hears the voice of hope, the stirring of the truth within his mind, the gentle rustling of the wings of peace.

Your own acknowledgment you are one Self, united with your Father, is a call to all the world to be at one with you. To everyone you meet today, be sure to give the promise of today's idea and tell him this:

You are one Self with me, united with our Creator in this Self. I honor you because of What I am, and What He is, Who loves us both as One.

Healing is a thought by which two minds perceive their oneness and become glad.

Author's Note: Being one Self in God and one with all the world is an idea that can be very hard to grasp while we believe in a world of duality. And even though it may not ever be completely understood while we seem to be in a body and in a world believing in the world of duality, all of which our eyes are showing us, we can begin to accept the idea that separation is a dream. Oneness, on its simplest level, implies that God's Truth is Universal. Whatever we believe in within the realm of time, timelessness and God's Truth is True and nothing else is true.

*We cannot solve our problems
with the same level of thinking
that created them.
Ice cannot be dissolved at 32 degrees;
its temperature has to be raised.*

Albert Einstein

YOUR LITTLE WILLINGNESS

The holy instant is the result of your determination to be holy. It is the "answer." The desire and the willingness to let it come precede its coming. You prepare your mind for it only to the extent of recognizing that you want it above all else. It is not necessary that you do more; indeed, it is necessary that you realize that you cannot do more. Do not attempt to give the Holy Spirit what He does not ask, or you will add the ego to Him and confuse the two. He asks but little. It is He Who adds the greatness and the might. He joins with you to make the holy instant far greater than you can understand. It is your realization that you need do so little that enables Him to give so much.

Trust not your good intentions. They are not enough. But trust implicitly your willingness, whatever else may enter. Concentrate only on this, and be not disturbed that shadows surround it. That is why you came. If you could come without them you would not need the holy instant. Come to it not in arrogance, assuming that you must achieve the state its coming brings with it. The miracle of the holy instant lies in your willingness to let it be what it is. And in your willingness for this lies also your acceptance of yourself as you were meant to be.

Your difficulty with the holy instant arises from your fixed conviction that you are not worthy of it. And what is this but the determination to be as you would make yourself? **God did not create His dwelling place unworthy of Him.** And if you believe He cannot enter where He wills to be, you must be interfering with His Will. You do not need the strength of willingness to come from you, but only from His Will.

You are perfectly safe as long as you are completely unconcerned about your readiness, but maintain a consistent trust in mine.

The holy instant does not come from your little willingness alone. It is always the result of your small willingness combined with the unlimited power of God's Will. You have been wrong in thinking that it is needful to prepare yourself for Him.

You merely ask the question. The answer is given. Seek not to answer, but merely to receive the answer as it is given. In preparing for the holy instant, do not attempt to make yourself holy to be ready to receive it. That is but to confuse your role with God's. Atonement cannot come to those who think that they must first atone, but only to those who offer it nothing more than simple willingness to make way for it. Purification is of God alone, and therefore for you. Rather than seek to prepare yourself for Him, try to think thus:

I who am host to God am worthy of Him. He who established His dwelling place in me created it as He would have it be. It is not needful that I make it ready for Him, But only that I do not interfere with His plan to restore to me my own awareness of my readiness, which is eternal. I need add nothing to His plan. But to receive it, I must be willing not to substitute my own in place of it.

And that is all. Add more, and you will merely take away the little that is asked. Remember you made guilt, and that your plan for the escape from guilt has been to bring Atonement to it, and make salvation fearful. And it is only fear that you will add, if you prepare yourself for love. Release yourself to Him Whose function is release. Give Him but what He ask, that you may learn how little is your part, and how great is His.

You are still convinced that your understanding is a powerful contribution to the truth, and makes it what it is. Yet we have emphasized that you need understand nothing. Salvation is easy just *because* it asks nothing you cannot give right now.

Forget not that it has been your decision to make everything that is natural and easy for you impossible. If you believe the holy instant is difficult for you, it is because you have become the arbiter of what is possible, and remain unwilling to give place to One Who knows. The whole belief in orders of difficulty in miracles is centered on this. Everything God wills is not only possible, but has already happened. And that is why the past has gone. It never happened in reality. Only in your mind, which thought it did, is its undoing needful.

My Father knows my holiness. Shall I deny His knowledge, and believe in what His knowledge makes impossible? Shall I accept as true what He proclaims as false? Or shall I take His Word for what I am, since He is my Creator, and the One Who knows the true condition of His Son?

Father, I was mistaken in myself, because I failed
to realize my Source from which I came.
I have not left that Source to enter in a body and to die.
My holiness remains a part of me, as I am part of You.
And my mistakes about myself are
dreams. I let them go today.
And I stand ready to receive Your Word
alone for what I really am.

You are only love, but when you deny this, you make what you are something you must learn to remember.

Author's Note: We are being asked to abandon all our preconceived ideas and concepts about ourselves, along with the belief that we know how to correct them. The correction process is not *of* us but *for* us. We need not understand, but only to become willing to abandon our assumptions and stay true to our convictions.

The "holy instant" removes us from the past, frees us from the future, and places us in the eternal present where God's peace and joy can be found.

ONLY PERCEPTION CAN BE SICK

I have said before that the Holy Spirit is the Answer. He is the Answer to everything, because He knows what the answer to everything is. The ego does not know what a real question is, although it asks an endless number. Yet you can learn this as you learn to question the value of the ego, and thus establish your ability to evaluate its questions. When the ego tempts you to sickness do not ask the Holy Spirit to heal the body, for this would merely be to accept the ego's belief that the body is the proper aim of healing. Ask, rather, that the Holy Spirit teach you the right perception of the body, for perception alone can be distorted. Only perception can be sick, because only perception can be wrong.

You see what you expect, and you expect what you invite. Your perception is the result of your invitation, coming to you as you sent for it.

Wrong perception is the wish that things be as they are not. You do not have to seek reality. It will seek you and find you when you meet its conditions. Its conditions are part of what it is. And this part only is up to you. The rest is of itself. You need do so little because your little part is so powerful that it will bring the whole to you. Accept, then, your little part, and let the whole be yours.

The body cannot heal, because it cannot make itself sick. It "needs" no healing. Its health or sickness depends entirely on how the mind perceives it, and the purpose that the mind would use it for.

Wholeness heals because it is of the mind. All forms of sickness, even unto death, are physical expressions of the fear of awakening. They are attempts to reinforce sleeping out of fear of waking. This is a pathetic way of trying not to see by rendering the faculties for seeing ineffectual. "Rest in peace" is a blessing for the living, not the dead, because rest comes from waking, not from sleeping. Sleep is withdrawing; waking is joining. Dreams are illusions of joining, because they reflect the ego's distorted notions about what joining is. Yet the Holy Spirit, too, has use for sleep, and can use dreams on behalf of waking if you will let Him.

You can rest in peace only because you are awake.

Healing is release from the fear of waking and the substitution of the decision to wake. The decision to wake is the reflection of the will to love, since all healing involves replacing fear with love. The Holy Spirit cannot distinguish among degrees of error, for if He taught that one form of sickness is more serious than another, He would be teaching that one error can be more real than another. His function is to distinguish only between the false and the true, replacing the false with the true.

The Bible enjoins you to be perfect, to heal all errors, to take no thought of the body as separate and to accomplish all things in my name. This is not my name alone, for ours is a shared identification. The Name of God's Son is One, and you are enjoined to do the works of love because we share this Oneness. Our minds are whole because they are one. If you are sick you are withdrawing from me. Yet you cannot withdraw from me alone. You can only withdraw from yourself *and* me.

SALVATION'S POWER

Pain is a wrong perspective. When it is experienced in any form, it is a proof of self-deception. It is not fact at all. There is no form it takes that will not disappear if seen aright, for pain proclaims God cruel. How could it be real in any form? It witnesses to God the Father's hatred of His Son, the sinfulness He sees in him, and His insane desire for revenge and death—Can such projections be attested to? Can they be anything but wholly false?

Pain is a sign illusions reign in place of truth. It demonstrates God is denied, confused with fear, perceived as mad, and seen as a traitor to Himself. If God is real, there is no pain. If pain is real, there is no God. For vengeance is not part of love. And fear, denying love and using pain to prove that God is dead, has shown that death is victor over life. Peace to such foolishness! The time has come to laugh at such insane ideas.

It is your thoughts alone that cause you pain. Nothing external to your mind can hurt or injure you in any way. There is no cause beyond yourself that can reach down and bring oppression. No one but yourself affects you. There is nothing in the world that has the power to make you ill or sad, or weak or frail. But it is you who have the power to dominate all things you see by merely recognizing what you are. As you perceive the harmlessness in them, they will accept your holy will as theirs. And what was seen as fearful now becomes a source of innocence and holiness.

Beware of the temptation to perceive yourself unfairly treated.

Lay down your arms, and come without defense into the quiet place where Heaven's peace holds all things still at last. Lay down all thoughts of danger and of fear. Let no attack enter with you. Lay down the cruel sword of judgment that you hold against your throat, and put aside the withering assaults with which you seek to hide your holiness.

Here will you understand there is no pain. Here does the joy of God belong to you. This is the day when it is given you to realize the lesson that contains all of salvation's power. It is this:

Pain is illusion; joy, reality. Pain is but sleep; joy is awakening. Pain is deception; joy alone is truth.

And so again we make the only choice that ever can be made. We choose between illusions and the truth, or pain and joy, or hell and Heaven. Let our gratitude unto our Teacher fill our hearts, as we are free to choose our joy instead of pain, our holiness in place of sin, the peace of God instead of conflict, and the light of Heaven for the darkness of the world.

Rest in His Love and protect your rest by loving.

If you bring forth what is within you, what you bring forth will save you. But if you do not bring forth what is within you, what you do not bring forth will destroy you.

Gospel of Thomas

HOSTAGE OR HOST?

Be not content with littleness. But be sure you understand what littleness is, and why you could never be content with it. Littleness is the offering you give yourself. You offer this in place of magnitude, and you accept it. Everything in this world is little because it is a world made out of littleness, in the strange belief that littleness can content you. When you strive for anything in this world in the belief that it will bring you peace, you are belittling yourself and blinding yourself to glory.

Littleness and glory are the choices open to
your striving and your vigilance.
You will always choose one at the expense of the other.

Yet what you do not realize, each time you choose, is that your choice is your evaluation of yourself. Choose littleness and you will not have peace, for you will have judged yourself unworthy of it. And whatever you offer as a substitute is much too poor a gift to satisfy you. It is essential that you accept the fact, and accept it gladly, that there is no form of littleness that can ever content you. You are free to try as many as you wish, but all you will be doing is to delay your homecoming. For you will be content only in magnitude, which is your home.

There is a deep responsibility you owe yourself, and one you must learn to remember all the time. The lesson may seem hard at first, but you will learn to love it when you realize that it is true and is but a tribute to your power. You who have sought and found littleness, remember this: Every decision you make stems from what you think you are, and represents the value that you put upon yourself. Believe the little can content you, and by limiting yourself you will not be satisfied. For your function is not little, and it is only by finding your function and fulfilling it that you can escape from littleness.

"Would you be hostage to the ego or host to God?" Let this question be asked you by the Holy Spirit every time you make a decision. For every decision you make does answer this, and invites sorrow or joy accordingly.

All honor is due the host of God. Your littleness deceives you, but your magnitude is of Him Who dwells in you, and in whom you dwell.

The Holy Spirit and the ego are the only choices open to you.
God created one, and so you cannot eradicate
it. You made the other, and so you can.
Only what God creates is irreversible and unchangeable.

WHAT IS DEATH?

Death is the central dream from which all illusions stem. Is it not madness to think of life as being born, aging, losing vitality, and dying in the end? We have asked this question before, but now we need to consider it more carefully. It is the one fixed, unchangeable belief of the world that all things in it are born only to die.

In this perception of the universe as God created it, it would be impossible to think of Him as loving. For who has decreed that all things pass away, ending in dust and disappointment and despair, can but be feared. He holds your little life in his hand but by a thread, ready to break it off without regret or care, perhaps today. Or if he waits, yet is the ending certain. Who loves such a god knows not of Love, because he has denied that life is real. Death has become life's symbol. His world is now a battleground, where contradiction reigns and opposites make endless war. Where there is death is peace impossible.

Death is the symbol of the fear of God. His Love is blotted out in the idea, which holds it from awareness like a shield held up to obscure the sun. The grimness of the symbol is enough to show it cannot coexist with God. It holds an image of the Son of God in which he is "laid to rest" in devastation's arms, where worms wait to greet him and to last a little while by his destruction. Yet the worms as well are doomed to be destroyed as certainly. And so do all things live because of death. Devouring is nature's "law of life." God is insane, and fear alone is real.

If death is real for anything, there is no life. Death denies life. But if there is reality in life, death is denied. No compromise in this is possible. There is either a god of fear or One of Love. The world attempts a thousand compromises, and will attempt a thousand more. Not one can be acceptable to God's teachers, because not one could

be acceptable to God. He did not make death because He did not make fear. Both are equally meaningless to Him.

The "reality" of death is firmly rooted in the belief that God's Son is a body. And if God created bodies, death would indeed be real. But God would not be loving. There is no point at which the contrast between the perception of the real world and that of the world of illusions becomes more sharply evident. Death is indeed the death of God, if He is Love. And now His Own creation must stand in fear of Him. He is not Father, but destroyer. He is not Creator, but avenger. Terrible His Thoughts and fearful His image. To look on His creations is to die.

"And the last to be overcome will be death." Of course! Without the idea of death there is no world. All dreams will end with this one. This is salvation's final goal; the end of all illusions. And in death are all illusions born. What can be born of death and still have life? But what is born of God and still can die? **The inconsistencies, the compromises, and the rituals the world fosters in its vain attempts to cling to death and yet to think love real are mindless magic, ineffectual and meaningless. God is, and in Him all created things must be eternal. Do you not see that otherwise He has an opposite, and fear would be as real as love?**

Teacher of God, your one assignment could be stated thus: Accept no compromise in which death plays a part. Do not believe in cruelty, nor let attack conceal the truth from you. What seems to die has but been misperceived and carried to illusion. Now it becomes your task to let the illusions be carried to the truth. Be steadfast but in this; be not deceived by the "reality" of any changing form. Truth neither moves nor wavers nor sinks down to death and dissolution. And what is the end of death?

Nothing but this: the realization that the Son of God is guiltless now and forever. Nothing but this. But do not let yourself forget it is not less than this.

As you look upon yourself and judge what you do honestly, you may be tempted to wonder how you can be guiltless. Yet consider this: You are not guiltless in time, but in eternity. You have made errors in the past, but there is no past. Always has no direction. Time seems to go in one direction, but when you reach its end it will roll up like a long carpet spread along the past behind you, and will disappear. As long as you believe the son of God is guilty you will walk along this carpet, believing that it leads to death. And this journey will seem long and cruel and senseless, for so it is.

Death is a thought that takes on many forms, often unrecognized. It may appear as sadness, fear, anxiety or doubt; as anger, faithlessness and lack of trust; concern for bodies, envy, and all forms in which the wish to be as you are not may come to tempt you. All such thoughts are but reflections of the worshipping of death as savior and as giver of release.

It is impossible to worship death in any form, and still select a few you would not cherish and would yet avoid, while still believing in the rest. For death is total. Either all things die, or else they live and cannot die. No compromise is possible. For here again we see an obvious position, which we must accept if we be sane; what contradicts one thought entirely cannot be true, unless its opposite is proven false.

God made not death. Whatever form it takes must therefore be illusion. This is the stand we take today. And it is given us to look past death and see the life beyond.

Our Father, bless our eyes today. We are Your
messengers, and we would look upon the glorious
reflection of Your Love which shines
in everything. We live and move in You alone.
We are not separate from Your eternal life.
There is no death, for death is not Your Will.
And we abide where You have placed us, in
the life we share with You and with all living
things, to be like You and part of You forever.
We accept Your Thoughts as ours, and our
will is one with Yours eternally.

Author's Note: God did not create death—we created the belief in it. And if death is an illusion, and the Holy Spirit assures us that it is, so must the body be, for bodies appear to die. All form, which includes not only the body but everything in the material world, is an illusion. The word illusion is commonly misunderstood. An illusion is something that appears to exist, but does not really exist at all, being only a perception in our mind. Illusions have never existed; not in the past or in this present moment. Nor does it mean they will cease to exist in the future. They have never existed, being only perceptions without our minds. Can you not see then that, if form is real on any level, death is indeed real?

ANOTHER CHANCE

Trials are but lessons that you failed to learn presented once again, so where you made a faulty choice before you now can make a better one, and thus escape all pain that what you chose before has brought to you. In every difficulty, all distress, and each perplexity Christ calls to you and gently says, "My brother, choose again."

He would not leave one source of pain unhealed, nor any image left to veil the truth. He would remove all misery from you whom God created altered into joy. He would not leave you comfortless, alone in dreams of hell, but would release your mind from everything that hides His face from you. His Holiness is yours because He is the only power that is real in you. His strength is yours because He is the Self that God created as His only Son.

The images you make cannot prevail against what God Himself would have you be. Be never fearful of temptation, then, but see it as it is—another chance to choose again, and let Christ's strength prevail in every circumstance and every place you raised an image of yourself before. For what appears to hide the face of Christ is powerless before His majesty, and disappears before His holy sight. The saviors of the world, who see like Him, are merely those who choose His strength instead of their own weakness, seen apart from Him. They will redeem the world, for they are joined in all the power of the Will of God. And what they will is only what He wills.

Learn, then, the happy habit of response to all temptation to perceive yourself as weak and miserable with these words:

I am as God created me. His Son can suffer nothing. And I "am" His Son.

Thus is Christ's strength invited to prevail, replacing all your weakness with the strength that comes from God and that can never fail. For in that choice are false distinctions gone, illusory alternatives laid by, and nothing left to interfere with truth.

Choosing depends on learning. And truth cannot be learned, but only recognized. Decisions are the outcome of your learning, for they rest on what you have accepted as the truth of what you are, and what your needs must be.

"Lead us not into temptation" means "Recognize your errors and choose to abandon them by following my guidance." Error cannot really threaten truth, which can always withstand it. Only the error is actually vulnerable. You are free to establish your kingdom where you see fit, but the right choice is inevitable if you remember this:

Spirit is in a state of grace forever. Your reality is only spirit. Therefore you are in a state of grace forever.

Only the mind can create because spirit has already been created, and the body is a learning device for the mind. Learning devices are not lessons in themselves. Their purpose is merely to facilitate learning.

YOUR COMPLETE DEPENDENCE

When the Atonement has been completed, all talents will be shared by all the Sons of God. God is not partial. All His children have His total Love, and all His gifts are freely given to everyone alike. "Except ye become as little children" means that unless you fully recognize your complete dependence on God, you cannot know the real power of the Son in his true relationship with the Father. The specialness of God's Sons does not stem from exclusion but from inclusion. All my brothers are special. If they believe they are deprived of anything, their perception becomes distorted. When this occurs the whole family of God, or the Sonship, is impaired in its relationships.

It should especially be noted that God has only *one* Son. If all his Creations are His Sons, every one must be an integral part of the whole Sonship. The Sonship in its Oneness transcends the sum of its parts. However, this is obscured as long as any of its parts is missing. That is why the conflict cannot ultimately be resolved until all the parts of the Sonship have returned. Only then can the meaning of wholeness in the true sense be understood. Any part of the Sonship can believe in error or incompleteness if he so chooses. However, if he does so, he is believing in the existence of nothingness. The correction of this error is the Atonement. (God is the Perfect Whole of Which we are a Perfect Part—God's One Son.)

Ultimately, every member of the family of God must return. The miracle calls him to return because it blesses and honors him, even though he may be absent in spirit. "God is not mocked" is not a warning but a reassurance. God *would* be mocked if any of His creations lacked holiness. The creation is whole, and the mark of wholeness is holiness. Miracles are affirmations of Sonship, which is a state of completion and abundance.

The miracle is the sign that the mind has chosen to be led by me in Christ's service. The abundance of Christ is the natural result of choosing to follow Him. All shallow roots must be uprooted, because they are not deep enough to sustain you. The illusion that shallow roots can be deepened, and thus made to hold, is one of the distortions on which the reverse of the Golden Rule rests.

The Golden Rule asks you do unto others as
you would have them do unto you.
This means that the perception of both must be accurate.
The Golden Rule is the rule for appropriate behavior.

You cannot behave appropriately unless you perceive correctly. Since you and your neighbor are equal members of one family, as you perceive both so you will do to both. You should look out from the perception of your own holiness to the holiness of others.

Miracles arise from a mind that is ready for them. By being united this mind goes out to everyone, even without the awareness of the miracle worker himself. The impersonal nature of miracles is because the Atonement itself is one, uniting all creations with their Creator. As an expression of what you truly are, the miracle places the mind in a state of grace. The mind then naturally welcomes the Host within and the stranger without. When you bring in the stranger, he becomes your brother.

Author's Note: "Do unto others as you would have them do unto you" is indeed the Golden Rule, for what we do unto others *is* done unto ourselves.

TO TEACH IS TO LEARN

The role of teaching and learning is actually reversed in the thinking of the world. The reversal is characteristic. It seems as if the teacher and the learner are separated, the teacher giving something to the learner rather than to himself. Further, the act of teaching is regarded as a special activity, in which one engages only a relatively small proportion of one's time. The course, on the other hand, emphasizes that to teach *is* to learn, so that teacher and learner are the same. It also emphasizes that teaching is a constant process; it goes on every moment of the day, and continues into sleeping thoughts as well.

To teach is to demonstrate. There are only two thought systems (the ego's, or God's; fear or Love), and you demonstrate that you believe one or the other is true all the time. From your demonstration others learn, and so do you. The question is not whether you will teach, for in that there is no choice. The purpose of the course might be said to provide you with a means of choosing what you want to teach on the basis of what you want to learn. You cannot give to someone else, but only to yourself, and this you learn through teaching. Teaching is but a call to witnesses to attest to what you believe. It is a method of conversation. This is not done by words alone. Any situation must be to you a chance to teach others what you are, and what they are to you. No more than that, but also never less.

The curriculum you set up is therefore determined exclusively by what you think you are, and what you believe the relationship of others is to you. Teaching but reinforces what you believe about yourself. Its fundamental purpose is to diminish self-doubt. This does not mean that the self you are trying to protect is real. But is does mean that the self you think is real is what you teach.

Everyone who follows the world's curriculum, and everyone here does follow it until he changes his mind, teaches solely to convince himself that he is what he is not. Herein is the purpose of the world. What else, then, would its curriculum be? Into this hopeless and closed learning situation, which teaches nothing but despair and death, God sends His teachers. And as they teach His lessons of joy and hope, their learning finally becomes complete.

Who are God's teachers? A teacher of God is anyone who chooses to be one. His qualifications consist solely of this: Somehow, somewhere he has made a deliberate choice in which he did not see his interests as apart from someone else's. Once he has done that, his road is established and his direction is sure. A light has entered the darkness. It may be a single light, but that is enough. He has entered an agreement with God even if he does not yet believe in Him. He has become a bringer of salvation. He has become a teacher of God.

Everything you teach you are learning. Teach only love, and learn that love is yours and you are love.

Teaching is done in many ways, above all by example. Teaching should be healing, because it is the sharing of ideas and the recognition that to share ideas is to strengthen them.

THE POWER OF JOINING

When you feel the holiness of your relationship is threatened by anything, stop instantly and offer the Holy Spirit your willingness, in spite of fear, to let Him exchange this instant for the holy one that you would rather have. He will never fail in this. But forget not that your relationship is one, and so it must be that whatever threatens the peace of one is an equal threat to the other. The power of joining its blessing lies in the fact that it is now impossible for you or your brother to experience fear alone, or to attempt to deal with it alone. Never believe that this is necessary, or even possible. Yet just as this is impossible, so is it equally impossible that the holy instant come to either of you without the other. And it will come to both at the request of either.

Whoever is saner at the time the threat is perceived should remember how deep is his indebtedness to the other and how much gratitude is due him, and be glad that he can pay his debt by bringing happiness to both. Let him remember this, and say:

*I desire this holy instant for myself, that I may
share it with my brother, whom I love.
It is not possible that I can have it
without him, or he without me.
Yet it is wholly possible for us to share it now. And so I
choose this instant as the one to offer to the Holy Spirit,
that His blessing may descend on us, and keep us both in peace.*

I want the peace of God—to say these words is nothing. But to mean these words is everything. If you could but mean them for just an instant, there would be no further sorrow possible for you in any form, in any place or time. Heaven would be completely given back to full awareness, memory of God entirely restored, and the resurrection of all creation fully recognized.

When you unite with me you are uniting without the ego, because I have renounced the ego in myself and therefore cannot unite with yours. Our union is therefore the way to renounce the ego in you. The truth in both of us is beyond the ego. Our success in transcending the ego is guaranteed by God, and I share this confidence for both of us and all of us. I bring God's peace back to all His children because I received it from Him for us all. Nothing can prevail against our united wills because nothing can prevail against God's.

*And if I need a word to help me, He will give
it to me. If I need a thought, that will He
also give. And if I need but stillness
and a tranquil, open mind, these are the gifts I will
receive of Him. He is in charge by my request.
And He will hear and answer me, because He
speaks for God my Father and His holy Son.*

Author's Note: It is only by extending God's Love to others that we become aware of His Love being given to us. This is the power of joining. And it is through its sharing that love increases.

THOSE WHO OFFER PEACE

You maker of a world that is not so, take rest and comfort in another world where peace abides. This world you bring with you to all the weary eyes and tired hearts that look on sin and beat its sad refrain. From you can come their rest. From you can rise a world they will rejoice to look upon, and where their hearts are glad. In you there is a vision that extends to all of them, and covers them in gentleness and light. And in this widening world of light the darkness that they thought was there is pushed away, until it is but distant shadows, far away, not long to be remembered as the sun shines them to nothingness. And all their "evil" thoughts and "sinful" hopes, their dreams of guilt and merciless revenge, and every wish to hurt and kill and die, will disappear before the sun you bring.

Would you not do this for the Love of God? And for *yourself*? For think what it would do for you. Your "evil" thoughts that haunt you now will seem increasingly remote and far away from you. And they go farther and farther off, because the sun in you has risen that they may be pushed away before the light. They linger for a while, a little while, in twisted forms too far away for recognition, and are gone forever. And in the sunlight you will stand in quiet, in innocence and wholly unafraid. And from you will the rest you found extend, so that your peace can never fall away and leave you homeless. Those who offer peace to everyone have found a home in Heaven the world cannot destroy. For it is large enough to hold the world within its peace.

In you is all of Heaven. Every leaf that falls is given life in you. Each bird that ever sang will sing again in you. And every flower that ever bloomed has saved its perfume and its loveliness for you.

What aim can supersede the Will of God and of His Son, that Heaven be restored to him for whom it was created as his only home? Nothing before and nothing after it. No other place; no other state nor time. Nothing beyond nor nearer. Nothing else. In any form. This can you bring to all the world, and all the thoughts that entered it and were mistaken for a little while. How better could your own mistakes be brought to truth than by your willingness to bring the light of Heaven with you as you walk beyond the world of darkness into light?

In the light of the real reason that He brings, as you follow Him, He will show you that there is no reason here at all.

Author's Note: Reason is synonymous with cause. God is the only Cause, as all reason is of His Holy Spirit.

Happiness is when what you think, what you say,
and what you do are in harmony with Love.

Mahatma Gandhi

ONE PROVISO

The ego is certain that love is dangerous, and this is always its central teaching. It never puts it this way; on the contrary, everyone who believes that the ego is salvation seems to be intensely engaged in the search for love. Yet the ego, though encouraging the search for love very actively, makes one proviso: Do not find it. Its dictates, then, can be summed up simply as: "Seek and do *not* find." This is the one promise the ego holds out to you, and the one promise it will keep. For the ego pursues its goal with fanatical insistence, and its judgment, though severely impaired, is completely consistent.

The search the ego undertakes is therefore bound to be defeated. And since it also teaches that it is your identification, its guidance leads you to a journey which must end in perceived self-defeat.

You must have noticed an outstanding characteristic of every end that the ego has accepted as its own. When you have achieved it, *it has not satisfied you.* This is why the ego is forced to shift ceaselessly from one goal to another, so that you will continue to hope it can yet offer you something.

Do you realize that the ego must set you on a journey which cannot but lead to a sense of futility and depressions? To seek and not to find is hardly joyous. Is this the promise you would keep? The Holy Spirit offers you another promise, and one that will lead to joy. For His promise is always "Seek and you *will* find," and under His guidance you cannot be defeated. His is the journey to accomplishment, and the goal He sets before you He will give you. For He will never deceive God's Son whom He loves with the Love of the Father.

You *will* undertake a journey because you are not at home in this world. And you *will* search for your home whether you realize where it is or not. If you believe it is outside you the search will be futile, for you will be seeking it where it is not. You do not remember how to look within for you do not believe your home is there. Yet the Holy Spirit remembers it for you, and He will guide you to your home because that is His mission. As He fulfills His mission He will teach you yours, for your mission is the same as His. By guiding your brothers home you are but following Him.

My Name, O Father, still is known to You.
I have forgotten It, and do not know where I
am going, who I am, or what it is I do.
Remind me, Father, now, for I am weary of the world
I see. Reveal what You would have me see instead.

Behold the Guide your Father gave you, that you might learn you have eternal life. For death is not your Father's Will nor yours, and whatever is true is the Will of the Father. You pay no price for life for that was given you, but you do pay a price for death, and a very heavy one. If death is your treasure, you will sell everything else to purchase it. And you will believe that you have purchased it, because you have sold everything else. Yet you cannot sell the Kingdom of Heaven. Your inheritance can neither be bought nor sold. There can be no disinherited parts of the Sonship, for God is whole and all His extensions are like Him.

The Holy Spirit guides you into life eternal, but
you must relinquish your investment in death,
or you will not see life though it is all around you.

THE ANSWER TO CONFLICTING GOALS

Seek you no further. You will not find peace except the peace of God. Accept this fact, and save yourself the agony of yet more bitter disappointments, bleak despair, and sense of icy hopelessness and doubt. Seek you no further. There is nothing else for you to find except the peace of God, unless you seek for misery and pain.

This is the final point to which each one must come at last, to lay aside all hope of finding happiness where there is none; of being saved by what can only hurt; and making peace of chaos, joy of pain, and Heaven out of hell. Attempt no more to win through losing, nor to die to live. You cannot but be asking for defeat.

Yet you can ask as easily for love, for happiness, and for eternal life in peace that has no ending. Ask for this, and you can only win. **To ask for what you have already must succeed. To ask for what is false be true can only fail.** Forgive yourself for vain imaginings, and seek no longer what you cannot find. For what could be more foolish than to seek and seek and seek again for hell, when you have but to look with open eyes to find that Heaven lies before you, through a door that opens easily to welcome you?

In the ego's language, "to have" and "to be" are different, but they are identical to the Holy Spirit. The Holy Spirit knows that you both "have" everything and "are" everything.

Freedom is given you where you beheld but chains and iron doors. But you must change your mind about the purpose of the world, if you would find escape. You will be bound till all the world is seen by you as blessed, and everyone made free of your mistakes and honored as he is. You made him not; no more yourself. And as you free the one, the other is accepted as he is.

What does forgiveness do? In truth it has no function, and does nothing. For it is unknown in Heaven. It is only hell where it is needed, and where it must serve a mighty function. Is not the escape of God's beloved Son from evil dreams that he imagines, yet believes are true, a worthy purpose? Who could hope for more, while there appears to be a choice to make between success and failure; love and fear?

Peace is the bridge that everyone will cross, to leave this world behind. But peace begins within the world perceived as different, and leading from this fresh perception to the gate of Heaven and the way beyond. Peace is the answer to conflicting goals, to senseless journeys, frantic, vain pursuits, and meaningless endeavors. Now the way is easy, sloping gently toward the bridge where freedom lies with the peace of God.

The peace of God is everything I want. The peace of God is my goal; the aim of all my living here, the end I seek, my purpose and my function and my life , while I abide where I am not at home.

WHEREVER I AM, THERE GOD IS

**Today's idea will eventually overcome completely the
sense of loneliness and abandonment all the separated
ones experience. Depression is an inevitable consequence
of separation. So are anxiety, worry, a deep sense of
helplessness, misery, suffering and intense fear of loss.**

When you are sad, *know this need not be.* Depression
comes from a sense of being deprived of something you
want and do not have. **Remember that you are deprived
of nothing except by your own decisions, and then decide
otherwise.** When you are anxious, realize that anxiety
comes from the capriciousness of the ego, *and know this
need not be.* You can be as vigilant against the ego's dictates
as for them. When you feel guilty your ego is in command,
because only the ego can experience guilt. *This need not be.*

The habit of engaging with God and His creations
is easily made if you actively refuse to let your mind slip
away. The problem is not one of concentration; it is the
belief that no one, including yourself, is worth consistent
effort. Side with me consistently against this deception,
and do not permit this shabby belief to pull you back.

The separated ones have invented many "cures"
for what they believe to be "the ills of the world." But
the one thing they do not do is to question the reality of
the problem. Yet its effect cannot be cured because the
problem is not real. The idea for today has the power
to end all this foolishness forever. And foolishness it is,
despite the serious and tragic forms it may take.

Deep within you is everything that is perfect, ready to
radiate through you and out into the world. It will cure all
sorrow and pain and fear and loss because it will heal the
mind that thought these things were real, and suffered out
of its allegiance to them.

What is not love is always fear, and nothing else.

**You can never be deprived of your perfect holiness
because its Source goes with you wherever you go. You
can never suffer because the Source of all joy goes with
you wherever you go. You can never be alone because the
Source of all life goes with you wherever you go. Nothing
can destroy your peace of mind because God goes with
you wherever you go.**

*The fear of God is causeless. But His Love
is Cause of everything beyond all fear, and
thus forever real and always true.*

What seems to be the fear of God is really the fear of
your own reality.

THE BRANCHING OF THE ROAD

When you come to the place where the branch in the road is quite apparent, you cannot go ahead. You must go either one way or the other. For now if you go straight ahead, you will go nowhere. The whole purpose of coming this far was to decide which branch you will take now. The way you came no longer matters. It can no longer serve. No one who reaches this far can make the wrong decision, although he can delay. And there is no part of the journey that seems more hopeless and futile than standing where the road branches, and not deciding on which way to go.

It is but the first few steps along the right way that seem hard, for you have chosen, although you still may think you can go back and make the other choice. This is not so. A choice made with the power of Heaven to uphold it cannot be undone. Your way is decided. There will be nothing you will not be told, if you acknowledge this.

And so you and your brother stand, here in this holy place, before the veil of sin that hangs between you and the face of Christ. Let it be lifted! Raise it together with your brother, for it is but a veil that stands between you. Either you or your brother alone will see it as a solid block, nor realize how thin the drapery that separates you now. Yet it is almost over in your awareness, and peace has reached you even here, before the veil. Think what will happen after. The Love of Christ will light your face, and shine from it into a darkened world that needs the light. And from this holy place He will return with you, not leaving it nor you. You will become His messenger, returning Him unto Himself.

The branch that bears no fruit will be cut
off and will wither away. Be glad!
The light will shine from the true Foundation of Life,
and your own thought system will stand corrected.

Think of the loveliness that you will see, who walk with Him! And think how beautiful will you and your brother look to the other! How happy you will be to be together, after such a long and lonely journey where you walked alone.

Those who would let illusions be lifted from their minds are
this world's saviors, walking the world with their Redeemer,
and carrying His message of hope and freedom and release
from suffering to everyone who needs a miracle to save him.

How easy is it to offer this miracle to everyone! No one who has received it for himself could find it difficult. For by receiving it, he learned it was not given him alone. Such is the function of the holy relationship; to receive together and give as you received. Standing before the veil, it still seems difficult. But hold out your hand, joined with your brother's, and touch this heavy-seeming block, and you will learn how easily your fingers slip through its nothingness. It is no solid wall. And only an illusion stands between you and your brother, and the holy Self you share together.

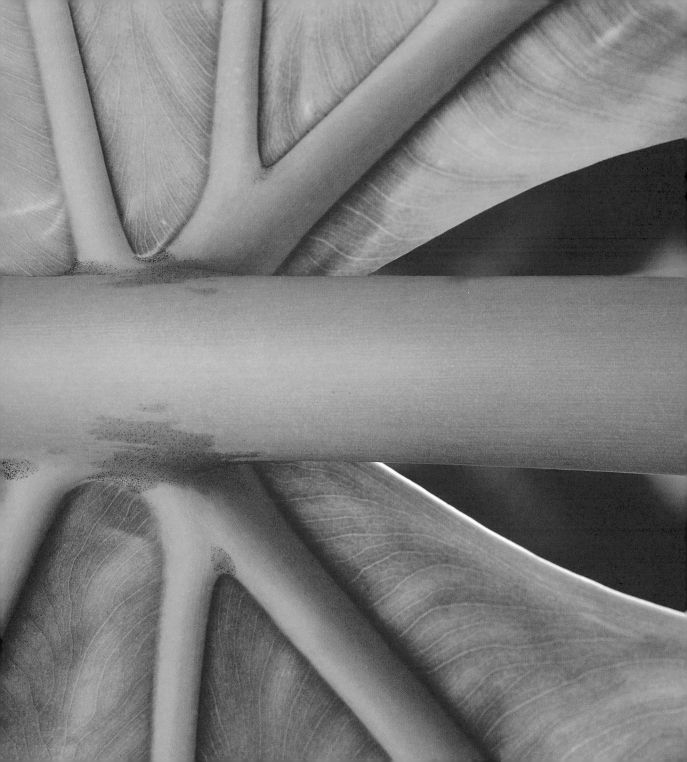

A CALL FROM LOVE TO LOVE

The Holy Spirit mediates between illusions and the truth. Since He must bridge the gap between reality and dreams, perception leads to knowledge through the grace that God has given Him, to be His gift to everyone who turns to Him for truth. Across the bridge that He provides are dreams all carried to the truth, to be dispelled before the light of knowledge. There are sights and sounds forever laid aside. And where they were perceived before, forgiveness has made possible perception's tranquil end.

The goal the Holy Spirit's teaching sets is just this end of dreams. For sights and sounds must be translated from the witnesses of fear to those of love. And when this is entirely accomplished, learning has achieved the only goal it has in truth. For learning, as the Holy Spirit guides it to the outcome He perceives for it, becomes the means to go beyond itself, to be replaced by the eternal truth.

He is your Guide to salvation, because He holds
the remembrance of things past and to come,
and brings them to the present. He holds this
gladness gently in your mind, asking only
that you increase it in His Name by sharing
it to increase His joy in you.

If you but knew how much your Father yearns to have you recognize your sinlessness, you would not let His Voice appeal in vain, nor turn away from His replacement for the fearful images and dreams you made. The Holy Spirit understands the means you made, by which you would attain what is forever unattainable. And if you offer them to Him, He will employ the means you made for exile to restore your mind to where it truly is at home.

From knowledge, where He has been placed by God, the Holy Spirit calls to you, to let forgiveness rest upon your dreams, and be restored to sanity and peace of mind. Without forgiveness will your dreams remain to terrify you. And the memory of all your Father's Love will not return to signify the end of dreams has come.

Accept your Father's gift. It is a Call from Love to Love, that It be but Itself. The Holy Spirit is His gift, by which the quietness of Heaven is restored to God's beloved Son. Would you refuse to take the function of completing God, when all He wills is that you be complete?

Father, how still today! How quietly do all things fall in
place! This is the day that has been chosen as the time in
which I come to understand the lesson that there is no need
that I do anything. In You is every choice already made.
In You has every conflict been resolved. In You
is everything I hope to find already given me.
Your peace is mine. My heart is quiet, and my mind
at rest. Your Love is Heaven, and Your Love is mine.

CHAPTER VI

The War Against Yourself

*The miracle dissolves error because the Holy Spirit
identifies error as false or unreal.
This is the same as saying that by perceiving light,
darkness automatically disappears.*

AN INWARD CONDITION

Projection makes perception. The world you see is what you gave it, nothing more than that. But though it is no more than that, it is not less. Therefore, to you it is important. It is the witness to your state of mind, the outside picture of an inward condition. As a man thinketh, so does he perceive. Therefore, seek not to change the world, but choose to change your mind about the world. Perception is a result and not a cause. And that is why order of difficulty in miracles is meaningless. Everything looked upon with vision is healed and holy. Nothing perceived without it means anything. And where there is no meaning, there is chaos.

Perception is a mirror, not a fact. And what I look on is my state of mind, reflected outward.

Damnation is your judgment on yourself, and this you will project upon the world. See it as damned, and all you see is what you did to hurt the Son of God. If you behold disaster and catastrophe, you tried to crucify him. If you see holiness and hope, you joined the Will of God to set him free. There is no choice that lies between these two decisions. And you will see the witness to the choice you made, and learn from this to recognize which one you chose. The world you see but shows you how much joy you have allowed yourself to see in yourself, and to accept as yours. And, if this is its meaning, then the power to give it joy must lie within you.

Projection makes perception, and you cannot see beyond it. Again and again have you attacked your brother, because you saw in him a shadow figure in your private world. And thus it is you must attack yourself first, for

what you attack is not in others. Its only reality is in your own mind, and by attacking others you are literally attacking what is not there.

The delusional can be very destructive, for they do not recognize they have condemned themselves.

You have no idea of the tremendous release and deep peace that comes from meeting yourself and your brothers totally without judgment. When you recognize what you are and what your brothers are, you will realize that judging them in any way is without meaning. In fact, their meaning is lost to you precisely *because* you are judging them. **All your difficulties stem from the fact that you do not recognize yourself, your brother or God.** To recognize means to "know again," implying that you knew before . . . God knows His children with perfect certainty. He created them by knowing them. He recognizes them perfectly. When they do not recognize each other, they do not recognize Him.

Author's Note: The ego's interpretation of the world, and the solution to all its many problems, is one where you seek outside yourself for understanding, correction, and truth. But the Holy Spirit's interpretation of the world is quite different, being that He teaches the solution to *all* problems that are perceived *without* are *within* the mind and nowhere else. Hence, "seek not to change the world but choose to change your mind about the world."

All the beauty we behold in the world is simply a reflection of mind on where we have become willing to see our own innocence.

Science is nothing but perception.

Plato

NO EXCEPTIONS

If you are trusting in your own strength, you have every reason to be apprehensive, anxious, and fearful. What can you predict or control? What is there in you that can be counted on? What would give you the ability to be aware of all the facets of any problem, and to resolve them in such a way that only good can come of it? What is there in you that gives you the recognition of the right solution, and guarantees that it will be accomplished?

Of yourself you can do none of these things. To believe that you can is to put your trust where trust is unwarranted, and to justify fear, anxiety, depression, anger, and sorrow. Who can put his faith in weakness and feel safe? Yet who can put his faith in strength and feel weak?

> *The children of God are entitled to the perfect comfort that comes from perfect trust.*
> *Until they achieve this, they waste themselves and their true creative powers on useless attempts to make themselves more comfortable by inappropriate means.*

God is your safety in every circumstance. His Voice speaks for Him in all situations and in every aspect of all situations, telling you exactly what to do to call upon His strength and His protection. There are no exceptions because God has no exceptions. And the Voice Which speaks for Him thinks as He does. It is not by trusting yourself that you will gain confidence. But the strength of God in you is successful in all things.

The recognition of your own frailty is a necessary step in the correction of your errors, but it is hardly a sufficient one in giving you the confidence you need, and to which you are entitled. You must also gain an awareness that confidence in your real strength is fully justified in every respect and in all circumstances.

Let go all the trivial things that churn and bubble on the surface of your mind, and reach down and below them to the Kingdom of Heaven. There is a place in you where there is perfect peace. There is a place in you where nothing is impossible. There is a place in you where the strength of God abides.

> *Remember that peace is your right, because you are giving your trust to the strength of God.*

To give up all problems to one Answer is to reverse the thinking of the world entirely. And that alone is faithfulness. Nothing but that really deserves the name. Yet each degree, however small, is worth achieving. Their many forms will not deceive you while you remember this. One problem, one solution. Accept the peace this simple statement brings.

Author's Note: In truth, there is only one problem, and only one solution. All problems, in all their many forms, "are all symbolic of something deeper: an unconscious guilt that exists at the level of the mind that can be traced all the way back to the original belief in separation from God and the massive guilt and fear that it generated." And the one solution is a miracle.

—from *Love Has Forgotten No One*, by Gary Renard

THE ONLY SANE SOLUTION

The ego tries to exploit all situations into forms of praise for itself in order to overcome its doubts. It will remain doubtful as long as you believe in its existence. You who made it cannot trust it, because in your right mind you realize it is not real. The only sane solution is not to try to change reality, which is indeed a fearful attempt, but to accept it as it is. You are part of reality, which stands unchanged beyond the reach of your ego but within easy reach of spirit. When you are afraid, be still and know that God is real, and you are His beloved Son in whom He is well pleased. Do not let your ego dispute this, because the ego cannot know what is as far beyond its reach as you are.

God knows you only in peace, and this "is" your reality.

God is not the author of fear. You are. You have chosen to create unlike Him, and have therefore made fear for yourself. You are not at peace because you are not fulfilling your function. God gave you a very lofty function that you are not meeting. Your ego has chosen to be afraid instead of meeting it. When you awaken you will not be able to understand this, because it is literally incredible. Do not believe the incredible now. Any attempt to increase its believeableness is merely to postpone the inevitable. **The word "inevitable" is fearful to the ego, but joyous to the spirit. God is inevitable, and you cannot avoid Him any more than He can avoid you.**

The ego is afraid of the spirit's joy, because once you have experienced it you will withdraw all protection from the ego, and become totally without investment in fear. Your investment is great now because fear is a witness to the separation, and your ego rejoices when you witness to it. Leave it behind! Do not listen to it and do not preserve it. Listen only to God, Who is as incapable of deception as is the spirit He created. Release yourself and release others. Do not present a false and unworthy picture of yourself to others, and do not accept such a picture of them yourself.

The ego has built a shabby and unsheltering home for you, because it cannot build otherwise. Do not try to make this impoverished house stand. Its weakness is your strength. Only God could make a home that is worthy of His creations, who have chosen to leave it empty by their own dispossession. Yet His home will stand forever, and is ready for you when you choose to enter it. Of this you can be wholly certain.

God is as incapable of creating the perishable as the ego is of making the eternal.

When you made visible what is not true, what *is* true became invisible to you. Yet it cannot be invisible in itself, for the Holy Spirit sees it with perfect clarity. It is invisible to you because you are looking at something else. Yet it is no more up to you to decide what is visible and what is invisible, than it is up to you to decide what reality is. What can be seen is what the Holy Spirit sees. The definition of reality is God's, not yours. He created it, and He knows what it is. You who knew have forgotten, and unless He had given you a way to remember you would have condemned yourself to oblivion.

IN BLESSING IT DEPARTS

The world you perceive is a world of separation. Perhaps you are willing to accept even death to deny your Father. Yet He would not have it so, and so it is not so. You still cannot will against Him, and that is why you have no control over the world you made. It is not a world of will because it is governed by the desire to be unlike God, and this desire is not will. The world you made is therefore totally chaotic, governed by arbitrary and senseless "laws," and without meaning of any kind. For it is made out of what you do not want, projected from your mind because you are afraid of it. Yet this world is only in the mind of its maker, along with his real salvation. Do not believe it is outside of yourself, for only by recognizing where it is will you gain control over it. For you do have control over your mind, since the mind is the mechanism of decision.

If you will recognize that all the attack you perceive is in your own mind and nowhere else, you will at last have placed its source, and where it begins it must end. For in this same place also lies salvation. The altar of God where Christ abideth is there. You have defiled the altar, but not the world. Yet Christ has placed the Atonement on the altar for you. Bring your perceptions of the world to this altar, for it is the altar to truth. There you will see your vision changed, and there you will learn to see truly. From this place, where God and His Son dwell in peace and where you are welcome, you will look out in peace and behold the world truly. Yet to find the place, you must relinquish your investment in the world as you project it, allowing the Holy Spirit to extend the real world to you from the altar of God.

It might be worth a little time to think once more about the value of this world. Perhaps you will concede there is no loss in letting go all thought of value here. The world you see is merciless indeed, unstable, cruel, unconcerned with you, quick to avenge and pitiless with hate. It gives but to rescind, and takes away all things that you have cherished for a while. No lasting love is found, for none is here. This is the world of time, where all things end.

> *The world will end when its thought system*
> *has been completely reversed.*
> *Until then, bits and pieces of its thinking*
> *will still seem sensible.*

The world will end in joy, because it is a place of sorrow. When joy has come, the purpose of the world has gone. The world will end in peace, because it is a place of war. When peace has come, what is the purpose of the world? The world will end in laughter, because it is a place of tears. Where there is laughter, who can longer weep? And only complete forgiveness brings all this to bless the world. In blessing it departs, for it will not end as it began. To turn hell into Heaven is the function of God's teachers, for what they teach are lessons in which Heaven is reflected. And now sit down in true humility, and realize that all God would have you do you can do. Do not be arrogant and say you cannot learn His Own curriculum. His Word says otherwise. His Will is done. It cannot be otherwise. And be you thankful it is so.

And so we trust in Him to send us miracles to bless the world, and heal our minds as we return to Him.

> *The end of the world is not its destruction,*
> *but its translation into Heaven.*
> *The reinterpretation of the world is the*
> *transfer of all perception into knowledge.*

Until forgiveness is complete,
the world does have a purpose.

WHAT IS THE EGO?

The ego is idolatry; the sign of limited and separated self, born in a body, doomed to suffer and to end its life in death. It is the "will" that sees the Will of God as enemy, and takes a form in which it is denied. The ego is the "proof" that strength is weak and love is fearful, life is really death, and what opposes God alone is true.

The ego is insane. In fear it stands beyond the Everywhere, apart from All, in separation from the Infinite. In its insanity it thinks it has become a victor over God Himself. And in its terrible autonomy it "sees" the Will of God has been destroyed. It dreams of punishment, and trembles at the figures in its dreams; its enemies, who seek to murder it before it can ensure its safety by attacking them.

The Son of God is egoless. What can he know of madness and the death of God, when he abides in Him? What can he know of sorrow and of suffering, when he lives in eternal joy? What can he know of fear and punishment, sin and guilt, of hatred and attack, when all there is surrounding him is everlasting peace, forever conflict-free and undisturbed, in deepest silence and tranquility?

What is the ego? But a dream of what you really are. A thought you are apart from your Creator and a wish to be what He created not. It is a thing of madness, not reality at all. A name for namelessness is all it is. A symbol of impossibility; a choice for options that do not exist.

To know reality is not to see the ego and its thoughts, its works, its acts, its laws and its beliefs, its dreams, its hopes, its plans for its salvation, and the cost belief in it entails. In suffering, the price for faith in it is so immense that crucifixion of the Son of God is offered daily at its darkened shrine, and blood must flow before the altar where its sickly followers prepare to die.

Yet will one lily of forgiveness change the darkness into light; the altar to illusions to the shrine of Life Itself. And peace will be restored forever to the holy minds which God created as His Son, His dwelling place, His joy, His love, completely His, completely one with Him.

The ego is a wrong-minded attempt to perceive yourself as you wish to be, rather than as you are. Yet you can know yourself only as you are, because that is all you can be sure of. Everything else "is" open to question.

Author's Note: The ego is the belief in separation. It is the desire for authorship, to dream of the impossible— Erasing God Out. The concept of the ego is no different than the concept of Satan or the devil, all being symbols of opposition to truth. They are nothing more than the projection of the personal thoughts system's guilt, projected outside of itself where it is no longer responsible for it. We become victims of these "evil forces" when we put our belief in such things. And the cost of this belief is powerlessness over choosing to experience peace, although it only takes a single shift of mind to realign our mind with Truth.

THE SELF-ACCUSED

Only the self-accused condemn. As you prepare to make a choice that will result in different outcomes, there is first one thing that must be overlearned. It must become a habit of response so typical of everything you do that it becomes your first response to all temptation, and to every situation that occurs. Learn this, and learn this well, for it is here delay of happiness is shortened by a span of time you cannot realize.

You never hate your brother for his sins, but only for your own. Whatever form his sins appear to take, it but obscures the fact that you believe them to be yours, and therefore meriting a "just" attack.

Why should his sins be sins, if you did not believe they could not be forgiven in you? Why are they real in him, if you did not believe that they are your reality? And why do you attack them everywhere except you hate yourself? Are *you* a sin? You answer "yes" whenever you attack, for by attack do you assert that you are guilty, and must give as you deserve. And what can you deserve but what you are? If you did not believe that you deserved attack, it never would occur to you to give attack to anyone at all. Why should you? What would be the gain to you? What could the outcome be that you would want? And how could murder bring you benefit?

Sins are in bodies. They are not perceived in minds. They are not seen as purposes, but actions. Bodies act, and minds do not. And therefore must the body be at fault for what it does. It is not seen to be a passive thing, obeying your commands, and doing nothing of itself at all. If you are sin you *are* a body, for the mind acts not. And purpose must be in the body, not the mind. The body must act on its own, and motivate itself. If you are sin you lock the mind within the body, and you give its purpose to its prison house, which acts instead of it. A jailer does not follow orders, but enforces orders on the prisoner.

Yet is the *body* prisoner, and not the mind. The body thinks no thoughts. It has no power to learn, to pardon, nor enslave. It gives no orders that the mind need serve, nor sets conditions that it must obey. It holds in prison but the willing mind that would abide in it. It sickens at the bidding of the mind that would become its prisoner. And it grows old and dies, because that mind is sick within itself. **Learning is all that causes change. And so the body, where no learning can occur, could never change unless the mind preferred the body change in its appearances, to suit the purpose given by the mind. For the mind can learn, and there is all change made.**

Let us be glad that you will see what you believe, and that it has been given you to change what you believe. The body will but follow. It can never lead you where you would not be. It does not guard your sleep, nor interfere with your awakening. Release your body from imprisonment, and you will see no one as prisoner to what you have escaped. You will not want to hold in guilt your chosen enemies, nor keep in chains, to the illusions of a changing love, the ones you think are friends. Open your mind to change, and there will be no ancient penalty exacted from your brother or yourself.

WHO IS THE PHYSICIAN?

The acceptance of sickness as a decision of the mind, for a purpose for which it would use the body, is the basis of healing. And this is so for healing in all forms. A patient decides that this is so, and he recovers. If he decides against recovery, he will not be healed. Who is the physician? Only the mind of the patient himself. The outcome is what he decides that it is. Special agents seem to be ministering to him, yet they but give form to his own choice. He chooses them in order to bring tangible form to his desire. And it is this they do, and nothing else. They are not actually needed at all. The patient could merely rise up without their aid and say, "I have no use for this." There is no form of sickness that would not be cured at once.

What is the single requisite for this shift in perception? It is simply this: *The recognition that sickness is of the mind, and has nothing to do with the body.*

What does this recognition "cost"? It cost the whole world you see, for the world will never again appear to rule the mind. For with this recognition is responsibility placed where it belongs; not with the world, but on him who looks on the world and sees it as it is not. He looks on what he chooses to see. No more and no less. The world does nothing to him. He only thought it did. Nor does he do anything to the world, because he was mistaken about what it is. Herein is the release from guilt and sickness both, for they are one. Yet to accept this release, the insignificance of the body must be an acceptable idea.

With this idea is pain forever gone. But with this idea goes also all confusion about creation. Does not this follow of necessity? Place cause and effect in their true sequence in one respect, and the learning will generalize and transform the world. The transfer value of one true idea has no end or limit. The final outcome of this lesson is the remembrance of God. What do guilt and sickness, pain, disaster and all suffering mean now? Having no purpose, they are gone. And with them also go all the effects they seemed to cause. Cause and effect but replicate creation. Seen in their proper perspective, without distortion and without fear, they re-establish Heaven.

*Atonement does not heal the sick, for that is not a cure.
It takes away the guilt that makes the sickness
possible. And that is cure indeed.
The guiltless mind cannot suffer. Being sane, the
mind heals the body because "it" has been healed.*

Who, then, is the therapist, and who is the patient? In the end, everyone is both. He who needs healing must heal. Physician, heal thyself. Who else is there to heal? And who else is in need of healing? Each patient who comes to a therapist offers him a chance to heal himself. He is therefore his therapist. And every therapist must learn to heal from each patient who comes to him. He thus becomes his patient.

Author's Note: Whenever we believe ourselves or others to be anything other than what God created, we bring suffering upon ourselves, although we can do no real damage, for our true Selves are unalterable. But we will have an entirely realistic illusion of pain and suffering. All our physical and emotional senses will confirm its seeming reality, but it is only a dream. All healing comes from the decision to follow the Holy Spirit's guidance. Although we are the ones who make the choice to be healed, the healing is given by One Who knows what healing is! Choosing to be healed is our only part in salvation.

God does not know of separation. What He knows is only that He has one Son. His knowledge is reflected in the ideal patient-therapist relationship. God comes to him who calls, and in Him he recognizes Himself.

HERE IN THE MIDST

Be lifted up, and from a higher place look down upon it. From there will your perspective be quite different. Here in the midst of it, it does seem real. Here you have chosen to be part of it. Here murder is your choice. Yet from above, the choice is miracles instead of murder. And the perspective coming from this choice shows you the battle is not real, and easily escaped. Bodies may battle but the clash of forms is meaningless. And it is over when you realize it never was begun. How can a battle be perceived as nothingness when you engage in it? How can the truth of miracles be recognized if murder is your choice?

When the temptation to attack rises to make your mind darkened and murderous, remember you *can* see the battle from above. Even in forms you do not recognize, the signs you know. There is a stab of pain, a twinge of guilt, and above all, a loss of peace. This you know well. When they occur leave not your place on high, but quickly choose a miracle instead of murder. And God Himself and all the lights of Heaven will gently lean to you, and hold you up. For you have chosen to remain where He would have you, and no illusion can attack the peace of God together with His Son.

Whatever form temptation seems to take, it always but reflects a wish to be a self that you are not.

Temptation has one lesson it would teach, in all its forms, wherever it occurs. It would persuade the holy Son of God he is a body, born in what must die, unable to escape its frailty, and bound by what it orders him to feel. It sets the limits on what he can do; its power is the only strength he has; his grasp cannot exceed its tiny reach. Would you be this, if Christ appeared to you in all His glory, asking you but this:

> *Choose once again if you would take your place*
> *among the saviors of the world, or remain*
> *in hell, and hold your brothers there.*
> *For He "has" come, and He "is" asking this.*

Perhaps you think the battleground can offer something you can win. Can it be anything that offers you a perfect calmness, and a sense of love so deep and quiet that no touch of doubt can ever mar your certainty? And that will last forever?

Those with the strength of God in their awareness could never think of battle. What could they gain but loss of their perfection? For everything fought for on the battleground is of the body; something it seems to offer or to own. No one who knows that he has everything could seek limitation, nor could he value the body's offerings. The senselessness of conquest is quite apparent from the quiet sphere above the battleground. Who with the Love of God upholding him could find the choice of miracles or murder hard to make?

Author's Note: The word "murder" is used to describe our judgments and the attack thoughts we project unto our brothers. Every thought other than the extension of God's Love could be referred to as murder. The act itself is not what needs to be healed. It is the judgments and the attack thoughts within our minds that need healing.

LOVE'S MESSENGERS

The attraction of guilt produces fear of love, for love would never look on guilt at all. It is the nature of love to look upon only the truth, for there it sees itself, with which it would unite in holy union and completion. As love must look past fear, so must fear see love not. For love contains the end of guilt, as surely as fear depends on it. **Love is attracted only to love. Overlooking guilt completely, it sees no fear. Being wholly without attack, it could not be afraid. Fear is attracted to what love sees not and each believes that what the other looks upon does not exist. Fear looks on guilt with just the same devotion that love looks on itself. And each has messengers which it sends forth, and which return to it with messages written in the language in which their going forth was asked.**

Love's messengers are gently sent, and return with messages of love and gentleness. The messengers of fear are harshly ordered to seek out guilt, and cherish every scrap of evil and of sin that they can find, losing none of them on pain of death, and laying them respectfully before their lord and master. Perception cannot obey two masters, each asking for messages of different things in different languages. **What fear would feed upon, love overlooks. What fear demands, love cannot even see.** The fierce attraction that guilt holds for fear is wholly absent from love's gentle perception. What love would look upon is meaningless to fear, and quite invisible.

Relationships in this world are the result of how the world is seen. And this depends on which emotion was called on to send its messengers to look upon it, and return with word of what they saw. Fear's messengers are trained through terror, and they tremble when their master calls on them to serve him. For fear is merciless, even to its friends. Its messengers steal guiltily away in hungry search

of guilt, for they are kept cold and starving and made very vicious by their master, who allows them to feast only upon what they return to him. No little shred of guilt escapes their hungry eyes. And in their savage search for sin they pounce on any living thing they see, and carry it screaming to their master, to be devoured.

Send not these savage messengers into the world, to feast upon it and to prey upon reality. For they will bring you word of bones and skin and flesh. They have been taught to seek for the corruptible, and to return with gorges filled with things decayed and rotted. To them such things are beautiful, because they seem to allay their savage pangs of hunger. For they are frantic with the pain of fear, and would avert the punishment of him who sends them forth by offering him what they hold dear.

The Holy Spirit has given you love's messengers to send instead of those you trained through fear. They are as eager to return to you what they hold dear as are the others. If you send them forth, they will see only the blameless and the beautiful, the gentle and the kind. They will be as careful to let no little act of charity, no tiny expression of forgiveness, no little breath of love escape their notice. And they will return with all the happy things they found, to share them lovingly with you. Be not afraid of them. They offer you salvation. Theirs are the messages of safety, for they see the world as kind.

If you send forth only the messengers the Holy Spirit gives you, wanting no messages but theirs, you will see fear no more. The world will be transformed before your sight, cleansed of all guilt and softly brushed with beauty. The world contains no fear that you laid not upon it. And none you cannot ask love's messengers to remove from it, and see it still. The Holy Spirit has given you His messengers to send to your brother and return to you with what love sees. They have been given to replace the hungry dogs of fear you sent instead. And they go forth to signify the end of fear.

Love, too, would set a feast before you, on a table covered with a spotless cloth, set in a quiet garden where no sound but singing and softly joyous whispering is ever heard. This is a feast that honors your holy relationship, and at which everyone is welcomed as an honored guest. And in a holy instant grace is said by everyone together, as they join in gentleness before the table of communion. And I will join you there, as long ago I promised and promise still. For in your new relationship am I made welcome. And wherever I am made welcome, there I am.

God's messengers are joyous, and their
joy heals sorrow and despair.
They are the proof that God wills perfect happiness for
all who will accept their Father's gifts as theirs.

Author's Note: The meaning of the Last Supper is seen here within this teaching. Jesus's last request was for all to "Drink the wine, Praise the God of all, and let the world be the world." Jesus's request was for us to be of good cheer, unite with our brothers (which is to praise God), and change only our minds about the world. Nothing else.

THE RECOGNITION OF SPIRIT

You see the flesh or recognize the spirit. There is no compromise between the two. If one is real the other must be false, for what is real denies its opposite. There is no choice in vision but this one. What you decide in this determines all you see and think is real and hold as true. On this one choice does all your world depend, for here have you established what you are, as flesh or spirit in your own belief. If you choose flesh, you never will escape the body as your own reality, for you have chosen that you want it so. But choose the spirit, and all Heaven bends to touch your eyes and bless your holy sight, that you may see the world of flesh no more, except to heal and comfort and to bless.

I am not a body, I am free. For I am still as God created me.

Salvation is undoing. If you choose to see the body, you behold a world of separation, unrelated things, and happenings that make no sense at all. This one appears and disappears in death; that one is doomed to suffering and loss. And no one is exactly as he was an instant previous, nor will he be the same as he is now an instant hence. Who could have truth where so much change is seen, for who is worthy if he be but dust? Salvation is undoing of all this. For constancy arises in the sight of those whose eyes salvation has released from looking at the cost of keeping guilt, because they chose to let it go instead.

Nothing so blinding as perception of form. For sight of form means understanding has been obscured.

You who believe that you can choose to see the Son of God as you would have him be, forget not that no concept of yourself will stand against the truth of what you are. Undoing truth would be impossible. But concepts are not difficult to change.

Are you invulnerable? Then the world is harmless in your sight. Do you forgive? Then is the world forgiving, for you have forgiven it its trespasses, so it looks on you with eyes that see as yours. Are you a body? So is all the world perceived as treacherous, and out to kill. Are you a spirit, deathless, and without the promise of corruption and the stain of sin upon you? So the world is seen as stable, fully worthy of your trust; a happy place to rest in for a while, where of heart? And what could hurt the truly innocent?

Your will be done, you holy child of God. It does not matter if you think you are in earth or Heaven. What your Father wills of you can never change. The truth in you remains as radiant as a star, as pure as light, as innocent as love itself. And you are worthy that your will be done!

Author's Note: Truth (God/Love/Spirit) is formless. Therefore, form of any kind, which is Spirit's complete opposite, must be illusion. Form not only includes all that the body's eyes behold, but what cannot be seen as well—such as energy and unseen forces. What can be measured and has the ability to shift or change lies in opposition to the truth. For truth is formless and remains perpetual.

*Forgiveness is impossible
if you believe bodies are real.*

Ernest Holmes

BEHIND THE DARK DOORS

In the darkness you have obscured the glory God gave you, and the power He bestowed upon His guiltless Son. All this lies hidden in every darkened place, shrouded in guilt and in the dark denial of innocence. Behind the dark doors you have closed lies nothing, because nothing can obscure the gift of God. It is the closing of the doors that interferes with recognition of the power of God that shines in you. Banish no power from your mind, but let all that would hide your glory be brought to the judgment of the Holy Spirit, and there undone. Whom He would save for glory *is* saved for it. He has promised the Father that through Him you would be released from littleness to glory. To what He promised God He is wholly faithful, for He shares with God the promise that was given Him to share with you.

The Holy Spirit asks of you but this: **bring to Him every secret you have locked away from Him. Open every door to Him, and bid Him enter the darkness and lighten it away. At your request He enters gladly. He brings the light to darkness if you make the darkness open to Him. But what you hide He cannot look upon.** He sees for you, and unless you look with Him He cannot see. The vision of Christ is not for Him alone, but for Him with you. Bring, therefore, all your dark and secret thoughts to Him, and look upon them with Him. He holds the light, and you the darkness. They cannot coexist when both of you together look on them. His judgment must prevail, and He will give it to you as you join your perception to His.

What do you want? Light or darkness, knowledge or ignorance are yours, but not both. Opposites must be brought together, not kept apart. For their separation is only in your mind, and they are reconciled by union, as you are.

In union, everything that is not real must disappear, for truth "is" union.

Joining with Him is seeing in the way in which you learn to share with Him the interpretation of perception that leads to knowledge. You cannot see alone. Sharing perception with Him Whom God has given you teaches you how to recognize what you see. It is the recognition that nothing you see means anything alone. Seeing with Him will show you that all meaning, including yours, comes not from double vision, but from the gentle fusing of everything into *one* meaning, *one* emotion and *one* purpose. God has one purpose which He shares with you. The single vision which the Holy Spirit offers you will bring this oneness to your mind with clarity and brightness so intense you could not wish, for all the world, not to accept what God would have you have. Behold your will, accepting it as His, with all His Love as yours.

All honor to you through Him, and through Him unto God.

YOUR ASSURANCE

Before your brother's holiness the world is still, and peace descends on it in gentleness and blessing so complete that not one trace of conflict still remains to haunt you in the darkness of the night. He is your savior from the dreams of fear. He is the healing of your sense of sacrifice and fear that what you have will scatter with the wind and turn to dust. In him is your assurance God is here, and with you now. While he is what he is, you can be sure that God is knowable and will be known to you. For He could never leave His Own creation. And the sign that this is so lies in your brother, offered you that all your doubts about yourself may disappear before his holiness. See in him God's creation. For in him his Father waits for your acknowledgment that He created you as part of Him.

Without you there would be a lack in God, a Heaven incomplete, a Son without a Father. There could be no universe and no reality. For what God wills is whole, and part of Him because His Will is one. Nothing alive that is not part of Him, and nothing is but is alive in Him. Your brother's holiness shows you that God is one with him and you; that what he has is yours because you are not separate from him nor from his Father.

What is in him is changeless, and your changelessness
is recognized in its acknowledgment.
The holiness in you belongs to him. And by
your seeing it in him, returns to you.

Choose, then, his body or his holiness as what you want to see, and which you choose is yours to look upon. Yet will you choose in countless situations, and through time that seems to have no end, until the truth be your decision. For eternity is not regained by still one more denial of Christ in him. And where is your salvation, if he is but a body? Where is your peace but in his holiness? And where is God Himself but in that part of Him He set forever in your brother's holiness, that you might see the truth about yourself, set forth at last in terms you recognized and understood?

You who believe it easier to see your
brother's body than his holiness,
be sure you understand what made this judgment.
Here is the voice of specialness heard clearly . . .

Author's Note: This lesson reminds us that our salvation lies with our brothers and sisters, who walk this journey with us, for it is within them that God has placed His Kingdom. How we perceive them is how we will perceive ourselves. Behold the body, and we have placed our faith in illusions. But recognize the spirit and our faith is placed in truth. What we perceive outward becomes trusted reality.

YOUR PITIFUL APPRAISAL

It will never happen that you must make decisions for yourself. You are not bereft of help, and Help that knows the answer. Would you be content with little, which is all that you alone can offer yourself, when He Who gives you everything will simply offer it to you? He will never ask what you have done to make you worthy of the gift of God. Ask it not therefore of yourself. Instead, accept His answer, for He knows that you are worthy of everything God wills for you. Do not try to escape the gift of God He so freely and so gladly offers you. He offers you but what God gave Him for you. You need not decide whether or not you are deserving of it. God knows you are.

Would you deny the truth of God's decision, and place your pitiful appraisal of yourself in place of His calm and unswerving value of His Son? Nothing can shake God's conviction of the perfect purity of everything that He created, for it *is* wholly pure. Do not decide against it, for being of Him it must be true. Peace abides in every mind that quietly accepts the plan God set for its Atonement, relinquishing its own. You know not of salvation, for you do not understand it. Make no decisions about what it is or where it lies, but ask the Holy Spirit everything, and leave all decisions to His gentle counsel.

The One Who knows the plan of God that God would have you follow can teach you what it is. Only His wisdom is capable of guiding you to follow it. Every decision you undertake alone but signifies that you would define what salvation *is* and what you would be saved *from*. The Holy Spirit knows that all salvation is escape from guilt. You have no other *enemy*, and against this strange distortion of the purity of the Son of God the Holy Spirit is your only friend. He is the strong protector of the innocence that sets you free. And it is His decision to undo everything that would obscure your innocence from your unclouded mind.

Let Him, therefore, be the only Guide that you would follow to salvation. He knows the way, and leads you gladly on it. With Him you will not fail to learn that what God wills for you *is* your will. Without His guidance you will think you know alone, and will decide against your peace as surely as you decided that salvation lay in you alone. Salvation is of Him to Whom God gave it for you. He has not forgotten it. Forget Him not and He will make every decision for you, for your salvation and the peace of God in you.

Be quiet in your faith in Him Who loves you, and would lead you out of insanity. Madness may be your choice, but not your reality. Never forget the Love of God, Who has remembered you. For it is quite impossible that He could ever let His Son drop from the loving Mind wherein he was created, and where his abode was fixed in perfect peace forever.

Say to the Holy Spirit only, "Decide for me," and it is done. For His decisions are reflections of what God knows about you, and, in this light, error of any kind becomes impossible.

Would I not rather join the thinking of the universe
than to obscure all that is really mine with my
pitiful and meaningless "private" thoughts?

YOUR RANGE OF CHOICE

Perception is consistent. What you see reflects your thinking. And your thinking but reflects your choice of what you want to see. Your values are determiners of this, for what you value you must want to see, believing what you see is really there. No one can see a world his mind has not accorded value. And no one can fail to look upon what he believes he wants.

Yet who can really hate and love at once? Who can desire what he does not want to have reality? And who can choose to see a world of which he is afraid? Fear must make blind, for this its weapon is: That which you fear to see you cannot see. Love and perception thus go hand in hand, but fear obscures in darkness what is there. What, then, can fear project upon the world? What can be seen in darkness that is real?

Truth is eclipsed by fear, and what remains is but imagined.

Fear has made everything you think you see—all separation, all distinctions, and the multitude of differences you believe make up the world. They are not there. Love's enemy has made them up. Yet love can have no enemy, and so they have no cause, no being and no consequence. They can be valued, but remain unreal. They can be sought, but they cannot be found. Today we will not seek for them, nor waste this day in seeking what cannot be found.

It is impossible to see two worlds which have no overlap of any kind. Seek for the one; the other disappears. But one remains. They are the range of choice beyond which your decision cannot go. The real and the unreal are all there are to choose between, and nothing more than these.

Begin your searching for the other world by asking for a strength beyond your own, and recognizing what it is you seek. You do not want illusions. And you come, emptying your hands of all the petty treasures of this world. You wait for God to help you, as you say:

It is impossible to see two worlds. Let me accept the strength God offers me and see no value in this world, that I may find my freedom and deliverance.

God will be there. For you have called upon the great unfailing power which will take this giant step with you in gratitude. Nor will you fail to see His thanks expressed in tangible perception and in truth. You will not doubt what you will look upon, for though it is perception, it is not the kind of seeing that your eyes alone have ever seen before. And you will know God's strength upheld you as you made this choice.

Dismiss temptation easily today whenever it arises, merely by remembering the limits of your choice. The unreal or the real, the false or true is what you see and only what you see. Perception is consistent with your choice, and hell or Heaven comes to you as one.

Accept a little part of hell as real, and you have damned your eyes and cursed your sight, and what you will behold is hell indeed. Yet the release of Heaven still remains within your range of choice . . . All you need say to any part of hell, whatever form it takes, is simply this:

It is impossible to see two worlds. I seek my freedom and deliverance, and this is not a part of what I want.

It's not what you look at that matters,
it's what you see.

Henry David Thoreau

CHAPTER VII

The Awakening/ *The* Journey Back Home

*Miracles reawaken the awareness that
the spirit, not the body, is the altar of truth.
This is the recognition that leads
to the healing power of the miracle.*

*I cannot imagine a God
who rewards and punishes
the objects of His creation
and is but a reflection
of human frailty.*

Albert Einstein

OUTSIDE OF HEAVEN

There is no life outside of Heaven. Where God created life, there life must be. In any state apart from Heaven life is illusion. At best it seems like life; at worst, like death. Yet both are judgments on what is not life, equal in their inaccuracy and lack of meaning. Life not in Heaven is impossible, and what is not in Heaven is not anywhere. Outside of Heaven, only the conflict of illusion stands; senseless, impossible and beyond all reason, and yet perceived as an eternal barrier to Heaven. Illusions are but forms. Their content is never true.

What you consider content is not content at all. It is merely form, and nothing else.

Salvation is the recognition that the truth is true, and nothing else is true. This you have heard before, but may not yet accept both parts of it. Without the first, the second has no meaning. But without the second, is the first no longer true. Truth cannot have an opposite. This cannot be too often said and thought about. For if what is not true is true as well as what is true, then part of truth is false. And truth has lost its meaning. Nothing but the truth is true, and what is false is false.

As God created you, you must remain unchangeable, with transitory states by definition false. And that includes all shifts in feeling, alterations in conditions of the body and the mind; in all awareness and in all response. This is the all-inclusiveness which sets the truth apart from falsehood, and the false kept separate from the truth, as what it is.

Is it not strange that you believe to think you made the world you see is arrogance? God made it not. Of this you can be sure. What can He know of the ephemeral, the sinful and the guilty, the afraid, the suffering and lonely, and the mind that lives within a body that must die? You but accuse Him of insanity, to think He made a world where such things seem to have reality. He is not mad. Yet only madness makes a world like this.

If this were the real world, God "would" be cruel. For no Father could subject his children to this as the price of salvation and "be" loving. "Love does not kill to save."

To think that God made chaos contradicts His will, invented opposites to truth, and suffers death to triumph over life; all this is arrogance. Humility would see at once these things are not of Him. And can you see what God created not? To think you can is merely to believe you can perceive what God willed not to be. And what could be more arrogant than this?

You love me, Father. You could never leave me desolate, to die within a world of pain and cruelty. How could I think that Love has left Itself? There is no will except the Will of Love. Fear is a dream, and has no will that can conflict with Yours. Conflict is sleep, and peace awakening. Death is illusion: life, eternal truth. There is no opposition to Your Will. There is no conflict, for my will is Yours.

Your safety lies in truth, and not in lies. Love is your safety. Fear does not exist. Identify with love, and you are safe. Identify with love, and you are home. Identify with love, and find your Self.

A WORD OF GRATITUDE

Each day a thousand treasures come to me with every passing moment. I am blessed with gifts throughout the day, in value far beyond all things of which I can conceive. A brother smiles upon another, and my heart is gladdened. Someone speaks a word of gratitude or mercy, and my mind receives this gift and takes it as its own. And everyone who finds the way to God becomes my savior, pointing out the way to me, and giving me his certainty that what he learned is surely mine as well.

A day devoted now to gratitude will add the benefit of some insight into the real extent of all the gains which you have made; the gifts you have received. Be glad today, in loving thankfulness, your Father has not left you to yourself, nor let you wander in the dark alone. Be grateful He has saved you from the self you thought you made to take the place of Him and His creation. Give Him thanks today.

Give thanks that He has not abandoned you, and that His Love forever will remain shining on you, forever without change. Give thanks as well that you are changeless, for the Son He loves is changeless as Himself. Be grateful you are saved. Be glad you have a function in salvation to fulfill. Be thankful that your value far transcends your meager gifts and petty judgments of the one whom God established as His Son.

Receive the thanks of God today, as you give thanks to Him. For He would offer you the thanks you give, since He receives your gifts in loving gratitude, and gives them back a thousand and a hundred thousand more than they were given. He will bless your gifts by sharing them with you. And so they grow in power and in strength, until they fill the world with gladness and with gratitude.

Receive His thanks, and you will understand how lovingly He holds you in His Mind, how deep and limitless His care for you, how perfect is His gratitude to you. Remember hourly to think of Him, and give Him thanks for everything He gave His Son, that he might rise above the world, remembering his Father and his Self.

I thank You, Father, for the many gifts that come to me today and every day from every Son of God. My brothers are unlimited in all their gifts to me. Now may I offer them my thankfulness, that gratitude to them may lead me on to my Creator and His memory.

Author's Note: We are saved only from our own judgments and condemnations. There is no other enemy. And we are saved for God's glory! This alone deserves the title of gratitude.

THE REAL ALTERNATIVE

Real choice is no illusion. But the world has none to offer. All its roads but lead to disappointment, nothingness and death. There is no choice in its alternatives. Seek not escape from problems here. The world was made so that problems could not *be* escaped. Be not deceived by all the different names its roads are given. They have but one end. Their end is certain, for there is no choice among them. All of them will lead to death.

The learning that the world can offer but one choice is the beginning of acceptance that there is a real alternative instead. To fight against this step is to defeat your purpose here. You did not come to learn to find a road the world does not contain. The search for different pathways in the world is but the search for different forms of truth. And this would *keep* the truth from being reached.

There is a choice that you have power to make when you have seen the real alternatives. Until that point is reached you have no choice, and you can but decide how you would choose the better to deceive yourself again. This course attempts to teach no more than that the power of decision cannot lie in choosing different forms of what is still the same illusion and the same mistake. All choices in the world depend on this; you choose between your brother and yourself, and you will gain as much as he will lose, and what you lose is what is given him. How utterly opposed to truth is this, when all the lesson's purpose is to teach that what your brother loses you have lost, and what he gains is what is given *you*.

He has not left His Thoughts! But you forgot His Presence and remembered not His Love. No pathway in the world can lead to Him, nor any worldly goal be one with His. What road in all the world will lead within, when every road was made to separate the journey from the purpose it must have unless it be but futile wandering? All

roads that lead away from what you are will lead you to confusion and despair. Yet has He never left His Thoughts to die, without their Source forever in themselves.

He has not left His Thoughts! He could no more depart from them than they could keep Him out. In unity with Him do they abide, and in their oneness both are kept complete. There is no road that leads away from Him. A journey from yourself does not exist. How foolish and insane it is to think that there could be a road with such an aim! Where could it go? And how could you be made to travel on it, walking there without your own reality at one with you?

Forgive yourself your madness, and forget all senseless journeys and all goal-less aims. They have no meaning. You cannot escape from what you are. For God is merciful, and did not let His Son abandon Him. For what He is be thankful, for in that is your escape from madness and from death. Nowhere but where He is can you be found. There *is* no path that does not lead to Him.

"You" are the means for God; not separate, nor with a life apart from His. His life is manifest in you who are His Son. Each aspect of Himself is framed in holiness and perfect purity, in love celestial and so complete it wishes only that it may release all that it looks upon unto itself.

Learn now, without despair, there is no hope of answer in the world. But do not judge the lesson that is but begun with this. Seek not another signpost in the world that seems to point to still another road. No longer look for hope where there is none. Make fast your learning now, and understand that you but waste time unless you go beyond what you have learned to what is yet to learn. For from this lowest point will learning lead to heights of happiness, in which you see the purpose of the lesson shining clear, and perfectly within your learning grasp.

BECAUSE OF THEM

Think but how holy you must be from whom the Voice for God calls lovingly unto your brother, that you may awaken in him the Voice that answers to your call! And think how holy he must be when in him sleeps your own salvation, with his freedom joined! However much you wish he be condemned, God is in him. And never will you know He is in you as well while you attack His chosen home, and battle with His host. Regard him gently. Look with loving eyes on him who carries Christ within him, that you may behold his glory and rejoice that Heaven is not separate from you.

Is it too much to ask a little trust for him who carries Christ to you, that you may be forgiven all your sins, and left without a single one you cherish still? Forget not that a shadow held between your brother and yourself obscures the face of Christ and memory of God. And would you trade them for an ancient hate? The ground whereon you stand is holy ground because of Them Who, standing there with you, have blessed it with their innocence and peace.

The blood of hatred fades to let the grass grow green again, and let the flowers be all white and sparkling in the summer sun. What was a place of death has now become a living temple in a world of light. Because of Them. It is Their presence which has lifted holiness again to take its ancient place upon an ancient throne. Because of Them have miracles sprung up as grass and flowers on the barren ground that hate had scorched and rendered desolate. What hate has wrought have They undone. And now you stand on ground so holy Heaven leans to join with it, and make it like itself.

And They come quickly to the living temple, where a home for Them has been set up. There is no place in Heaven holier. And They have come to dwell within the temple offered Them, to be Their resting place as well as yours.

What hatred has released to love becomes the brightest light in Heaven's radiance. And all the lights in Heaven brighter grow, in gratitude for what has been restored.

Around you angels hover lovingly, to keep away all darkened thoughts of sin, and keep the light where it has entered in. Your footprints lighten up the world, for where you walk forgiveness gladly goes with you. No one on earth but offers thanks to one who has restored his home, and sheltered him from bitter winter and the freezing cold.

Now is the temple of the living God rebuilt as host again to Him by Whom it was created. Where He dwells, His Son dwells with Him, never separate. And They give thanks that They are welcomed at last. Where stood a cross stands now the risen Christ, and ancient scars are healed within His sight. An ancient miracle has come to bless and to replace an ancient enmity that came to kill. In gentle gratitude does God the Father and the Son return to what is Theirs, and will forever be. Now is the Holy Spirit's purpose done. For They have come! For They have come at last!

Let my own feeble voice be still, and let me hear the mighty Voice of Truth Itself assure me that I am God's perfect Son.

Author's Note: The teaching of this lesson cannot be overemphasized. Jesus is trying to help us recognize that our salvation lies within our brothers and sisters—for God's Kingdom resides within them, as it does within us. Any form of attack upon another is an attack upon God's Kingdom. How we look on them is how we shall look upon ourselves. We are saved from our own judgments that we have placed upon others when we become willing to see their holiness, for in seeing their holiness, we see our own.

LOVE ALWAYS ANSWERS

Sit quietly and look upon the world you see, and tell yourself: The real world is not like this. It has no buildings and there are no streets where people walk alone and separate. There are no stores where people buy an endless list of things they do not need. It is not lit with artificial light, and night comes not upon it. There is no day that brightens and grows dim. There is no loss. Nothing is there but shines, and shines forever.

The world you see must be denied, for sight of it is costing you a different kind of vision. You cannot *see* both worlds, for each of them involves a different kind of seeing, and depends on what you cherish. The sight of one is possible because you have denied the other. Both are not true, yet either one will seem as real to you as the amount to which you hold it dear. And yet their power is not the same, because their real attraction to you is unequal.

You do not really want the world you see, for it has disappointed you since time began. The homes you built have never sheltered you. The roads you made have led you nowhere, and no city that you built has withstood the crumbling assault of time. Nothing you made but has the mark of death upon it. Hold it not dear, for it is old and tired and ready to return to dust even as you made it. This aching world has not the power to touch the living world at all. You could not give it that, and so, although you turn in sadness from it, you cannot find in it the road that leads away from it into another world.

Yet the real world has the power to touch you even here, because you love it. And what you call with love will come to you. Love always answers, being unable to deny a call for help, or not to hear the cries of pain that rise to it from every part of this strange world you made but do not want. All that you need to give this world away in glad exchange for what you did not make is willingness to learn that the one you made is false.

You have been wrong about the world because you have misjudged yourself. From such a twisted reference point, what could you see? All seeing starts with the perceiver, who judges what is true and what is false. And what he judges false he does not see. You who would judge reality cannot see it, for whenever judgment enters, reality has slipped away. The out of mind is out of sight, because what is denied is there but is not recognized. Christ is still there, although you know Him not. His Being does not depend upon your recognition. He lives within you in the quiet present, and waits for you to leave the past behind and enter into the world He holds out to you in love.

Whenever you are tempted to undertake a useless journey that would lead away from light, remember what you really want, and say:

The Holy Spirit leads me unto Christ, and where else would I go? What need have I but to awake in Him?

We cannot sing redemption's hymn alone. My task is not complete until I have lifted every voice with mine. And yet it is not mine, for as it is my gift to you, so was it the Father's gift to me, given through His Spirit. The sound of it will banish sorrow from the mind of God's most holy Son, where it cannot abide. Healing in time is needed, for joy cannot establish its eternal reign where sorrow dwells. **You dwell not here, but in eternity. You travel but in dreams while safe at home. Give thanks to every part of you that you have taught how to remember you. Thus does the Son of God give thanks unto his Father for his purity.**

SOONER OR LATER

To your most holy Self all praise is due for what you are, and for what He is Who created you as you are. Sooner or later must everyone bridge the gap he imagines exists between his selves. Each one builds this bridge, which carries him across the gap as soon as he is willing to expend some little effort on behalf of bridging it. His little efforts are powerfully supplemented by the strength of Heaven, and by the united will of all who make Heaven what it is, being joined within it. And so the one who would cross over is literally transported there.

Your bridge is builded stronger than you think, and your foot is planted firmly on it. Have no fear that the attraction of those who stand on the other side and wait for you will not draw you safely across. For you will come where you would be, and where your Self awaits you.

*His Kingdom has no limits and no end, and there is
nothing in Him that is not perfect and eternal.
All this is "you," and nothing outside of this "is" you.*

We share one life because we have one Source, a Source from which perfection comes to us, remaining always in the holy minds which He created perfect. As we were, so are we now and will forever be. A sleeping mind must awaken, as it sees its own perfection mirroring the Lord of Life so perfectly it fades into what is reflected there. And now it is no more a mere reflection. It becomes the thing reflected, and the light which makes reflection possible. No vision now is needed. For the awakened mind is one that knows its Source, its Self, its Holiness.

I will go with you to the Holy One, and through my perception He can bridge the little gap. **Your gratitude to your brother is the only gift I want. I will bring it to God for you, knowing that to know your brother is to know God.** If you are grateful to your brother, you are grateful to God for what He created. Through your gratitude you come to know your brother, and one moment of real recognition makes everyone your brother because each of them is of your Father. **Love does not conquer all things, but it does set all things right.** Because you are the Kingdom of God, I can lead you back to your own creations. You do not recognize them now, but what has been dissociated is still there.

As you come closer to a brother you approach me, and as you withdraw from him I become distant to you. Salvation is a collaborative venture. It cannot be undertaken successfully by those who disengage themselves from the Sonship, because they are disengaging themselves from me. God will come to you only as you will give Him to your brothers. Learn first of them and you will be ready to hear God. That is because the function of Love is one.

*Teach no one that he is what you would not want to be.
Your brother is the mirror in which you
see the image of yourself . . .*

Author's Note: The gap perceived between our personal minds and the Mind of God is bridged by the Holy Spirit when we ask for help. The miracle that is received demonstrates the transformation from the limited and conceptual and egotistical self-identity to the limitless Self created by God. It is the realization that we can't, but He can and He will and He does.

THE WAY THE TRUTH POINTS OUT

Let us turn to Him who leads the way and makes our footsteps sure. To Him we leave these lessons, as to Him we give our lives henceforth. For we would not return again to the belief in sin that made the world seem ugly and unsafe, attacking and destroying, dangerous in all its ways, and treacherous beyond the hope of trust and the escape from pain.

His is the only way to find the peace that God has given us. It is His way that everyone must travel in the end, because it is this ending God Himself appointed. In the dream of time it seems to be far off. And yet, in truth, it is already here; already serving us as gracious guidance in the way to go. Let us together follow in the way that truth points out to us. And let us be the leaders of our many brothers who are seeking for the way, but find it not.

And to this purpose let us dedicate our minds, directing all our thoughts to serve the function of salvation. Unto us the aim is given to forgive the world. It is the goal that God has given us. It is His ending to the dream we seek, and not our own. For all that we forgive we will not fail to recognize as part of God Himself. And thus His memory is given back, completely and complete.

It is our function to remember Him on earth, as it is given us to be His Own completion in reality. So let us not forget our goal is shared, for it is the remembrance which contains the memory of God, and opens the way to Him and to the Heaven of His peace. And shall we not forgive our brother, who can offer this to us? He is the way, the truth and the life that shows the way to us. In him resides salvation, offered us through our forgiveness, given unto him.

We will not end this year without the gift our Father promised to His holy Son. We are forgiven now. And we

are saved from all the wrath we thought belonged to God, and found it was a dream. We are restored to sanity, in which we understand that anger is insane, attack is mad, and vengeance merely foolish fantasy. We have been saved from wrath because we learned we were mistaken. Nothing more than that. And is a father angry at his son because he failed to understand the truth?

We come in honesty to God and say we did not understand, and ask Him to help us to learn His lessons, through the Voice of His Own Teacher. Would He hurt His Son? Or would He rush to answer him, and say, "This is My Son, and all I have is his"? Be certain He will answer thus, for these are His Own words to you. And more than that can no one ever have, for in these words is all there is, and all that there will be throughout all time and in eternity.

The power set in you in whom the Holy Spirit's goal has been established is so far beyond your little conception of the infinite that you have no idea how great the strength that goes with you.

There are those who have reached God directly, retaining no trace of worldly limits and remembering their own identity perfectly. These might be called the Teachers of teachers because, although they are no longer visible, their image can yet be called upon. And they will appear when and where it is helpful for them to do so. To those to whom such appearances would be frightening, they give their ideas. No one can call on them in vain. Nor is there anyone of whom they are unaware.

*Salvation is a paradox indeed! What could it be except a happy dream?
I ask you but that you forgive all things that no one ever did; to overlook what
is not there, and not to look upon the unreal as reality. You are but asked to
let your will be done, and seek no longer for the things you do not want.*

THE PROMISE OF SALVATION

Salvation is a promise, made by God, that you would find your way to Him at last. It cannot but be kept. It guarantees that time will have an end, and all the thoughts that have been born in time will end as well. God's Word is given every mind which thinks that it has separate thoughts, and will replace these thoughts of conflict with the thought of peace.

The Thought of peace was given to God's Son the instant that his mind had thought of war. There was no need for such a Thought before, for peace was given without opposite, and merely was. But when the mind is split there is a need of healing. So the Thought that has the power to heal the split became a part of every fragment of the mind that still was one, but failed to recognize its oneness. Now it did not know itself, and thought its own identity was lost.

Salvation is undoing in the sense that it does nothing, failing to support the world of dreams and malice. Thus it lets illusions go. By not supporting them, it merely lets them quietly go down to dust. And what they hid is now revealed; an altar to the holy Name of God whereon His Word is written, with the gifts of your forgiveness laid before it, and the memory of God not far behind.

I need but look upon all things that seem to hurt me, and with perfect certainty assure myself, "God wills that I be saved from this," and merely watch them disappear. I need but keep in mind my Father's Will for me is only happiness, to find that only happiness has come to me. And I need but remember that God's Love surrounds His Son and keeps his sinlessness forever perfect, to be sure that I am saved and safe forever in His Arms. I am the Son He loves. And I am saved because God in His mercy *wills* it so.

Let us come daily to this holy place, and spend a while together. Here we share our final dream. It is a dream in which there is no sorrow, for it holds a hint of all the glory given us by God. The grass is pushing through the soil, the trees are budding now, and birds have come to live within their branches. Earth is being born again in new perspective. Night has gone, and we have come together in the light.

From here we give salvation to the world, for it is here salvation was received. The song of our rejoicing is the call to all the world that freedom is returned, that time is almost over, and God's Son has but an instant more to wait until his Father is remembered, dreams are done, eternity has shined away the world, and only Heaven now exists at all.

What can I seek for, Father, but Your Love?
Perhaps I think I seek for something else;
a something I have called by many names. Yet is
Your Love the only thing I seek, or ever sought.
For there is nothing else that I could ever really
want to find. Let me remember You.
What else could I desire but the truth about myself?

This is your will, my brother. And you share this will with me, and with the One as well Who is our Father. **To remember Him is Heaven. This we seek. And only this is what it will be given us to find.**

BRINGING FANTASY TO TRUTH

Remember that the Holy Spirit is the Answer, not the question. Hear, then, one answer of the Holy Spirit to all the questions the ego raises: You are a child of God, a priceless part of His Kingdom, which He created as part of Him. Nothing else exists and only this is real. You have chosen a sleep in which you have had bad dreams, but the sleep is not real and God calls you to awake. There will be nothing left of your dream when you hear Him, because you will awaken. Your dreams contain many of the ego's symbols and they have confused you. Yet that was only because you were asleep and did not know. When you wake you will see the truth around you and in you, and you will no longer believe in dreams because they will have no reality for you. Yet the Kingdom and all that you have created there will have great reality for you, because they are beautiful and true.

You are at home in God, dreaming of exile but perfectly capable of awakening to reality.

The separation was not a loss of perfection, but a failure in communication. A harsh and strident form of communication arose as the ego's voice. It could not shatter the peace of God, but it could shatter yours. God did not blot it out, because to eradicate it would be to attack it. Being questioned, He did not question. He merely gave the Answer. His Answer is your Teacher.

The betrayal of the Son of God lies only in illusions, and all his "sins" are but his own imagining. His reality is forever sinless. He need not be forgiven but awakened. In his dreams he has betrayed himself, his brothers and his God. Yet what is done in dreams has not really been done. It is impossible to convince the dreamer that this is

so, for dreams are what they are because of their illusions of reality. Only in waking is the full release from them, for only then does it become perfectly apparent that they had no effect upon reality at all, and did not change it. Fantasies change reality. That is their purpose. They cannot do so in reality, but they can do so in the mind that would have reality be different.

Salvation requires the acceptance of but one thought; you are as God created you, not what you made of yourself. Whatever evil you may think you did, you are as God created you. Whatever mistakes you made, the truth about you is unchanged. Creation is eternal and unalterable. Your sinlessness is guaranteed by God. You are and will forever be exactly as you were created. Light and joy and peace abide in you because God put them there.

You are what God created or what you made. One Self is true; the other is not there. Try to experience the unity of your one Self. Try to appreciate Its holiness and the Love from which It was created. Try not to interfere with the Self which God created as you, by hiding Its majesty behind the tiny idols of evil and sinfulness you have made to replace It. Let It come into Its Own. Here you are; This is You. And light and joy and peace abide in you because this is so.

Author's Note: Upon waking from a nighttime dream, it becomes apparent that what we thought happened did not occur. We had only believed in and reacted to figures in a dream. It is when we wake that we realize we have never left our beds; we are safe at home in Love's embrace with nothing to be feared at all. In truth, we remain asleep throughout both day and night—with no waking. The only difference in the two is the figures perceived within the dreams. We are asleep until we awaken in God, regardless of the state of mind in which we perceive.

*The Kingdom is perfectly united
and perfectly protected, and the
ego will not prevail against it.*

I AM SUSTAINED BY THE LOVE OF GOD

Here is the answer to every problem that will confront you, today and tomorrow and throughout time. In this world, you believe you are sustained by everything but God. Your faith is placed in the most trivial and insane symbols: pills, money, "protective" clothing, influence, prestige, being liked, knowing the "right" people, and an endless list of forms of nothingness that you endow with magical powers.

All these things are your replacements for the Love of God. All these things are cherished to ensure a body identification. They are songs of praise to the ego. Do not put your faith in the worthless. It will not sustain you.

Only the Love of God will protect you in all circumstances. It will lift you out of every trial, and raise you high above all the perceived dangers of this world into a climate of perfect peace and safety. It will transport you into a state of mind that nothing can threaten, nothing can disturb, and where nothing can intrude upon the eternal calm of the Son of God.

Put not your faith in illusions. They will fail you. Put all your faith in the Love of God within you; eternal, changeless and forever unfailing. This is the answer to whatever confronts you today. Through the Love of God within you, you can resolve all seeming difficulties without effort and in sure confidence. Tell yourself this often today. It is a declaration of release from the belief in idols. It is your acknowledgment of the truth about yourself.

*There never was a time an idol brought you anything
except the "gift" of guilt. Not one was bought except
at cost of pain, nor was it ever paid by you alone.*

Let the idea for today sink deep into your consciousness. Repeat it, and think about it. Let related thoughts come to help you recognize its truth, and allow peace to flow over you like a blanket of protection and surety. Let no idle and foolish thoughts enter to disturb the holy mind of the Son of God. Such is the Kingdom of Heaven. Such is the resting place where your Father has placed you forever.

God is with me. He is my home, wherein I live and move, the Spirit which directs my actions, offers me Its Thoughts, and guarantees my safety from all pain. He covers me with kindness and with care, and holds in love the Son He shines upon, who also shines on Him. How still is he who knows the truth of what He speaks today!

*If you knew Who walks beside you on
the way that you have chosen,
fear would be impossible.*

Author's Note: Life can only be sustained *by* Life, and God alone *is* Life. It is only because "Love is" that "we are."

THE SIGN OF CHRISTMAS

Fear not to recognize the whole idea of sacrifice as solely of your making. And seek not safety by attempting to protect yourself from where it is not. Your brothers and your Father have become very fearful to you. And you would bargain with them for a few special relationships, in which you think you see some scraps of safety. Do not try longer to keep apart your thoughts and the Thought that has been given you. When they are brought together and perceived where they are, the choice between them is nothing more than a gentle awakening, and as simple as opening your eyes to daylight when you have no more need of sleep.

The sign of Christmas is a star, a light in darkness. See it not outside yourself, but shining in the Heaven within, and accept it as the sign the time of Christ has come. He comes demanding nothing. No sacrifice of any kind, of anyone, is asked by Him. In His Presence the whole idea of sacrifice loses all meaning. For He is Host to God. And you need but invite Him in Who is there already, by recognizing that His Host is One, and no thought alien to His Oneness can abide with Him there. Love must be total to give Him welcome, for the Presence of Holiness creates the holiness that surrounds it. No fear can touch the Host Who cradles God in the time of Christ, for the Host is as holy as the perfect Innocence which He protects, and Whose power protects Him.

This Christmas give the Holy Spirit everything that would hurt you. Let yourself be healed completely that you may join with Him in healing, and let us celebrate our release together by releasing everyone with us. Leave nothing behind, for release is total, and when you have accepted it with me you will give it with me. All pain and sacrifice and littleness will disappear in our relationship, which is as innocent as our relationship with our Father, and as powerful. Pain will be brought to us and disappear in our presence, and without pain there can be no sacrifice. And without sacrifice there love *must* be.

You who believe that sacrifice is love must learn that sacrifice is separation from love. For sacrifice brings guilt as surely as love brings peace. **Guilt is the condition of sacrifice as peace is the condition for the awareness of your relationship with God. Through guilt you exclude your Father and your brothers from yourself. Through peace your invite them back, realizing that they are where your invitation bids them be.** Who can try to resolve the "conflict" of Heaven and hell in him by casting Heaven out and giving it the attributes of hell, without experiencing himself as incomplete and lonely?

As long as you perceive the body as your reality, so long will you perceive yourself as lonely and deprived. And so long will you also perceive yourself as a victim of sacrifice, justified in sacrificing others. For who could thrust Heaven and its Creator aside without a sense of sacrifice and loss? And who could suffer sacrifice and loss without attempting to restore himself? Yet how could you accomplish this yourself, when the basis of your attempts is the belief in the reality of the deprivation? Deprivation breeds attack, being the belief that attack is justified. And as long as you would retain the deprivation, attack becomes salvation and sacrifice becomes love.

So is it that, in all your seeking for love, you seek for sacrifice and find it. Yet you find not love. It is impossible to deny what love is and still recognize it. The meaning of love lies in what you have cast outside yourself, and it has no meaning apart from you. It is what you prefer to keep that has no meaning, while all that you would keep away holds all the meaning of the universe, and holds the universe together in its meaning. Unless the universe were joined in you it would be apart from God, and to be without Him *is* to be without meaning.

In the holy instant the condition of love is met, for minds are joined without the body's interference, and where there is communication there is peace. **The Prince of Peace was born to re-establish the condition of love by teaching that communication remains unbroken even if the body is destroyed, provided that you see not the body as the necessary means of communication. And if you understand this lesson, you will realize that to sacrifice the body is to sacrifice nothing, and communication, which must be of the mind, cannot be sacrificed. Where, then, is sacrifice? The lesson I was born to teach, and still would teach to all my brothers, is that sacrifice is nowhere and love is everywhere. For communication embraces everything, and in the peace it re-establishes, love comes of itself.**

I can give up but what was never real. I
sacrifice illusions; nothing more.
And as illusions go I find the gifts illusions tried
to hide, awaiting me in shining welcome,
and in readiness to give God's ancient messages to me.

Let no despair darken the joy of Christmas, for the time of Christ is meaningless apart from joy. Let us join in celebrating peace by demanding no sacrifice of anyone, for so you offer me the love I offer you. What can be more joyous than to perceive we are deprived of nothing? Such is the message of the time of Christ, which I give you that you may give it and return it to the Father, Who gave it to me. For in the time of Christ communication is restored, and He joins us in the celebration of His Son's creation.

God offers thanks to the holy host who would receive Him, and lets Him enter and abide where He would be. And by your welcome does He welcome you into Himself, for what is contained in you who welcome Him is returned to Him. And we but celebrate His Wholeness as we welcome Him into ourselves. Those who receive the Father are one with Him, being host to Him Who created them. And by allowing Him to enter, the remembrance of the Father enters with Him, and with Him they remember the only relationship they ever had, and ever want to have.

This is the time in which a new year will soon be born from the time of Christ. I have perfect faith in you to do all that you would accomplish. Nothing will be lacking, and you will make complete and not destroy. Say, then, to your brother:

I give you to the Holy Spirit as part of myself.
I know that you will be released unless I
want to use you to imprison myself.
In the name of my freedom I choose your release,
because I recognize that we will be released together.

So will the year begin in joy and freedom. There is much to do, and we have been long delayed. Accept the holy instant as this year is born, and take your place, so long left unfulfilled, in the Great Awakening. Make this year different by making it all the same. And let all your relationships be made holy for you. This is our will.

Author's Note: "Make this year different by making it all the same," means: "Make this year different by giving 'only' the gift of Love."

WHAT ALWAYS HAS BEEN TRUE

What is the Will of God? He wills His Son to have everything. And this He guaranteed when He created him *as* everything. It is impossible that anything be lost, if what you *have* is what you *are*. This is the miracle by which creation became your function, sharing it with God. It is not understood apart from Him, and therefore has no meaning in this world.

Cause and effect are one, not separate. God wills you to learn what always has been true: that He created you as part of Him, and this must still be true because ideas leave not their source. Such is creation's law; that each idea the mind conceives but adds to its abundance, never takes away. This is as true of what is idly wished as what is truly willed, because the mind can wish to be deceived, but cannot make it be what it is not. And to believe ideas can leave their source is to invite illusions to be true, without success. For never will success be possible in trying to deceive the Son of God.

To use the power God has given you as He would have it used is natural. It is not arrogant to be as He created you, nor to make use of what He gave to answer all His Son's mistakes and set him free. But it is arrogant to lay aside the power that He gave, and choose a little senseless wish instead of what He wills. The gift of God to you is limitless. There is no circumstance it cannot answer, and no problem which is not resolved within its gracious light.

Abide in peace, where God would have you be. And be the means whereby your brother finds the peace in which your wishes are fulfilled. Let us unite in bringing blessing to the world of sin and death. For what can save each one of us can save us all. There is no difference among the Sons of God. The unity that specialness denies will save them all, for what is one can have no specialness. And everything belongs to each of them. No wishes lie between a brother and his own. To get from one is to deprive them all. And yet to bless but one gives blessing to them all as one.

Your ancient Name belongs to everyone, as theirs to you. Call on your brother's name and God will answer, for on Him you call. Could He refuse to answer when He has already answered all who call on Him? A miracle can make no change at all. But it can make what always has been true be recognized by those who know it not; and by this little gift of truth but let to be itself, the Son of God allowed to be himself, and all creation freed to call upon the Name of God as One.

What God calls One will be forever One, not separate.
His Kingdom is united; thus it was
created, and thus will it ever be.

*You dwell in peace as limitless as its Creator, and
everything is given those who would remember Him.
Over His home the Holy Spirit watches, sure that
its peace can never be disturbed.*

THE END OF CHOICE

What makes this world seem real except your own denial of the truth that lies beyond? What but your thoughts of misery and death obscure the perfect happiness and the eternal life your Father wills for you? And what could hide what cannot be concealed except illusion? What could keep from you what you already have except your choice to see it not, denying it is there?

The Thought of God created you. It left you not, nor have you ever been apart from it an instant. It belongs to you. By it you live. It is your Source of life, holding you one with it, and everything is one with you because it left you not. The Thought of God protects you, cares for you, makes soft your resting place and smooth your way, lighting your mind with happiness and love. Eternity and everlasting life shine in your mind, because the Thought of God has left you not, and still abides with you.

Who would deny his safety and his peace, his joy, his healing and his peace of mind, his quiet rest, his calm awakening, if he but recognized where they abide? Would he not instantly prepare to go where they are found, abandoning all else as worthless in comparison with them? And having found them, would he not make sure they stay with him, and he remain with them?

Deny not Heaven. It is yours today, but for the asking.

Nor need you perceive how great the gift, how changed your mind will be before it comes to you. Ask to receive, and it is given you. Conviction lies within it. Till you welcome it as yours, uncertainty remains. Yet God is fair. Sureness is not required to receive what only your acceptance can bestow.

Ask with desire. You need not be sure that you request the only thing you want. But when you have received, you will be sure you have the treasure you have always sought. What would you then exchange for it? What would induce you now to let it fade away from your ecstatic vision? For this sight proves that you have exchanged your blindness for the seeing eyes of Christ; your mind has come to lay aside denial, and accept the Thought of God as your inheritance.

We count on God, and not upon ourselves, to give us certainty. And in His Name we practice as His Word directs we do. His sureness lies beyond our every doubt. His love remains beyond our every fear. The Thought of Him is still beyond all dreams and in our minds, according to His Will.

Do you really believe you can make a voice that can drown out God's? Do you really believe you can devise a thought system that can separate you from Him? Do you really believe you can plan for your safety and joy better than He can?

You need be neither careful nor careless; you need merely cast your cares upon Him because He careth for you. You are His care because He loves you.

Author's Note: To deny our Oneness with God is to defend illusions and our belief in separation, deepening our belief in their reality. However, we can and should deny illusions the ability to have any power over us and hurt us. We are free to choose which we will defend, but only in serving truth will our minds and our will be free.

IT IS UP TO YOU

It is still up to you to choose to join with truth or with illusion. But remember that to choose one is to let the other go. Which one you choose you will endow with beauty and reality, because the choice depends on which you value more. The spark of beauty or the veil of ugliness, the real world or the world of guilt and fear, truth or illusions, freedom or slavery—it is all the same! For you can never choose except between God and the ego. Thought systems are but true or false, and all their attributes come simply from what they are. Only the Thoughts of God are true. And all that follows from them comes from what they are, and is as true as is the holy Source from which they came.

Complexity is nothing but a screen of smoke,
which hides the very simple fact that
no decision can be difficult.

My holy brother, I would enter into all your relationships, and step between you and your fantasies. Let my relationship to you be real to you, and let me bring reality to your perception of your brothers. They were not created to enable you to hurt yourself through them. They were created to create with you. This is the truth that I would interpose between you and your goal of madness. Be not separate from me, and let not the holy purpose of Atonement be lost to you in dreams of vengeance. Relationships in which such dreams are cherished have excluded me. Let me enter in the Name of God and bring you peace, that you may offer peace to me.

When you have accepted your mission to extend peace you will find peace, for by making it manifest you will see it. Its holy witnesses will surround you because you called upon them, and they will come to you. I have heard you call upon them, and they will come to you. I have heard your call and I have answered it, but you will not look upon me nor hear the answer that you sought. That is because you do not yet want *only* that. Yet as I become more real to you, you will learn that you do want only that. And you will see me as you look within, and we will look upon the real world together. Through the eyes of Christ, only the real world exists and only the real world can be seen. **As you decide, so will you see. And all that you see but witnesses to your decision.**

Father, it is Your peace that I would give, receiving it from You. I am Your Son, forever just as You created me, for the Great Rays remain forever still and undisturbed within me. I would reach to them in silence and in certainty, for nowhere else can certainty be found. Peace be to me, and peace to all the world. In holiness were we created, and in holiness do we remain.

Author's Note: You might ask yourself the question: Why bother, if nothing I do or don't do can alter truth? If the outside world is all illusionary and solely a projection of my mind, why bother? In answering this question it would be helpful to remember that in everything we do, we are seeking for the peace we thought we had lost. Peace is not only our natural inheritance, it is our natural state of being. It is inevitable that we will seek for peace in any situation where we believe we have lost it. So the only true question to ask yourself is: Will I continue to seek for peace outside myself where it can never be found, or will I turn within to find it? This is the only choice we need make— all else is given us. It is our practice of turning inward that will bring about our awareness of Truth and offer us God's blueprint for our returning home to Love.

*If you chase two rabbits,
you will not catch either one.*
—Russian proverb

THE TURNING POINT/
INTO CHRIST'S PRESENCE
WILL WE ENTER NOW

This is a day of silence and of trust. It is a special time of promise in your calendar of days. It is a time Heaven has set apart to shine upon, and cast a timeless light upon this day, when echoes of eternity are heard. This day is holy, for it ushers in a new experience; a different kind of feeling and awareness. You have spent long days and nights in celebrating death. Today you learn to feel the joy of life.

This is another crucial turning point in the curriculum. We add a new dimension now; a fresh experience that sheds a light on all that we have learned already, and prepares us for what we have yet to learn. It brings us to the door where learning ceases, and we catch a glimpse of what lies past the highest reaches it can possibly attain. It leaves us here an instant, and we go beyond it, sure of our direction and our only goal.

Today it will be given you to feel a touch of Heaven, though you will return to paths of learning. Yet you have come far enough along the way to alter time sufficiently to rise above its laws, and walk into eternity a while. This you will learn to do increasingly, as every lesson, faithfully rehearsed, brings you more swiftly to this holy place and leaves you, for a moment, to your Self.

He will direct your practicing today, for what you ask for now is what He wills. And having joined your will with His this day, what you are asking must be given you. Nothing is needed but today's idea to light your mind, and let it rest in still anticipation and in quiet joy, wherein you quickly leave the world behind.

From this day forth, your ministry takes on a genuine devotion, and a glow that travels from your fingertips to those you touch, and blesses those you look upon. A vision reaches everyone you meet, and everyone you think of, or who thinks of you. For your experience today will so transform your mind that it becomes the touchstone for the holy Thoughts of God.

Today we will embark upon a course you have not dreamed of. But the Holy One, the Giver of the happy dreams of life, Translator of perception into truth, the holy Guide to Heaven given you, has dreamed for you this journey which you make and start today, with the experience this day holds out to you to be your own.

Into Christ's Presence will we enter now, serenely unaware of everything except His shining face and perfect Love. The vision of His face will stay with you, but there will be an instant which transcends all vision, even this, the holiest. This you will never teach, for you attained it not through learning. Yet the vision speaks of your remembrance of what you knew that instant, and will surely know again.

Christ vision has one law. It does not look upon a body,
and mistake it for the Son whom God created.
It beholds a light beyond the body; an idea
beyond what can be touched, a purity
undimmed by errors, pitiful mistakes,
and fearful thoughts of guilt from dreams
of sin. It sees no separation. And it looks
on everyone, on every circumstance,
all happenings and all events, without the
slightest fading of the light it sees.

THE WILLINGNESS TO PERCEIVE NOTHING ELSE

The world as you perceive it cannot have been created by the Father, for the world is not as you see it. God created only the eternal, and everything you see is perishable. Therefore, there must be another world that you do not see. The Bible speaks of a new Heaven and a new earth, yet this cannot be literally true, for the eternal are not re-created.

To perceive anew is merely to perceive
again, implying that before,
or in the interval between, you were not perceiving at all.

Every loving thought that the Son of God ever had is eternal. The loving thoughts his mind perceives in this world are the world's only reality. They are still perceptions, because he still believes that he is separate. Yet they are eternal because they are loving. And being loving they are like the Father, and therefore cannot die. The real world can actually be perceived. All that is necessary is a willingness to perceive nothing else.

You have made many ideas that you have placed between yourself and your Creator, and these beliefs are the world as you perceive it. Truth is not absent here, but it is obscure. You do not know the difference between what you have made and what *you* have created. To believe that you can perceive the real world is to believe that you can know yourself. You can know God because it is His Will to be known. The real world is all that the Holy Spirit has saved for you out of what you have made, and to perceive only this is salvation, because it is the recognition that reality is only what is true.

We are not inconsistent in the thoughts that we present in our curriculum. Truth must be true throughout, if it be true. It cannot contradict itself, nor be in parts uncertain and in others sure. You cannot walk the world apart from God, because you could not be without Him. He is what your life is. Where you are He is. There is one life. That life you share with Him. Nothing can be apart from Him and live.

There is a light in you which cannot die; whose presence is so holy that the world is sanctified because of you. All things that live bring gifts to you and offer them in gratitude and gladness at your feet. The scent of flowers is their gift to you. The waves bow down before you, and the trees extend their arms to shield you from the heat, and lay their leaves before you on the ground that you may walk in softness, while the wind sinks to a whisper round your holy head.

The light in you is what the universe longs to behold. All living things are still before you, for they recognize Who walks with you. The light you carry is their own. And thus they see in you their holiness, saluting you as savior and as God. Accept their reverence, for it is due to Holiness Itself, which walks with you, transforming in Its gentle light all things unto Its likeness and Its purity.

This is the way salvation works. As you step back, the light in you steps forward and encompasses the world. It heralds not the end of sin in punishment and death. In lightness and in laughter is sin gone, because its quaint absurdity is seen. It is a foolish thought, a silly dream, not frightening, ridiculous perhaps, but who would waste an instant in approach to God Himself for such a senseless whim?

Yet you have wasted many, many years on just this foolish thought. The past is gone, with all its fantasies. They keep you bound no longer. The approach to God is near. And in the little interval of doubt that still remains, you may perhaps lose sight of your Companion, and mistake Him for the senseless, ancient dream that now is past.

"Who walks with me?" This question should be asked a thousand times a day, till certainty has ended doubting and established peace. Today let doubting cease. God speaks for you in answering your question with these words:

I walk with God in perfect holiness. I light the world,
I light my mind and all the minds which
God created one with me.

I thank You, Father, for Your plan to save me from the hell I made. It is not real. And you have given me the means to prove its unreality to me. The key is in my hand, and I have reached the door beyond which lies the end of dreams. I stand before the gate of Heaven, wondering if I should enter and be at home. Let me not wait again today. Let me forgive all things, and let creation be as You would have it be and as it is. Let me remember that I am Your Son, and opening the door at last, forget illusions in the blazing light of truth, as memory of You returns to me.

There will be great joy in Heaven on your
homecoming, and the joy will be yours.
For the redeemed son of man is the guiltless Son of
God, and to recognize him is your redemption.

It was only a matter of being willing to believe in a Power greater
than myself. Nothing more was required of me to make my beginning.
I saw that growth could start from that point upon a foundation
of complete willingness. Would I have it? Of course I would.

Bill Wilson

THE FORGOTTEN SONG

Listen,—perhaps you catch a hint of an ancient state not quite forgotten; dim, perhaps, and yet not altogether unfamiliar, like a song whose name is long forgotten, and the circumstances in which you heard completely unremembered. Not the whole song has stayed with you, but just a little wisp of melody, attached not to a person or a place or anything particular. But you remember, from just this little part, how lovely was the song, how wonderful the setting where you heard it, and how you loved those who were there and listened with you.

The notes are nothing. Yet you have kept them with you, not for themselves, but as a soft reminder of what would make you weep if you remembered how dear it was to you. You could remember, yet you are afraid, believing you would lose the world you learned since then. And yet you know that nothing in the world you learned is half so dear as this. **Listen,** and see if you remember an ancient song you knew so long ago and held more dear than any melody you taught yourself to cherish since.

Beyond the body, beyond the sun and stars, past everything you see and yet somehow familiar, is an arc of golden light that stretches as you look into a great and shining circle. And all the circle fills with light before your eyes. The edges of the circle disappear, and what is in it is no longer contained at all. The light expands and covers everything, extending to infinity, forever shining and with no break or limit anywhere. Within it everything is joined in perfect continuity. Nor is it possible to imagine that anything could be outside, for there is nowhere that this light is not.

This is the vision of the Son of God, whom you know well. Here is the sight of him who knows his Father. Here is the memory of what you are; a part of this, with all of it within, and joined to all as surely as all is joined in you. Accept the vision that can show you this, and not the body. You know the ancient song, and know it well. Nothing will ever be as dear to you as is this ancient hymn of love the Son of God sings to his Father still.

And now the blind can see, for that same song they sing in honor of their Creator gives praise to them as well. The blindness that they made will not withstand the memory of this song. And they will look upon the vision of the Son of God, remembering who he is they sing of. What is a miracle but this remembering? And who is there in whom this memory lies not? **The light in one awakens it in all. And when you see it in your brother, you *are* remembering for everyone.**

Then let our brothers lean their tired heads against our shoulders as they rest a while. We offer thanks for them. For if we can direct them to the peace that we would find, the way is opening at last to us. An ancient door is swinging free again; a long forgotten word re-echoes in our memory, and gathers clarity as we are willing once again to hear.

God gives thanks to you, His Son,
for being what you are; His Own completion
and the Source of love, along with Him.
Your gratitude to Him is one with His to you.
For love can walk no road except the way of gratitude,
and thus we go who walk the way to God.

Salvation is for the mind, and it is attained through peace!
This is the only thing that can be saved
and the only way to save it.

*Jesus said, "When you make the two one, and when you make
the inside like the outside and the outside like the inside, and
the above like the below, and when you make the male and female
one and the same ... then you will enter the Kingdom of God."*

Gospel of Thomas

THE LORD'S PRAYER

Seek and *find* His message in the holy instant, where all illusions are forgiven. From there the miracle extends to bless everyone and to resolve all problems, be they perceived as great or small, possible or impossible. There is nothing that will not give place to Him and to His Majesty. To join in close relationship with Him is to accept relationships as real, and through their reality to give over all illusions for the reality of your relationship with God. Praise be to your relationship with Him and to no other. The truth lies there and nowhere else. You choose this or nothing.

The Word of God has no exceptions. It is this that makes it holy and beyond the world. Decide for God, and everything is given you at no cost at all. Decide against Him, and you chose nothing, at the expense of the awareness of everything.

Forgive us our illusions, Father, and help us to accept our true relationship with You,
in which there are no illusions, and where none can ever enter.
Our holiness is Yours. What can there be in us that needs forgiveness when Yours is perfect?
The sleep of forgetfulness is only the unwillingness to remember Your forgiveness and Your Love.
Let us not wander into temptation, for the temptation of the Son of God is not Your Will.
And let us receive only what You have given, and accept but this into the minds which You created and which You love.

Amen.

FINAL THOUGHTS

It has been one of my greatest joys to publish this book to share with all the world. I never dreamed I would be standing where I am now, for darkness had ruled so much of my life. It is a testament to His miracle.

I would like to close as I began, recognizing that *every step we take brings us a little nearer. Let us raise our hearts from dust to life, as we remember salvation is promised us, and that this course was sent to open up the path of light to us, and teach us, step by step, how to return to the eternal Self we thought we lost.* Y'shua's teachings in *A Course in Miracles* has set me free. He helped awaken in me the true meaning of life—God's Love. He has shown me a love without conditions; true joy and peace that surpass all understanding, and a love that honors me as I share it with you. I hope you found within these pages something to take with you, some understanding and peace of mind.

Make the time to place love above all else, and may forgiveness lead the way. For with this choice, we wake from sleep, dreams are transformed into reality, and nothingness is exchanged for everything. Let us behold the great gift God appointed as the means for us to find our way home to Him at last—His Holy Spirit, the Voice for Love. Heaven will remain to be God's only will for you, and it is only this that I will for all as well.

In the 11th hour of the final edits of this book, my dearest mother made her transition into God's Light. Through all of the many years of suffering and pain, with thoughts of fear and conflict she experienced in her final years, she helped remind me of a most precious lesson. It only takes a "holy instant" to release and surrender, to join with and to awaken into God. And that she did indeed. In her final days she let go, and trust became her guiding light. Her last breath gave to me my own. I now accept Atonement for myself and am forevermore one with her and all the world: June, 1931–April, 2014.

All blessings to you.

With love. Your brother, Brad Oliphant

Brad's entire collection of photography work can be viewed at www.BradOliphantPhotography.com

NOTES

This section contains standard designations of page numbers, quoted references, or direct paraphrases from *A Course in Miracles** or its related pamphlets.

Course references are signified below:

T: *Text*

W: *Workbook*

M: Manual for Teachers

PR: Preface

S: *The Song of Prayer* pamphlet

C: Clarification for terms

R: Review

in: Introduction

II. The holiest of . . . : a present love: T-26.IX.6.

VI. As you look . . . what you seek: T-12.VII.7.

XII. The sounds of . . . : of *God's son*: W-94.

XIII. *The Son of God is You*: W-64.

XIII. *You stand in light . . . remain throughout eternity*: W-94.

INTRODUCTION

XVI. *The journey that . . . to further darkness*: T-14.VI.1.

XVII. . . . *all terms are . . . a delaying maneuver*: C-in.2.

XVIII. . . . "nothing that is true need be explained": T-7.I.6.

XVIII. *Divine Abstraction*: T-4.VII.5.

XVIIII. " . . . an untrained mind can accomplish nothing": W-in.

XVIII. "compares what you . . . : accord as false": T-1.I.50.

XVIII. *The power of decision . . . of this world*: T-7.VII.9.

XIX. "the world is . . . but by truth": T-3.VII.6.

XIX. "The enemy is you as is the Christ": S-1.II.6.

XXI. "It emphasizes application . . . rather than theology: PR.

XXI. "a universal theology . . . possible but necessary: PR.

XXI. *This is a . . . peace of God*: T-in.

XXI and XXII. *It makes a . . . in every respect*: PR.

XXII–XXIII. *Remember only this . . . that is required*: W-in.

XXIII. We recognize we . . . *so am I*: W-R.5.in.

XXIV. To see me . . . : *born to give*: T-15.X.2, 3.

XXIV. Each miracle of joining is a mighty herald of eternity: T-20.V.1.

XXV. Simply do this . . . : unto your God: W-189.

XXV. *Heaven itself is . . . as their own*: W-133.

CHAPTER I

1. *Miracles honor you . . . restore your sanity*: T-1.I. #33.

2. Prayer is the . . . Father and himself: S-1.in.1–2.

2. Prayer is a . . . contained in this: S-1.I.1, 4.

2. Prayer for specifics . . . content with less: S-1.IV.3.

2. Prayer is a . . . disappears in Him: S-1.I.5.

2. *You have sought . . . been given you*: S-1.I.3.

2. Herein lies the . . . and receives everything: S-1.I.7.

3. *The only meaningful . . . have everything*: T-3.V.6.

5. A miracle is . . . remedy it brings: W–"What is a miracle?"

5. *The miracle is useless . . . had no effects*: T-28.II.11.

5. A miracle contains . . . miracle of love: W–"What is a miracle?"

5. *Miracle-minded forgiveness . . . does not matter*: T-2.V.A.16.

*All content and page numbers are taken from the third edition of the course.

5. The miracle is . . . thought was there: W–"What is a miracle?"

5. **Miracles demonstrate that . . . the real world:** T-12.VII.1.

5. Miracles fall like . . . life has immortality: W–"What is a miracle?"

6. **Your worth is . . .** *this delusion lasts:* T-4.I. 7.

6. The Holy Spirit . . . is it yours: T-12.VI. 2.

6. Spirit need not . . . *of God Himself:* T-4.I.3, 4, 12.

6. **You whose mind . . . wills for you:** T-13.XI.5, 7.

9. **Forget not that . . .** No belief is neutral: T-24.in.1–2.

9. *Every thought you . . . thought is impossible:* W-16.

9. Everyone has . . . what He knows: T-24.in.2.

9. *Peace is an . . . Health is inner peace:* T-4.III.1.

9. **Knowledge is not . . . you have Knowledge:** T-8.I.1.

9. *The great peace . . . aware of it:* T-6.II.12.

10. **I am God's Son . . . abides His Own:** W–"What am I?"

10. Father, I was created . . . Son of God: W-326.

10. The statement "God created man . . . *There is nothing else*: T-3.V.7.

10. *Spirit am I . . . save the world:* W-97.

10. I am as . . . *is the world's:* W.162.

13. **When you meet . . .** what you are: T-8.III.4–7.

13. *Father, You gave . . . Name is Yours:* W-266.

15. Those who remember . . . *peace will come:* T-14.XI.12–13, 15, 5, 14.

15. **Your task is . . . from its reality:** T-16.IV.6.

16. **This world you . . .** peace a while: W-182.

16. *In time, we . . . coexist with God:* T-2.V.A.17–(7).

16. **Be quiet in . . . perfect peace forever:** T-14.III.15.

16. *Love waits on . . . have not lost:* T-13.VII.9.

16. Eternity is an idea. . . *eternal is now:* T-5.III.5.

19. **You can do . . .** *me to heal:* T-2.V.A.18.

19. God is praised . . . guidance through you: T-4.VII.8.

19. *Step back in faith . . . with the rest:* W-155.

19. As God sent . . . peace and union: T-8.IV.3.

20. **The meaning of . . .** *you peace forever:* T-20.VI.1–4.

23. **The emphasis of this course . . .** this is necessary: M-24.6.

23. *Heaven is your home . . . be in you:* T-12.VI.7.

23. **Heaven is chosen . . .** nothingness is recognized: W-138

23. *What is Heaven . . . of its creation?:* T-26.IV.3.

23. The Bible repeatedly . . . your whole mind: T-4.VII.6–7.

23. *To be in the Kingdom . . . attention on it:* T-7.III.4.

24 and 25. We are the joint will. . . as you are: T-8.VI.1–10.

25. *As you perceive . . . only an awakening:* T-13.I.7.

28. This is a course in mind training: T-1.VII.4.

28. *This is a course . . are teach you:* T-16.III.4.

28. **The purpose of your learning . . .** as you are: W-R.1.in.

28. Yet your willingness . . .your own teacher: T-11.VIII.3.

28. The Holy Spirit . . . *what to seek:* T-13.XI.6.

28. The Holy Spirit . . . not look back: T-14.II.1–3.

31. **Forget not that . . .** he is not: T-24.VI 4.

31. You cannot understand . . . Holy Spirit sees: T-5.III.8.

31. **Can you imagine . . . and nothing more:** T-15.I.1.

31. *Father, we would . . . You created us:* W-249.

31. All healing is . . . world can know: T-13.VIII.1.

31. My mind is . . . only the past: W-8.

31. It is the reason . . . is not there: W-7.

31. *Give the past . . . represent, and why:* T-17.III.7.

31. Unless the past . . . it is gone: W-289.

31. *Take this very . . . wholly without condemnation:* T-15.I.9.

31. *Healing must be complete. . . mar its welcome:* T-13.III.9.

32. There is a positive . . . assault promotes fear: T-6.I.1–2.

32. The real meaning of the crucifixion . . . model for learning: T-6.I.3.

32. *The ultimate purpose . . . rid of guilt*: T-13.II.1.

32. **The crucifixion did . . .** in any way: T-3.I.1–2.

32. and 33. Assault can ultimately . . . **will teach amiss:** T-6.I.4–7.

33. **Very simply, the resurrection . . . across the world:** M-28.1–2.

33. **The crucifixion cannot be shared . . . it was intended:** T-6.I.12–14.

33. *Each day, each . . . unhappy or happy:* T-14.III.4.

34. **There is nothing . . . be at peace:** T-18.VI.1–4, 9–11, 14.

34. *Inward is sanity . . . is outside you:* T-18.I.7.

35. *Healing is the . . . minds that separate:* T-28.III.2.

36. **There is a . . . has no meaning:** M-1.3, 2.

36. *God's guiltless Son . . . of his Father:* T-13.VI.8.

36. **Ask for light . . . joy and yours:** T-5.II.11.

36. **Can you offer guilt . . . and also this:** T-14.VIII.2.

CHAPTER II

39. *Miracles transcend the . . . why they heal:* T-1.1.#17.

40. **Forgiveness recognizes what . . .** *as it is:* W–"What is forgiveness?"

40. **The unforgiving are . . .** become his choice: P-2.VI.1.

40. **Forgiveness is unknown . . . return to Him:** PR–"What it says."

40. *Once forgiveness has been accepted . . . you already have:* T-3.V.6.

40. **As prayer is . . .** anyone except yourself: S-2.I.4.

41. *Forgiveness is not . . . then forgive it:* T-27.II.2.

41. **Sin is insanity . . .** *that are untrue:* W–"What is sin."

41. **Sin is the . . .** recognize my Self: W–247.

41. **How long, O son of God . . .** *have never sinned:* T-25.II.10.

41. **You who were . . .** *forgive will remember:* W-68.

42. *Forgiveness opens up . . . open to yourself:* W-134.

42. **Would you not . . .** *wakening in Him:* W-68.

42. **Judgment was made . . .** of His Son: W-3.11.

45. **Where learning ends . . .** peace awaits you: T-18.IX.11–14.

45. **Forgiveness is the means. . .** *in my heart:* W-336.

46. **Christ is God's . . .** you at last: W–"What is Christ?"

46. *The Holy Spirit . . . idea "of" God:* T-5.III.2.

46. **The Holy Spirit . . .** except Christ's face?: W–"What is Christ?"

46. *Christ waits for your acceptance . . . peace with Him:* T-11.IV.7.

46. **There is no need . . . their own illusions:** C-5.1–2.

46. *The sight of . . . walk with Him:* T-24.V.7.

47. **Is he God's . . .** Love of God: C-5.6.

47. **Christ is at . . .** *to His Son:* T-11.IV.6.

47. **Not one does Christ forget. . . .** *as He does:* W-160.

48. **From knowledge and . . .** and as us: PR–"What is says."

48. **Forgiveness is the healing of perception of separation:** T-3.V. 9.

48. *This is the shift . . . lets it disappear:* C-4.6.

51. **Christ's vision is . . .** each of us: PR–"What is says."

51. **Christ's vision is . . .** sanctity in God: W-159.

52. **Comparison must be . . .** to each one?: T-24 II.1, 4–5.

52. **The special love relationship . . .** it must be: T-16.V.2.

52. **Specialness is a . . .** it is healed: T-24.IV.1–2.

52. **The special ones . . .** partly to forgive: T-24.III.7, 1.

52. *You cannot enter . . . love is like:* T-13.X.11.

55. **In the Holy . . .** *relationship with you:* T-15.VIII.6.

55. **The Voice of the Holy Spirit . . . reminds you of:** T-5.II.7.

55. **Do as God's Voice directs. . . . your function here:** W-186.

55. *You will never . . . be wholly joined:* T-11.II.6.

56. **Can you imagine . . .** beauty and forgiveness: T-17.II.

57. *I ask Your blessing . . . Your holy Son:* W-269.

57. **Ask not to . . .** your unforgiving mind: T-14.IV.3.

60. **Who is the . . .** states the truth: W-61.

60. *In this world . . . it of Himself:* T-14.IX.5.

60. **It is your . . .** *may be happy:* W-62.

60. **Forgiveness has a Teacher . . .** He created him: S-2.III.7.

60. *Do you believe . . . leave with me?:* T-18.III.4.

63. **God does not forgive . . .** *I forgive myself:* W-46.

63. **God does not forgive . . .** up to Him: R-W-60.

63. *Innocence is not . . . it is total:* T-3.II.2.

63. **Here is the answer! . . .** it to you: W-122.

63. *Those who would . . . is removed forever:* T-18.III.6.

64. **Ask and He will answer** . . . . this is so: M–"As for the rest."

64. *Have faith in Him . . . are His Son:* W-232.

67. **The ego seeks** . . . reality of dreams: T-17.III.6–9.

67. *The past that . . . what always was:* T-14.IX.1.

67. **The way to God** . . . *Him at last:* W-256.

68. Today's idea, completely . . . *trust in Him:* W-126.

69. **The cost of giving** . . . to hold dear: T-14.III.5.

70. Atonement is for . . . but *for* you: T-9.IV.1–2.

70. *You cannot be . . . made them necessary:* T-14.XI.7.

70. **The ego, too,** . . . your function is: T-9.IV.4–6.

70. *If all but . . . remains is eternal:* T-17.III.5.

70. My trust in you . . . theirs is wanting: T-4.VI.6.

CHAPTER III

73. *A miracle is . . . neighbor's worth simultaneously*: T.1.1. 18.

74. We have repeated . . . **salvation unto you:** T-21.II.1–3.

74. *The power of . . . cause of restoration:* T-14.VI.5.

74 and 75. Be willing, for . . . **effect and Source:** T-21.II.8–11.

75. *God is the . . . causeless cannot be:* T-14.III.8.

75. Each day, each . . . and creation unified: W-271.

76. To extend is . . . to do this: T-2.I.1–2, 4.

76. Correction has one . . . *are like Him:* M-18.3.

76. **The issue of** . . . where it is: T-3.VI.8–9.

78. **Here is the** . . . *God created me*: W-139.

79. If the sole . . . solution of undoing: T-5.V.7.

80. What keeps the . . . **attempts to teach:** W-132.

80. **What is the World?** . . . certainty has gone: W–"What is the World."

80 and 81. A lesson earlier . . . be released alone: W-132.

81. **You cannot give** . . . *peace of God:* T-31.VII.2, 3, 5.

83. All temptation is . . . **you are saved:** W-70.

83. *The enemy is you, as is the Christ:* S-1.II.6.

83. **The seeming cost** . . . for healing lies: W-70.

83. **The secret of salvation** . . . free of it: T-27.VIII.10–11, 13.

84 and 85. The ego, like . . . *you to Him:* T-15.I.2–4, 6, 7–8, 10.

87. It is hard . . . will always be: T-2.I.5.

87. You *are* the . . . not know now: T-5.II.4.

87. Any split in . . . belief in separation: T-6.II.1.

87. *The wholeness of . . . to heal it:* T-6.V.C.8–9.

87. *You will find Heaven . . . you really want:* W-131.

88. It has been . . . you remember Him: M-20.1–6.

91. God Himself gave . . . *God for me:* T-5.VII.4–6.

91. **The ego tries** . . . *as a creator:* T-6.V.B.6, 8.

91. The Holy Spirit's . . . never to undermine: T-8.VIII.8.

92. **Faith is the** . . . **purpose for itself:** T-19.I.10–11, 15–16.

95. *God does not . . .* up to Heaven: W-193.

95. *Have no fear . . . is for you:* T-28.I.15.

95. Heaven itself is . . . God for you: T-12.VIII.5.

96. Gratitude is a . . . *of all creation:* W-195.

99. **You who want** . . . *is His Gift:* T-1.VI.1–5.

99. Perfect love is all-encompassing . . . have no opposite": T-in.1.

100. **Anything in this** . . . one is best: T-26.VI.1.

100. Brother, take not . . . where you go: T-23.II.22.

100. Lead not your . . . Him on His: T-26.VI.2–3.

100. *Let your mind . . . appointed for you:* T-14.VIII.3.

100. We gather at . . . not his own: W-125.

101. You may not . . . to God's answer: W-71.

102. Father, You are . . . safe returning home: W-324.

102. I will use . . . of true perception: W-87.(73).

102. *I will there . . . not my will:* W-73.

102. Understanding is light . . . behalf of God: T-5.III.6.

102. Nothing will change . . . light *is* understanding: T-9.V.6.

102. *Only be quiet . . . Word of God:* W-125.

104. Grace is an . . . I will release: W-169.

104. *God is, and . . . real as love?:* M-27.6.

105. Nothing real can . . . peace of God: T-in.1.

CHAPTER IV

107. *There is no . . . love are maximal:* T-1.I.#1.
108. *There is a . . . has allotted you:* T-25.VIII.2, 4, 13.
108. What could you . . . *demands for sacrifice:* W-135.
108. "Vengeance is mine . . . part of God: T-5.VI.7.
111. What fear has . . . and is undone: T-5.IV.1.
111. *"The wicked shall perish" . . . cannot even understand:* T-5.VI.9.
111. Every loving thought . . . is their purification: T-5.IV.3.
111. *Miracles are everyone's . . . is necessary first:* T-1.I.7.
111. How can you . . . are with you: T-5.IV.8.
112. Nothing beyond yourself . . . perception of it: T-10.in.1–2
112. *You who are . . . only in eternity:* T-5.III.10.
112. God does not . . . *deciding against Himself:* T-10.in.3.
115. Vision will come . . . you to see: T-20.VIII.1–2, 6, 10–11.
115. You will first . . . *dream of love:* T-13.VII.9.
115. *Child of God . . . only true usefulness:* T-1.VII.2.
116. *Here is the . . . of the world:* W-323.
116. *God gives but . . . He with you:* W-185.
116. *From Him you . . . be perfectly accomplished:* W-77.
116. *You are entitled . . . we celebrate today!:* T-13.XI.11.
116. Say His name . . . upon your holiness: W-183.
118. Everyone here has . . . will be justified: T-25.III. 6–9.
118. Sin is the . . . *You with it:* W-259.
119. *What I have . . . I may see:* W-52. 97.
120. What can it . . . just to everyone: T-25.IX.1–3, 5, 7–8.
120. *Everything you think . . . Spirit is lacking:* T-5.IV.7.
120. When a brother . . . lose your way: T-9.III.5–6.
121. The little problems . . . *"is" his due:* T-25.IX.9–10.
121. I will never . . . as you do: T-5.IV.6.
123. The holy instant . . . outside His Fatherhood: T-18.VIII.11.
123. *The holy instant . . . frame of time:* T-17.IV.11.
123. What is the . . . of its holiness: T-21.VIII.5.
123. *If God's Will . . . are in Him:* T-8.IV.1.
123. God's Will for . . . apart from His: W-116. (101.)
123. *This holy instant . . . gives me peace:* W-365.
124. Forget not that . . . *fear beside him:* T-19.IV.D.8, 11–13.
124. To love my . . . return to Him: W-246
124. Let me forget . . . is my own: W-288.
124. *What could restore . . . You as well:* W-335.
127. God, Who encompasses . . . only like itself: T-4.VII.5.
127. When I said . . . and only meaning: T-7.III.1.
127. I have said . . . our inherent equality: T-1.VII 5.
127. Awe should be . . . potential in you: T-1.II.3, 1, 3.
128. We have observed . . . Son is saved: W-76.
128. *Father, I wake . . . .* and my own: W-346.
130. *Humility is strength . . . He does know:* T-16.I.4.
130. *Humility will never . . . not of you:* T-18.IV.III.
130. *Of your ego . . . them truer perception:* T-4.I.12.
130. *I am the . . . it is true:* W-61.
130. *Be humble before . . . plan but His:* T-15.IV.3.
130. *Truth is humble . . . and in love:* W-152.
132. The Last Judgment . . . cannot but continue: T-2.VIII.2–3.
132. *If it is . . . judge for you:* T-12.VII.12.
132. Everyone will ultimately . . . in the Atonement: T-2. VIII.4–5.
132 and 133. Is each one . . . wait for Him: M–"Is Each One To Be Judged In The End?"
133. You who believed . . . this be fearful?: T-9.IV.9, 12.
133. Christ's Second Coming . . . His only joy: W–"What Is The Second Coming?"
133. *You are still . . . are My Son:* W–"What Is the Last Judgment?"
135. I have given . . . think with God: R-1.W–51. (2–4).
135. *Since the purpose . . . opposite of truth:* W-57. (33).
135. God did not . . . I really abide: R–1. W-53. (14).
135. *The world you . . . has no meaning:* W-14.

205. To think that . . . **arrogant than this?:** W-152.

205. *You love me . . . will is Yours:* W-331.

205. Your safety lies . . . find your Self: W–"What is the body."

206. Each day a . . . mine as well: W-315.

206. A day devoted . . . and his Self: W-123.

206. *I thank You . . . and His memory:* W-315.

209. **Real choice is . . . lead to Him:** T-31.IV.2.6, 8–11.

209. *You are the means . . . upon unto itself:* T-25.I.4, 7, 5.

209. **Learn now, without . . . your learning grasp:** T-31.IV.4.

210. **Think but how . . . come at last!:** T-26.IX.1–3, 6–8.

210. *Let my own . . . God's perfect Son:* W-118.

213. Sit quietly and . . . awake in Him?: T-13.VII.1–5, 14–15.

214. To your most . . . *this* "is" *you:* T-16.III.8–9, 7.

214. **We share one life . . . Self, its Holiness:** W-167.

214. I will go . . . Love is one: T-4.VI.7–8.

214. *Teach no one . . . image of yourself:* T-7.VII.3.

216. Let us turn . . . and in eternity: W–Final Lessons. in.

216. *The power set . . . goes with you:* T-17. VII. 7.

216. There are those . . . they are unaware: M-26.2.

219. **Salvation is a . . . not far behind:** W–"What is salvation?"

219. *I need but . . . "wills" it so:* W-235.

219. Let us come . . . exists at all: W–"What is salvation?"

219. *What can I . . . us to find:* W-231

220. **Remember that the . . . beautiful and true:** T-6.IV.1, 6.

220. *You are at . . . awakening to reality:* T-10.I.2.

220. The separation was . . . is your Teacher: T-6.IV.12.

220. The betrayal of . . . reality be different: T-17.I.1.

220. **Salvation requires the . . . this is so:** W-93.

221. *The Kingdom is . . . prevail against it:* T-4.III.1.

223. Here is the answer . . . **truth about yourself:** W-50.

223. *There never was . . . by you alone:* T-30.V.10

223. Let the idea . . . **placed you forever:** W-50.

223. God is with . . . He speaks today!: W-222.

223. *If you knew . . . would be impossible:* T-18.III.3.

224. **Fear not to . . . comes of itself:** T-15.XI.1–7.

225. *I can give up . . . messages to me:* W-322.

225. Let no despair . . . is our will: T-15.XI.8–10.

226. **What is the . . .** *it ever be:* T-26.VII.11, 13, 18–20, 15.

226. *You dwell in . . . never be disturbed:* T-23.10.

227. What makes this . . . to His Will: W-165.

229. Do you really . . . He loves you: T-5.VII.1.

230. It is still up to you . . . which they came. T-17.III.9.

230. *Complexity is nothing . . . can be difficult:* W-133.

230. My holy brother . . . peace to me: T-17.III.10.

230. When you have . . . to your decision: T-12.VII.11.

230. Father, it is . . . *peace through us:* W-360.

230. **This is a . . . surely know again:** W-157.

234. **The world as . . . what is true:** T-11.VII.1–2, 4.

234. We are not inconsistent . . . *one with me:* W-156.

235. I thank you . . . returns to me: W-342.

235. *There will be . . . is your redemption:* T-13.II.9.

236. Listen,—perhaps you . . . **remembering for everyone:** T-21.I.6–10.

236. Then let our . . . way to God: W-195.

237. *Salvation is for . . . to save it:* T-12.III.5, 10.

238. Seek and *find . . . which You love:* T-16.VII.11–12.

238. The Word of God . . . this or nothing: M-13, 7.8.

238. *Forgive us our . . . which you love*: Amen: T-16. VIII.12.

GLOSSARY OF *A COURSE IN MIRACLES* TERMINOLOGY, BY AMY TORRES

ATONEMENT The final undoing (of the dream of separation); the culmination of miracles, holy instants, forgiveness and salvation; the Holy Spirit's correction of wrong-minded thinking (error, mistake, belief in what is not true) that we could actually separate from God's Mind.

BRIDGE The Holy Spirit provides the bridge from our self-concept to the Self that God created; the Holy Spirit is our communication link back home, to the Oneness of God in Heaven. Through a process of forgiveness, the Holy Spirit helps us bridge the little gap from perception to reality; from guilt to innocence; from time to timelessness, space to formlessness, illusion to truth, separation to unity.

CHRIST The Greatness within us; the Living Loving Light we are as one Son; our unified identity as the Son of God (also called the Sonship and Self).

CRUCIFIXION An extreme example of attack. Derived from the Latin word *crucifixio* or *crucifixus*, meaning "fixed to a cross." An ancient method of execution in which the victim's hands and feet were bound and nailed to a cross. This punishment was intended to torture and disgrace the recipient. Jesus was crucified. He explains in the Course that we continue to crucify ourselves every day by thinking we are sinners. As long as we choose the ego as our teacher, we doom ourselves to a life of punishing

judgment, sin, guilt, fear, anger, hatred, attack, humiliation, and the like. Therefore, crucifixion is attack in any form—toward another or ourselves. If this seems dramatic, on a more ordinary level crucifixion includes irritation, chronic dissatisfaction, disappointment, loneliness, hunger, anything that is less than perfect wholeness, absolute love, peace, and joy. Remember, attack always originates in the ego mind. The message of the crucifixion is perfectly clear: *Teach only love for that is what you are.*

DEATH Death is just the ego's idea of finality. It serves the ego's scheme to try to prove its existence by using death to prove there is life. If someone or something can die, then it must have lived. This is ego logic. God's Mind is Life Eternal; therefore, anything that dies is not real. Death is simply an idea that we could be anything other than God—we can dream about this, fantasize about it, forget we came up with the idea, but nothing will make it true (Note M-27: What is Death?).

DREAM A figment of the ego's imagination; a deliberate forgetting of our Source; a selective unremembering (of our true identity).

EGO A belief that ideas (the Son of God) can leave their source. "What is the ego? But a dream of what you really are. A thought you are apart from your Creator and a wish to be what He created not. It is a thing of madness, not reality at all" (CoT-2). "The ego is a wrong-minded attempt to perceive yourself as you wish to be, rather that as you are" (T-3. IV. 2–3).

ERROR The wrong-minded ego belief that we have separated from God's One Mind. The Holy Spirit's response to the ego belief in sin and punishment is correction of an error, a mistake in thinking. "Right-mindedness listens to the Holy Spirit, forgives the world, and through Christ's vision sees the real world in its place. This is the final vision, the last perception, the condition in which God takes the final step Himself. Here time and illusions end together. Wrong-mindedness listens to the ego and makes illusions; perceiving sin and justifying anger, and seeing guilt, disease, and death as real. Both this world and the real world are illusions because right-mindedness merely overlooks, or forgives, what never happened. Therefore it is not the One-mindedness of the Christ Mind, whose will is one with God's" (Note CoT. 1).

FORGIVENESS The recognition that what we thought our brother did to us has not occurred; a process of undoing which leads us to recognize what we already have/who we already are. Forgiveness accesses God's Loving Light and helps us remember Living Light as our true identity. The practical application of forgiveness is, literally, "for giving"—by giving every thought, belief, opinion, idea, and judgment that we hold to the Holy Spirit to wipe the slate clean and reveal God's word written beneath our own. Forgiveness heals the perception of separation. "Forgiveness is the means by which we will remember. Through forgiveness the thinking of the world is reversed. The forgiven world becomes the gate of Heaven, because by its mercy we can at last forgive ourselves. Holding no one prisoner to guilt, we become free. Acknowledging Christ in all our brothers, we recognize His presence in ourselves. Forgetting all our misperceptions, and with nothing from the past to hold us back, we can remember God" (Preface: What It Says, last paragraph).

GOD'S TEACHERS Anyone who chooses to put Self before self-concept; anyone who chooses to follow the Holy Spirit's guidance and be a conduit for miracles.

HEALING The outcome of forgiveness; the natural result of choosing to be a miracle receiver and transmitter—in other words, a miracle worker. All healing is essentially the release from fear. "The body is healed because you came without it, and joined the Mind in which all healing rests. The body cannot heal, because it cannot make itself sick. It needs no healing. Its health or sickness depends entirely on how the mind perceives it, and the purpose that the mind would use it for" (T-19. I. 2:7./T-19.I. 3:1–3).

HEAVEN Infinity; an infinite extending of Love. Heaven is the metaphorical dwelling place of God's Son. Heaven is the natural state of mind in which God's Son lives—Loving Light.

HELL The ego uses time to stay out of the Eternal Present, which is God's domain. To the ego, Heaven is hell because it strips the ego of its identity and reveals that the ego does not exist at all. So the ego threatens us with hell and "eternal damnation" to distract us from the Truth, which is we have not sinned, have nothing to feel guilty about, and have nothing to fear. As the Text says, "You are at home in God, dreaming you are in exile but perfectly capable of awakening to reality" (T-10. I. 2:1).

HOLY The Wholeness and Unity of God's Mind..

HOLY INSTANT The present; a glimpse into Timelessness and the peace, love, and joy which is our birthright. ". . . a miniature of Heaven" (T-17.IV.11:1).

HOLY TRINITY The Father, the Son (which symbolizes Jesus and all his brothers—including you!), and the Holy Spirit; a Oneness which originates with the Father Who is the prime Creator.

IDOL A substitute for God—could be animal, vegetable, mineral, chemical, human, energy, anything that tries to limit Limitlessness, define the Indefinable, and confine Boundless Freedom. (See "I am sustained by God")

ILLUSION The ego's out-picturing of sin, guilt, and fear. Out-picturing thoughts always results in duality and form; in other words, time and space, you and me, right and wrong, good and bad, black and white, and so on. Out-picturing is another way of saying image making or form. "Nothing so blinding as perception of form. For sight of form means understanding has been obscured" (T-22. III. 6:7).

LIFE All That Is; infinite, eternal Loving Light. (*A Course in Miracles* calls the Holy Spirit the Voice for Life Itself.)

LOVE God's Mind infinitely, eternally extending His Peace and Joy.

MAGIC The belief in anything other than God's Love. Magic witnesses to separation and seems to make the error real—seems to prove we are human beings living on planet earth. The Holy Spirit uses true perception to direct the mind back to its Source and turn everything in our corporeal experience into a symbol of God's Love.

MIND God is God's One Thought of Unified Infinite, Eternal Love, Peace, and Joy (as opposed to mind, which means "ego mind"). Mind is synonymous with Spirit—in *A Course in Miracles* they mean the same thing. "Oneness is simply the idea that God is. And in His Being, He encompasses all things. No mind holds anything but Him. We say 'God is,' and then we cease to speak, for in that knowledge words are meaningless. There are no lips to speak them, and no part of mind sufficiently distinct to feel it is now aware of something not itself. It has united with its Source. And like its Source Itself, it merely is" (W-169).

MIRACLE Miracles are natural expressions of love. The real miracle is the Love that inspires them. Everything that comes from God's Love is a miracle. All miracles are equal—there is no such thing as a "harder" or "bigger" miracle. All expressions of God's Love are maximal. The use of miracles as spectacles to induce belief in God is a misunderstanding of their purpose. Miracles collapse time, giving us access to Eternal Love briefly, in order to reestablish our true identity. Miracles defy physical law, bringing more love both to the giver and receiver. Miracles are thoughts of Love (T-1: The Meaning of Miracles).

MURDER In this world, murder is the intentional (and unlawful) killing, by violent means, of one human being by another. Metaphysically, murder is what the ego is pretending it has done to God, and, even more irrationally, what it believes God wants to do to it. Murder is a useful concept for the ego because it assumes that bodies are real and that life is of the body—both of which are untrue, and as the Course states many times, "Only the truth is true." (Therefore, God is Divine Abstraction—formless and eternal, among other qualities.)

PERCEPTION Believing in images, mirages, illusions, magic, body senses. Perception is the opposite of God's knowledge. "Knowledge is truth, under one law, the law of love or God . . . The world of perception, on the other hand, is a world of time, of change, of beginning and endings. It is based on perception, not on fact. (Preface) Perception is the result of projection and produces the ego's idea of reality through the five senses (what we experience via the body as eyesight).

PRAYER Prayer is a request that you recognize what you already are. It is not supplication or imploring to have specific request granted. That kind of prayer is very limited and egocentric—it decides what is best and then dictates to God what should happen. Real prayer is opening to Truth. Real prayer results in healing and miracles for many more than the direct people involved—there is an abundant ripple effect that flows through all of humanity. Through prayer love is received, and through miracles love is expressed.

PROJECTION Egoistic imagination out-picturing a "world," "bodies," and "personal identities" on a screen of space and time; the ultimate purpose of projection is always to get rid of guilt.

REALITY The Truth of God's Mind; Infinite, Eternal, Unified, Living, Loving Light, Peace, Joy, and Innocence. Our True Home, the Knowledge of Being and Creativity.

REASON Contrary to ego logic, reason is how the Holy Spirit clears the way so that you can receive salvation. Reason sees through form to the one error the ego masks as many (its belief that is separated from God). Reason lights up the path to truth to correct the ego's error.

RESURRECTION Awakening to the Truth of Oneness. "Your resurrection is your reawakening. I am the model for rebirth, but rebirth is merely the dawning on your mind of what is already in it" (T-6. I. 7: 1–2). "Very simply, the resurrection is the overcoming or surmounting of death. It is a reawakening or a rebirth; a change of mind about the meaning of the world" (M-28. 1: 1–2).

SACRIFICE A belief in separation, which leads to believing in scarcity, deprivation, and loss. Sacrifice always involves the body, because it is only the body that can seem to be vulnerable, hurt, wounded, and, ultimately, to die.

SALVATION Salvation is the undoing of the ego thought system. "Salvation requires the acceptance of just one thought; you are as God created you, not what you made of yourself" (W-93). "How simple is salvation! All it says is what was never true is not true now, and never will be. The impossible has not occurred, and can have no effects. And that is all" (T31.I.1: 1-4).

SELF Son of God, Christ, Sonship, God's one ever-extending child, all brothers as One, as opposed to the ego's "self-concept," which is a figment of its own imagination, a puny idea that it could usurp God's power and somehow become God itself.

SELF-CONCEPT The ego's attempt to deny God's One Holy Self by making up an idea of a separate self (which it then incarnates in a body, trying to strengthen its false sense of identity, individuality, and autonomy in form).

SIN The belief in separation; a lack of love; a mistake, an error in thinking.

SON OF GOD All of us; Self; Sonship; God's One Child. "The Son of God is you" (W-64).

SONSHIP The all-inclusive Self, Christ, Son of God. The understanding that all humans are actually One; without exception, every single person is a brother.

TEMPTATION Anything that substitutes as an idol or magic for God's Love. "Whatever form temptation seems to take, it always but reflects a wish to be a self that you are not" (T-31.VII.12:1). "Temptation has one lesson it would teach, in all its forms, wherever it occurs. It would persuade the holy Son of God he is a body, born in what must die, unable to escape its frailty, and bound by what it orders him to feel" (T-31.VIII.1:1–2).

TRUTH The Course tells us many times, only "the truth is true." Absolute reality. The Holy Spirit shines the light of truth which dispels the ego's darkness and illuminates Reality. The truth is that God, Who is beyond description, is Formless, Changeless, Infinite, Eternal Love. This Love is abstract and bodiless—the world does not exist!

WORLD The ego dream that we could be somewhere other than at Home in Heaven; the ego belief that infinity can be split into space and materialize as a celestial body.